# Exchange and Development

# Exchange and Development

Peter A. Cornelisse

*Professor of Public Finance, Emeritus, Erasmus University, Rotterdam, the Netherlands*

Erik Thorbecke

*Graduate School Professor, H.E. Babcock Professor of Economics, Emeritus, Cornell University, USA*

**Edward Elgar**

Cheltenham, UK • Northampton, MA, USA

Published by
Edward Elgar Publishing Limited
The Lypiatts
15 Lansdown Road
Cheltenham
Glos GL50 2JA
UK

Edward Elgar Publishing, Inc.
William Pratt House
9 Dewey Court
Northampton
Massachusetts 01060
USA

A catalogue record for this book
is available from the British Library

Library of Congress Control Number: 2010922147

Mixed Sources
Product group from well-managed
forests and other controlled sources
www.fsc.org Cert no. SA-COC-1565
© 1996 Forest Stewardship Council
FSC

ISBN 978 1 84980 310 6 (cased)

Printed and bound by MPG Books Group, UK

# Contents

# Figures

# Boxes

# Preface and acknowledgements

This volume has evolved and matured over an extended period of time. The motivation for writing this book was our feeling that the exchange process was not only fundamental to socio-economic development and progress but also influenced by it. Research involvement in, and empirical observations from a large number of developing countries made us aware of the enormous diversity of existing forms of exchange and transactions.

While some transactions occur within markets, others are barter or virtual exchanges within a family and still others take place within firms or organizations, we were particularly impressed by the variety of transactions within each of these categories. We asked ourselves why such a bewildering number of forms of exchange could be observed simultaneously in different settings of the developing world. What seemed even more surprising was the existence of multiple forms of exchange for essentially the same product, such as credit. We gradually realized that economic transactions evoke and reflect structural differences between developing and developed economies; they also help determine the nature, state and pace of development. It is somewhat surprising that most approaches to development economics and policy making do not place more emphasis on the importance of thorough, in-depth analyses of economic transactions.

Why are there so many exchange structures and why do some actors choose, or are contrived, to operate within a specific exchange structure? An answer to this question required us to explore and analyze and dig deeply into the physiology of the exchange process. Since transactions represent the roots and the culmination of any exchange activity, an analytical framework was needed to explain their formation. We realized that transactions occur within what we call exchange configurations. This conceptual framework allows the tracing back of the form and content of transactions to their building blocks or elements of exchange, that is, the *item* exchanged; the *actors* involved in decisions related to the exchange; and the *environment* – physical, social, technological, legal and political – within which the actors operate. Characteristics of these elements, in different combinations, determine distinct types of exchange relations and help explain their operation. We term an entire constellation – consisting of a particular combination of characteristics of elements of exchange, the decision process actors go through, and the resulting transactions – an exchange configuration. Exchange configurations can be thought of as channels through which specific transactions are effectuated. Actors, given their own attributes, the properties of the item transacted and the environment they face, will choose to operate in (or will design) that configuration and corresponding transaction that minimize perceived transaction costs.

In the course of writing this book we realized how much was taken for granted in the analysis of exchange. For example, we found well over a hundred different definitions of 'market' – perhaps the most fundamental concept underlying the exchange process. In studying the evolution of the process of exchange over the last couple of millennia, it became clear that the form taken by exchange configurations and their resulting transactions changed with economic development – gradually away from inter-personal, family or community-based transactions and increasingly towards impersonal market transactions. The dynamics of growth and development cannot be well understood without unveiling the link between exchange and development. We hope that the conceptual framework presented in this volume will encourage and assist further research attempting to bridge exchange and development.

As development economists – involved in research projects in Asia, Latin America and Africa – we had many opportunities to observe various forms of economic exchange in developing countries and the operation of a variety of local markets, such as for domestic food and cash crops in Indonesia, rice exchange in Taiwan, the multiple settings through which rural informal credit is channelled in sub-Saharan Africa, the dealings in black markets of foreign exchange in Turkey and Peru, dealings in a cotton market in Burkina Faso, a market for seasonal labour in Ivory Coast, in primary wheat markets and Islamic banking in Pakistan, to name only a few. It took a special effort to formulate a conceptual framework capable of explaining the bewildering number of distinct exchange configurations and transactions at the heart of the above specific forms of exchange. The same applied with particular force to a closely related matter, namely the behavioural routines of informal actors.

One reason it took a long time for this project to mature into a book is that for most of the time the two authors operated from their home bases, Cornell University and Erasmus University. Another reason is that our insights grew by leaps and bounds, sometimes with considerable time intervals in between. Other research projects in which we were separately engaged gained priority on several occasions. Still, while these projects caused immediate delay, they regularly also helped to improve and widen our understanding of exchange processes.

The list of individuals who inspired, influenced and helped us in the con-
ception of this book is long. We can only mention a few. Erik Thorbecke is
most grateful for the many enlightening discussions he has had with Alain
de Janvry and Elisabeth Sadoulet on the present theme, starting with the
conference they jointly organized at Cornell University in 1993 on 'State,
Market, and Civil Organizations: New Theories and New Practices'.
Also during the 1990s Erik Thorbecke wrote a couple of monographs
with two of his graduate students, under the auspices of the Institute for
Policy Reform in Washington DC on, respectively, 'The Evolution of
Exchange' with Rimjhim Mehra (now Aggarwal), and 'Rural Informal
Credit Configurations' with Stefano Paternostro. Both of these themes
are rehearsed and elaborated upon in this volume. As is clearly revealed
in the volume, we owe a debt of gratitude to the architects of the 'New
Institutional Economics'. While drawing on their contributions we feel
that we have added some key insights such as the concept of exchange
configuration.

Peter Cornelisse wants to thank all those persons who, sometimes
unknowingly, had an impact on the project by offering their insights. The
first to be mentioned is Theo van Galen, close collaborator in the Pakistani
wheat-marketing project referred to in the main text, who tragically died
much too young. Commenting on the Exchange and Development project
at a very early stage – when our ideas were only being formed – Theo
insisted on the need for a full integration of the time dimension. Justus
Veenman (Erasmus University) pointed out a certain degree of correspondence between the exchange-configuration approach and Boudon's
theory of social change. On various occasions he also emphasized that
economics is a social science and that economic behaviour cannot be
understood without taking account of extra-economic aspects, such as
cultural and sociological aspects. By the time Wouter Steffelaar and Peter
Cornelisse had completed their study of 'Islamic banking in practice: the
case of Pakistan', his point had been driven home. John Groenewegen
(Technical University Delft) saved us time and energy by introducing us
to the recent and most relevant literature on learning processes. And, last
but not least, we are most grateful to Elma van de Mortel, who helped us
in accessing the vast literature on institutional economics.

We thank all these individuals for their help and interest in our project.
But they are not to be blamed if we took wrong turns.

Erik Thorbecke, Ithaca, NY
Peter Cornelisse, Rotterdam
April, 2010

# 1. Introduction and overview

## 1.1 WHY CONSIDER EXCHANGE AND DEVELOPMENT?

Exchange is a fundamental component of economic behaviour. Moreover, exchange determines the state and pace of economic development. An exchange-free 'Robinson Crusoe economy' – where individual needs are only met through own production, and own consumption is the only outlet for an individual's production – cannot rise above subsistence level. Exchange allows (1) specialization and division of labour; (2) exploitation of economies of scale in production; (3) improved combination and allocation of factors of production; (4) the transmission of information and innovations; and (5) reaping the result of transactions, thereby providing incentives to economic actors. Each of these functions offers crucial opportunities for improving productivity. Thus, market and non-market exchange is of pivotal importance in the determination of income, the structure and organization of production, satisfaction of needs, income distribution and internal and external equilibrium in developing and developed countries alike.

But the impact of exchange relations extends beyond an interpretation of development in economic terms such as income per head and security and distribution of personal income. Also the wider concept of human development – incorporating additional aspects such as level and distribution of education and information, state of health, justice and freedom[1] – is influenced by exchange relations. Moreover, as will be argued in subsequent chapters, aspects of economic as well as human development in their turn impact on exchange, thereby creating dynamic loops of self-propelling development.

In light of the above, it is surprising that, for a long time, the literature on economic exchange has been rather sparse. In large parts of the economics literature there has been a tendency to treat markets as abstract, featureless phenomena. This neglect can be attributed mostly to the dominant position of the pure neoclassical theory during the greater part of the past century. In neoclassical theory, exchange is assumed to be essentially frictionless and, therefore, of little consequence. Under this assumption there is indeed little to be gained from in-depth analyses of economic exchange. But the perspective alters drastically when it is realized that economic exchange as it occurs in the real world is a laborious and costly process with uncertain and imperfect outcomes.

Of course, the situation has improved in recent years. A host of studies in the structure–conduct–performance and industrial organization tradition has contributed to a better understanding of the impact that market structure has on firms engaged in transactions. Game theory has unveiled the mechanism underlying the behaviour of economic actors under well-defined conditions, and experimental economics has pointed at unexpected attitudes and reactions of actors when taking economic decisions. Further, the transaction costs literature has demonstrated how various types of transaction costs impact on actors' preferences for one or another transactional framework, called governance structure. Contributions in these and other fields, such as institutional and evolutionary economics, have definitely deepened the profession's understanding of different aggregate forms of exchange and of decision processes followed by economic actors. As a result of the new insights, views of development processes and, with them, development policies have changed.

But some crucial aspects of exchange have still been largely overlooked. For even if we now have better insights as to why some transactions are concluded in a market and others within a firm; or, how industrial structures affect decision making by managers of firms; or, why economic actors sometimes prefer cooperation over competition; it is still mostly unclear why so many vastly different types of transactions can be observed in the real world and which factors determine their shape. In other words, important aspects of economic exchange have remained largely unexplored. So, keeping in mind the fact that exchange is of vital importance to development, there are good reasons for examining exchange in more detail and trying to come to grips with such questions as, how does exchange come about, and which are its underlying elements? First of all, transactions are the uncontested basic unit of analysis in economics.[2] Therefore, an improved understanding of the factors influencing the characteristics of transactions has analytical merit. Secondly, a better insight into the roots of transactions can clarify certain important aspects of the development process and thereby raise the effectiveness of development policies. Especially in a period where structural adjustment, market liberalization, privatization and globalization are receiving increased attention, a more systematic approach to the study of exchange is becoming necessary.

The above paragraphs describe in a nutshell what motivated us to write this book. The main objective of this volume is to provide an analytical framework within which the process of exchange can be investigated and clarified. Because of the strong relation between exchange and development, the great majority of the illustrative cases we present below refer to developing countries. But it should be emphasized at the outset that the framework we propose has a universal character applying to developing as well as to developed countries.

## 1.2 THE NEED FOR AN ANALYTICAL FRAMEWORK FOR THE STUDY OF EXCHANGE

Despite the centrality of exchange to economics, it is not easy to find a conceptual framework of exchange that is able to reflect the diversity of transactions that occur in the real world. Exchange that takes place within formal markets is best studied within the economics literature.[3] In fact, the literature includes a most impressive variety of theoretical and empirical studies of market transactions of varying degree of sophistication, relating to all sorts of commodities, services and factors of production and concluded under widely differing conditions. The best among them prove to be of great theoretical and practical value by contributing significantly to the understanding of the operation of prototypical, specific and individual markets.

But these studies tend to have limited coverage and applicability; an overarching framework is lacking. The origins of the differences in decision procedures, form and content of various market transactions remain largely unclear and the question remains to what extent conclusions derived in one market apply in another. An exception, of course, is the transaction costs literature which is expressly concerned with the causes underlying different transactional forms. It shows for certain well-known categories of transactions – market transactions, intra-firm and intra-family transactions – under which conditions economic actors prefer one category over another. But in real life there are untold numbers of different sub-categories of transactions within each of the three categories above, especially within market transactions. The ideal framework for the study of exchange should be able to explain this wide variation of transactions within the main modes. It should provide answers to such questions as: What can we say about the decision processes that lead up to categories of transactions at different levels of disaggregation? Which are the factors underlying the decisions, and are their numbers manageable? And, last but not least, which are the forces of change that propel the dynamics of exchange decisions, and, thereby, the process of economic development?

Moreover, insufficient attention is generally paid to exchange that takes place outside formal markets. In developing countries, in particular, forms of non-market exchange are both socially and economically important. These include non-monetary insurance arrangements, labour exchanges, reciprocal 'gift' exchanges, patronage relations, intra-family transactions, and a variety of other social and cultural mechanisms that work to distribute goods and services among members of a community. Such non-market or semi-market forms are often treated either as if they are insignificant or as if they are distinct from and unconnected to market institutions. As North (1990, p. 11) notes with reference to such organizational forms as the medieval manor and the suq (bazaar market) of the Middle East and North Africa, 'Not only does [neoclassical theory] not characterize these organizations' exchange process very well, it does not explain the persistence for millennia of what appear to be inefficient forms of exchange.'

The purpose of this book is to present a comprehensive analytical framework and to apply it in search for answers to the above questions. As indicated, special attention will be paid to exchange patterns in developing countries. So, with a view to the massive importance of family farms and family businesses in the developing world, we expressly consider non-market (intra-family and intra-firm) transactions next to market transactions. The need for such an approach can be illustrated by a relatively simple example, namely, the decisions typically taken within a family farm regarding various types of transactions. Virtual exchange takes place within the farm household, as household members are allocated tasks relating to farm production and household care. Production inputs like family labour, land, draft animals and machines may be employed entirely for own (family-organized) production, but may also be offered (rented out) to other users in separate markets. Similarly, food produced on the family farm may be consumed entirely by family members, but the family may also decide to sell at least part of it. The point here is, of course, that families often have a choice among different forms of exchange; to disregard one or more of the options would invalidate the analysis. Thus, our premise is that these matters can only be adequately addressed when market and non-market transactions are both included within a unified framework that considers them as being alternative modes of exchange, and that provides means of understanding why such alternative modes exist, how they are selected, how they operate and which relations exist between them. In particular, the main contribution of the analytical framework developed in this volume is to suggest a methodology capable of identifying typologies of exchange configurations within market and non-market settings.

In the following chapters we also examine the prevalence of 'segmented' pockets of exchange, with different price levels for similar goods and factors one finds so often in less-developed countries. From numerous case studies, it is clear that there is significantly less integration of exchange configurations in developing countries than in developed countries. Thus, attention will be paid to the differences between formal and informal, and legal and illegal (black) markets and between traditional and modern forms of exchange. An understanding of the functioning of developing economies and of the obstacles and opportunities for economic growth requires insight into the elements underlying the transactions occurring in the developing world.

## 1.3　THE CONCEPT OF 'EXCHANGE CONFIGURATIONS'

The conceptual framework developed here is that of 'exchange configurations'. It allows the tracing back of the form and content of transactions and of the preparatory decision processes to their building blocks. We call these building blocks 'elements of exchange'. They are (1) the *item* exchanged; (2) the *actors* engaged in decisions related to the exchange; and (3) the *environment* – physical, social, technological, legal and political – within which the actors operate. We postulate that the characteristics of these elements, in different combinations, shape distinct types of exchange relations and help explain their operation. We term an entire constellation – consisting of a particular combination of characteristics of elements of exchange, the decision process actors go through, and the resulting transactions – an exchange configuration. Exchange configurations can be thought of as channels through which specific transactions are effectuated (see Box 1.1 for an illustration). Actors, given their own attributes, the properties of the item transacted and the environment they face, will choose to operate in (or will design) that configuration and corresponding transaction that minimizes perceived transaction costs.

Each of the three elements needs to be broken down into an array of characteristics. The *item* at the heart of a transaction can be a commodity (intermediate or final), a service, a labour service, financial fund, land or foreign exchange. Differences in the nature of these items influence the corresponding transactions. In fact, a more detailed, disaggregated distinction is often necessary to capture and reflect real-life transactions and the corresponding exchange configurations within which they originated. For example, agricultural commodities differ in many respects – such as

## BOX 1.1     AN EXAMPLE OF AN EXCHANGE CONFIGURATION

Now let us imagine a concrete situation. A small farmer's household in a Nigerian village has suffered a death in the family and desperately needs to borrow some funds for the funeral rites. In principle, different potential lenders could be approached. In this typical setting the potential lenders are likely to consist of the village branch of a rural bank or a micro-finance institution (both formal lenders) and a number of alternative informal lenders, i.e. professional moneylenders; Rotating Savings and Credit Associations (ROSCAs); traders, shopkeepers and merchants; friends and family.

How would this household decide which source of credit or which lender to approach? The farmer will realize quickly that he is essentially sealed off from formal credit institutions that require collateral and written contracts. This farmer possesses some land but no title. By customary law the land belongs to the village chief who allocates lifetime cultivating rights. Also, because the farmer is illiterate, the thought of a written binding contract is more than he can contemplate.

What about the informal lenders? The farmer has in the past received credit from a trader for a part of his crop to be delivered after harvest time. But the trader will not extend credit on different terms. Most ROSCAs operate in such a way that $N$ members contribute at regular intervals a pre-specified sum $S$ to a cash pool $NS$, which is then allocated to each member in turn until all have received the pool. Even if the farmer is a member of a ROSCA, he cannot count on receiving the pool prior to the funeral. The next alternative is the moneylender. But the interest rate quoted is unusually high even for this group of lenders, because the moneylender is not well acquainted with the farmer and cannot assess his reputation. This leaves the last alternative: 'friends and family'. Lenders from this group know him well and can assess his reputation; they can exercise a high degree of monitoring at virtually no extra costs and exert pressure on him if necessary. Moreover, as in the past the farmer has helped a neighbour and a relative with a loan under similar circumstances, he has a moral claim to reciprocity.

To the farmer a transaction in the latter configuration is the most attractive one among the feasible alternatives. The transaction he concludes is open-ended and has no explicit interest rate, repayment date and written contract.

perishability, uses and continuity of production – from other products. Often such more detailed properties appear to be of crucial importance for the shape of transactions.

Attributes of *actors* consist of preferences and objectives and other attributes, many of which can be used as instruments in pursuing the objectives. For individual actors such instruments include income, wealth, skills, education, social position and information. Other attributes – like age, gender, marital status – do not easily lend themselves for use as instruments, but they have a strong impact on the formation of intra-family transactions, especially in traditional societies. Other types of actors, such as firms and non-profit organizations, are characterized by attributes that differ partly from those of individual actors. Many producers, consumers, traders and investors are market actors; a branch manager of a vertically integrated firm and members of a farm household, operating within a firm and a family, respectively, are examples of non-market actors.

The *environment* is the third element of an exchange configuration. Some characteristics of the environment impose constraints on actors' decisions and their choice of transactions, others offer opportunities or provide protection, and still others combine these functions. Characteristics relating to the legal environment (such as property rights, laws and regulations), behavioural codes inspired by norms and values generally accepted in a given society, and characteristics of the physical environment (soil and climate characteristics as well as infrastructure) all have a direct and indirect impact on actions culminating in transactions. Further, the overall level of development of a region or country, as a determinant of purchasing power and the volumes exchanged, affects the degree of specialization that a market can support. Finally, the available technological shelf acts as a bound on the feasible range of market decisions.

Even this brief, provisional description already suggests that each of the three exchange elements has dozens, if not hundreds, of intrinsic characteristics that may conceivably be relevant for the formation of one or another type of transaction. These large numbers of characteristics and the even larger numbers of possible combinations of characteristics raise the question of whether exchange configurations are a manageable analytical instrument. Another problem to be faced is that many characteristics are not readily quantifiable as they are more qualitative in nature. This is particularly true of some of the dimensions of the environment, such as cultural aspects, the policy and legal framework, and the socio-economic structure. After analyzing both of these crucial issues in detail in this volume, we conclude that an operationally useful number of distinct and manageable exchange configurations can be identified and that the essentially qualitative nature of some of the characteristics of the elements does not present an insurmountable obstacle in defining them.

It must be emphasized at the outset that the exchange-configuration approach is an analytical framework rather than a full-scale theory. An economic theory aims to explain certain economic phenomena in a certain setting by specifying the relations expected to hold among a limited number of selected variables and data. The exchange-configuration approach helps in identifying the crucial characteristics of exchange elements underlying specific transactions and, in so doing, often suggests which theory is particularly appropriate for an explanation of the outcomes. But it is above all an invitation to take a novel look at transactions; to examine what causes transactions to be as they are and to note that the explanation of characteristics of transactions often lies in the details. The exchange-configuration approach offers clues for the identification of the factors that cause undesirable outcomes (be it from a private actor's or from a socio-economic point of view) and for the search for instruments to improve results. It assists in identifying the origins of forces that are capable of altering existing patterns of exchange and in locating the points of impact of these forces. It is also a constant reminder of the overwhelming importance of actors – as decision makers, learners, innovators – in shaping and changing patterns of exchange affecting thereby the state and pace of socio-economic development. It shows why governments, while essential in creating the basic conditions for development, cannot enforce development. Finally, it illustrates the importance of non-economic factors in an economic analysis and confirms once again that economics is a social science.

## 1.4   THE OBJECTIVES OF THIS BOOK

In an era when structural adjustment, privatization, globalization and the world-wide recession are receiving increased emphasis, a more systematic approach to the study of exchange and its impact on development is becoming necessary. This book is intended to provide the tools with which to better understand the nature and variety of the transactions that take place both within and outside of markets.

The approach proposed here is based on the concept of exchange configurations. It postulates that transactions (individual transactions and groups of homogeneous transactions) derive their form and content from the characteristics of only three types of elements of exchange: the item exchanged, the exchange environment and the actors involved in the transactions. Once a framework has been established and the characteristics of the exchange elements have been identified, the relationship between these characteristics and the shape, content and performance of market and non-market transactions can be explored. In sum, the concept of exchange configurations is an attempt to define a systematic, realistic and operational approach to the study of exchange.

A large number of different market and non-market exchange configurations typical of those found in the developing world and covering a wide spectrum of settings including national and regional staple foods markets, rural informal and formal credit, labour, land configurations and family farms are presented and analyzed. In particular, the process through which transactions are formed is scrutinized. The performance of exchange configurations is evaluated and linked to the overall development process. The evolution of exchange systems throughout history is rehearsed and its contribution to socio-economic development highlighted.

While the exchange-configuration approach is a general approach applying to developed and less developed countries alike, the cases discussed in the book relate mostly to the latter group of countries. By specifying distinct real-life exchange configurations and the key characteristics of exchange elements that constitute them, it is possible to state which characteristics are constraining exchange performance and concentrate reform efforts in these areas, and to predict more accurately when certain types of market reform will lead to perverse results. A better understanding of which characteristics of elements are the cause of market rigidity and friction will allow a policy maker to identify institutional or policy changes that could relax these constraints.

In addition, the exchange-configuration approach can shed light on a range of other questions such as: What is the root of differences between exchange configurations in developing and developed countries? How has the evolution of exchange, from community-based, largely non-market configurations in early stages of development to greater reliance on markets at later stages, contributed to development? What accounts for the greater segmentation and fragmentation of exchange configurations in developing countries? What are the most important factors determining the operation of exchange configurations? Do these factors vary for different types of exchanges, or is there one set of determinants that applies more or less universally? Can anything be learned about exchange in one developing country from studies in other developing countries, and from studies related to developed countries? Why do some types of exchange continue to occur outside the market within a firm or a family (such as a farm family) rather than within markets? What are the scope for and limitations of government policies in economic exchange? And, what is the role of economic actors in development processes?

## 1.5   OVERVIEW OF THE FOLLOWING CHAPTERS

Chapter 2 sets out to describe the essence of the exchange-configuration approach. For simplicity of presentation it limits itself to a static interpretation (the time factor is introduced in Chapter 6 and a fully dynamic version is presented in Chapter 7). While the exchange-configuration approach is based on only three elements of exchange (the item exchanged, the actors involved and the exchange environment), the discussion reveals that each of the elements must be divided into subcategories. Subsequently the subcategories need to be represented by a number of meaningful characteristics (or dimensions) in order to be able to explain the properties of the exchange under study. Thus, for example, the item exchanged needs to be specified as a commodity, service or factor of production. Subsequently, the commodity must be identified as an agricultural or an industrial commodity, or as a raw material, intermediate commodity or a consumer or investment good. Finally, the characteristics of the particular item have to be specified. This process of specification of the three elements is fairly straightforward in the great majority of cases, but it requires care and attention to detail as the form and content of the corresponding transactions sometimes appear to depend on rather fine distinctions.

A section of Chapter 2 presents a formal description of the actors' decision-making process. Actors, taking account of the relevant dimensions of the exchange elements, have to decide whether or not to go ahead with a transaction, and, in the first case, have to decide on the form and content of the transaction. The latter decision is strongly influenced by experience with prevailing, similar transactions. But when characteristics of exchange elements change, there may be reasons to deviate from past patterns and design and negotiate for transactions with different form and/or content. The perceived costs of this adaptation process will of course have to be weighed against the expected benefits. This discussion also helps to bring out an exclusive property of actors that sets them clearly apart from the other two elements of exchange: only actors can activate transactions and decide on change. Examples describing the formation of market transactions are based on illustrative cases of primary wheat-market configurations in Pakistan. Another section is devoted to a discussion of the characteristics of the form and content of market and non-market configurations.

The material presented is then used for a comparison of exchange configurations in developing and developed countries. It is shown how typical differences between the dimensions of exchange elements in these two groups of countries translate into different characteristics of market and non-market transactions. Finally, after having considered the strong relations that interconnect different exchange configurations, the findings of this chapter are summarized graphically in Figure 2.2.

Chapter 3 presents terms, concepts and theories selected from various strands of the economics literature which are used in subsequent chapters where the exchange-configuration approach is built step by step. These concepts help to turn exchange configurations into an operationally useful tool in capturing real-life exchange settings. The terms presented are generally familiar to economists and non-economists alike, but it is important to indicate which more specific meaning is attached to them in this book. The concepts and theories presented here have been selected because of their explanatory power with respect to a wide range of crucial aspects of transactions.

Terms like exchange, transactions, contracts and markets are used frequently throughout this book. But, even if the terms are common, their meaning is not always clear. This applies with particular force to 'markets' as a survey of the literature reveals. In our view, market transactions are self-contained, occur relatively frequently and provide information to third parties. Transactions that do not possess these key properties belong to other (exchange) categories than markets. In the discussion of the above-mentioned terms, the consequences of certain complicating aspects are also considered. Thus, for example, when writing about contracts, attention is given to the fact that contracts cannot always be complete and take account of all eventualities due to imperfect foresight.

We use parts of the new institutional economics (NIE) literature as an underpinning of the decision-making processes preceding transactions. Key concepts in this connection are uncertainty and risk as defined by Knight (1921). Uncertainty derives not only from certain states-of-the-world that cannot be predicted and for which the probability distribution of outcomes is unknown, but also from the fact that actors are unable to process all relevant information due to cognitive limitations. As a result actors cannot obtain optimal results. Given this realization, they typically use 'satisficing' behaviour, accepting outcomes that meet certain minimum standards. Uncertainty is a disagreeable and unwelcome phenomenon, not only in connection with transactions. This is why institutions are extremely useful as they help to reduce uncertainty by structuring human behaviour. North distinguishes between formal institutions (shaped and enforced by public authorities) like laws and regulations and informal institutions like customs and traditions.

The purpose of transaction cost economics (TCE), as developed by Williamson, is to explain the existence of alternative modes of organizing transactions. Examples of such modes, or 'governance structures', are markets, firms, hybrids, families and public bureaus. Predictably the main argument of TCE revolves around the concept of transaction costs, that is the costs of preparing, executing and adjusting contracts. Transactions are characterized by the prevalence of different mixes of complicating factors. These complicating factors are uncertainty, asset specificity and frequency, in combination with human characteristics like limited rationality and opportunism. Actors can reduce the impact of these factors, in particular the transactions costs they imply, by placing transactions under the most appropriate governance structure. Thus, there is a certain correspondence between TCE and the exchange-configuration approach. Roughly speaking, the former uses transaction costs to explain alternative aggregate modes of transactions, whereas the latter uses the same concept (next to elements of exchange) to explain the multitude of transactional forms within the aggregate modes.

The last two sections of Chapter 3 introduce dynamic aspects of actors' behaviour. Section 3.4 presents a brief discussion of the structure–conduct–performance (SCP) approach. This approach stipulates that the structure of the market in which firms operate determines the opportunities and limitations firms face regarding their conduct (that is, their tactical and strategic moves) which, in turn, determines their performance. The argument, which is limited to the operation of firms in a market context, can be generalized to fit the exchange-configuration approach. This section illustrates the immense importance of the capacity of actors to learn, evaluate, innovate and decide. Section 3.5 explores this unique capacity in more detail. It shows among others that organizations are in a remarkably good position to learn.

Chapter 4 contains a systematic discussion of the three exchange elements, more particularly of the characteristics of their subgroups and components. In so doing, it illustrates the vital differences between the elements, but it also provides ample opportunity to point at the close connections that sometimes exist between and among elements. For example, labour services, as items exchanged, are closely connected with their suppliers, an actor group. Further, because of this close connection, inherently dangerous work threatens the safety of workers. So governments enact rules and regulations (a component of the exchange environment) to protect workers from hazardous work conditions, another connection between two elements.

The item exchanged appears to be a very powerful determinant of the form and content of transactions. It is not coincidental that markets are traditionally named after the items traded within them. Section 4.3 lists and discusses a great variety of dimensions of subgroups of products, services and factors of production, often accompanied by an explanation of how a particular dimension of an item affects transactions. The variety of items is much too wide to allow an extensive discussion of each. However, an exception is made for credit (as a factor of production) which is examined in some detail. The pivotal characteristics of credit are (1) the lender repays the borrower at a later date, and (2) the borrower is free to transform whatever has been provided in loan. As lenders run considerable risk, they will seek security from borrowers, preferably in the form of material collateral that allows a straightforward value assessment. But the majority of individual borrowers in developing countries cannot offer more than their reputation as collateral. Obviously this type of collateral can be assessed only by those who know the borrowers and who can monitor their actions. As a result we see that each of two categories of borrowers (with and without material collateral) do business with one of two categories of lenders, that is formal credit suppliers like banks (money creating financial intermediaries, subject to registration, regulation and monitoring by monetary authorities and to public-policy measures) and informal lenders like employers, shopkeepers, professional moneylenders and friends and family. In other words, the two well-known characteristics of the item 'credit' appear to differentiate between different actor groups on either side of credit markets and thus to give rise to entirely different (formal and informal) exchange configurations.

The exchange environment typically consists of multiple components. Specific items and actor groups that play a role in certain types of transactions can be identified and singled out through a simple process of disaggregation and their relevant characteristics suggest themselves in most cases without much difficulty. The exchange environment is more unruly in this regard. It is rarely immediately clear without preliminary research which specific properties of the various components may have a significant impact on the transactions under study. Section 4.4 is concerned with a discussion of three clusters of environmental components. The first cluster consists of the cultural, political and legal components. These components define the institutional environment that is meant to structure human behaviour, including behaviour relating to exchange. Their impact on transaction costs and on the pace of development has recently attracted much attention. Secondly, we discuss the physical and technological environment. The rural–urban dichotomy and the extent and quality of the infrastructure figure among the most important aspects of the physical environment. Regarding the technological component it is observed that developing countries have a limited capacity to absorb and apply modern production techniques. The result is that isolated pockets applying state-of-the-art technology co-exist with production units using traditional techniques. The third cluster consists of the socio-economic environment defined mainly by the state of economic development.

Actors are discussed in Section 4.5. Actor groups can be distinguished according to their status and position (such as firms and other organizations, individuals, family members) and to their economic function (such as lenders, borrowers, employers, workers, exporters, importers, consumers, savers, investors). In many cases both distinctions apply. Each actor group evidently plays a different role in exchanges, so it stands to reason that the prominent characteristics also differ with these roles. Still, while the combinations of characteristics differ with the roles, it appears that general categories of characteristics apply to and are relevant in each type of role. We distinguish five such categories of actors' attributes which are discussed in some detail: (1) number, density, institutional and organizational form and bargaining power; (2) assets, liabilities, entitlements and income; (3) objectives, preferences and personal beliefs and attributes; (4) relations and instruments (related to 1 and 2); and (5) information and attitude towards risk and uncertainty.

Actors take a unique position among the elements of exchange. They collect and process information about the relevant dimensions of the three elements of exchange and, if they are satisfied with the form and content, they activate transactions. Transactions depend entirely on this capacity. But there is more. Besides being decision makers actors are also learners and innovators. They can change organizational forms, improve their skills, save, borrow, purchase investment goods, invest time, money and effort in technological progress, and so on. In other words, they can alter certain characteristics of exchange elements in order to improve the outcomes of transactions in which they participate. In short, actors play a crucial, active part in the dynamics of exchange.

The main objective of Chapter 5 is to demonstrate how different combinations of environmental settings, characteristics of items and attributes of actors can be identified which together yield relatively distinct and homogeneous transactions and corresponding exchange configurations. The process required to capture distinctive exchange configurations consists of selecting the most important elements among the large set reviewed in Chapter 4, namely, those that have the greatest discriminatory power and are most strongly associated with other elements – so that they can act as representative proxies for the latter with which they are correlated.

Two key obstacles have to be overcome in this process of deriving a set of representative exchange configurations. The first obstacle is the multi-dimensional nature of many of the elements. For example, actors in their decision-making process are influenced by a whole set of attributes such as income, assets, education, size of household, preferences and degree of risk aversion. In turn, the physical and locational setting within which actors enter into exchange transactions is composed of multiple dimensions. Obviously, for analytical purposes, it is neither possible nor desirable to take on board all of the attributes of actors and dimensions of the environment. Only those elements that are most representative and robust should be selected in capturing a specific exchange setting. A second obstacle is that many of the dimensions and aspects of elements can only be measured in an imperfect way – implying that in a number of cases qualitative or categorical estimates have to be used.

Fortunately both obstacles can be surmounted because of two key properties shared by many elements, namely, that they tend to (1) have non-continuous and often bi-modal distributions, and (2) be highly inter-related. These properties and the fact that it is costly to design new forms of transactions (thereby limiting the number of alternative forms) are crucial in deriving typologies of exchange configurations for different items in different settings.

The main contribution of Chapter 5 is to develop a methodology yielding a number of distinct and operationally useful exchange configurations. Firstly, we argue in Section 5.2 that the number of configurations is limited and therefore manageable. Secondly, in 5.3 we apply the methodology to derive a set of relatively typical product-exchange configurations from seven characteristics of exchange elements reflecting the setting prevailing in the developing world. These different configurations are described including the process through which transactions are determined in each case.

Chapter 6 is devoted to an analysis of exchange configurations at various stages of development and their evolution. An essentially comparative static approach is adopted comparing the typical exchange configurations prevailing during three phases of development (early, middle and mature) and setting the stage for the dynamic approach to the evolution of exchange configurations in Chapter 7. The analysis starts with a discussion of forms of exchange in subsistence-oriented economies – by far the dominant form throughout much of past history. Under the conditions existing in such societies (few means to control the natural environment and extremely high costs of external exchange) a communal approach to production and consumption offered the best chance of survival. Codes of behaviour and traditions that varied with the type of organization (for example based on reciprocity or redistribution) supported intra-communal exchange.

Markets are a relatively modern phenomenon; even today the transition towards market exchange is ongoing in many parts of the world. The origins of the general transition process from barter to market exchange are the subject of much speculation. In fact, market exchange may have developed more or less independently in various places well before physical market places emerged in Lydia and Greece around 500 BC. Similarly, as described in Section 6.3, there are various ways in which market exchange, after having been introduced in a society, can encroach upon community-oriented exchange. Different theories are reviewed speculating on the conditions leading to market transition and the factors contributing to communities switching from community-based to market transactions

A key contemporary issue concerns the decisions taken by individual present-day actors, such as rural households in developing countries, whether or not to participate in market exchange. It appears that several characteristics of exchange elements need to be considered in answering the above question. First of all, a farm household's decision to sell part of its output depends on the magnitude of its marketable surplus which depends, in turn, on household characteristics such as size, age and gender distribution, area of land owned, and access to draft animals. Further, when risks caused by pests, diseases and vagaries of the weather cannot be insured, less efficient production technologies that limit variation in output become more attractive (smallholders select a technology with a lower expected mean but also lower variance). The marketable surplus is reduced further when households do not have access to rural credit. Finally, such characteristics as poor infrastructure, incomplete information and limited competition widen the width of the band between the prices consumers pay and the prices received by farm households. The wider the band, the unlikelier it is that households participate in these markets as their net profits fall accordingly.

Section 6.4 is devoted to an exercise in comparative statics analyzing how changes in the exchange elements affect the form and content of transactions and the corresponding exchange configurations within which they occur. Three broad phases of development are reviewed. On the basis of two main sets composed of a few discriminating and interconnected elements, a number of typical and distinct exchange configurations prevailing in each of these phases could be identified. The first set combines *technology* (a component of the exchange environment) with *form of organization* (a characteristic of actors). Two states are distinguished: modern and traditional. The second set combines *geographical location* (another component of the environment) with *nature of product* (describing the item exchanged). Here a two-level distinction is made between rural and urban on the one hand and agricultural and non-agricultural on the other.

In the early development phase family-farm configurations applying traditional technologies and forms of organizations and operating in a rural, agricultural setting dominate. The distinctive characteristics of the exchange elements and of the ensuing, often inward-looking transactions are summarized in Figure 6.2. Other actors like cottage enterprises and urban firms in the handicrafts also employ traditional technologies. Modern enterprises are relatively rare.

The great majority of present-day developing countries have reached by now the middle development phase displaying a dual–dual structure in which rural and urban and traditional and modern sectors claim significant shares. When examining and comparing the characteristics of exchange elements in the latter two sectors one understands that tensions of a combined economic, social and cultural nature can easily flare up in this phase. Figure 6.3 gives details.

Finally, the mature development phase describes the dimensions of exchange elements of present-day developed countries. The traditional sector has practically vanished. Governments have reached a considerable size as their administrative capacity has increased vastly. Social-security schemes have been introduced, thereby eroding the role of social networks (families, clans, neighbourhoods) for mutual assistance.

The dynamic forces driving exchange figurations, which are only hinted at in earlier chapters, are the exclusive subject of discussion of Chapter 7. They derive their immense importance from the fact that they are also the forces propelling economic development. The number of these forces of change appears to be fairly large; they also differ considerably in terms of origin, nature and impact. So, in order to facilitate the discussion, the first task is to form categories of forces of changes that are homogeneous in origin and nature. We distinguish, for this purpose, between endogenous and exogenous dynamic forces on the one hand, and between intended (or premeditated) and unintended dynamic forces on the other. Endogenous forces emanate from decisions by actors in the exchange configuration(s) under consideration; exogenous forces have a different origin. Intended forces (in contrast with unintended forces) derive from premeditated decisions and acts intended to affect transactions. The four-way distinction that results (see Figure 7.1) is a useful guideline for the ensuing discussion as it yields easily recognizable categories of dynamic forces. They are: (1) actors' strategies and tactics (endogenous and intended); (2) public policies (exogenous and intended); (3) loops or feedbacks in exchange systems (endogenous and unintended); and (4) shocks (exogenous and unintended).

The intended forces of change can be described as the private and public policy measures relating to transactions. From the point of view of the exchange-configuration approach they are more interesting than the other forces. Intended forces are meant to change the transactions' form and/or content. They also reflect dissatisfaction with the outcomes of prevailing transactions which indicates, in turn, that some form of evaluation of these outcomes preceded the private or policy actions. Section 7.3 describes how different groups of policy makers can learn from the evaluation of various types of transactions.

The discussion of actors' strategies and tactics adds a new and vital dimension to the characteristics of the exchange element actors. We argued earlier that actors stand apart from the other elements because only they can breathe life into transactions. Here, we highlight the additional role of actors as learners, transformers and innovators effectuated through the strategic and tactical moves they undertake. Strategic moves in the exchange-configuration approach are defined as the moves that alter aspects of exchange elements; tactical moves take the prevailing exchange elements as given. It follows that strategic moves are especially powerful as they change the rules of the game and create a new transactional setting. Different actors have different instruments at their disposal to implement their strategies and tactics. In particular, firms can draw on a wide array of instruments. Figure 7.3, which presents a selection of instruments, also shows that instruments vary with the type of transactions.

Government policies aimed at transactions are complementary in a number of ways to the measures used by private actors. Thus we see, for example, that the strategic instruments of private actors impact primarily on the exchange elements actors and items exchanged. On the other hand, the instruments of governments affect the environment. The difference in the orientation of actions by private actors vis-à-vis policy measures undertaken by governments derives, of course, from the complementary task of public institutions in market economies. Another extremely important difference relates to the impact on transactions. Governments are indispensable for a proper functioning of market economies and they can wield enormous power, but their influence on transactions is only an indirect one. The final decisions regarding transactions are taken exclusively by actors.

Exchange configurations – especially market-exchange configurations

– affect each other through a variety of loops or feedbacks. The latter form a separate group of forces of change as they are endogenous (they emanate from decisions by actors), but unintentional. Examples are external effects (positive or negative), multiplier effects (idem), the flows of information that markets generate and changes in attitude brought about by the confrontation of segments of the population with alien values as markets expand.

Shocks are exogenous and unintended by nature; they just happen. They are, therefore, less interesting from an analytical point of view than the other dynamic forces. Still, they are not to be overlooked. Some shocks – such as wars, revolutions, natural disasters and demographic developments – have a large-scale, lasting and penetrating effect on many transactions. The effect of micro shocks – like a death in a family, a fire or burglary – can also be dramatic, but is more limited in range.

Chapter 7 ends with a presentation of six historical cases, spanning two millennia, illustrating the dynamics of exchange. The cases include the rise of market places and manors, the commercial revolution, town guilds and commercial and industrial capitalism. The description of these cases demonstrates the great variety of form that dynamic forces can take in the real world and especially also the revolutionizing energy they can unleash. The cases further show how endogenous forces of change grow in importance over time relative to exogenous forces.

Finally, in Chapter 8, we present some selective concluding messages to illustrate a number of aspects of the interdependence between exchange and development and of applications of the exchange-configuration approach. The messages cover the following six themes: (1) the interrelationship between the process of exchange and economic development; (2) the significant differences between the exchange process in poor countries and in rich countries and some characteristics of the exchange process in countries at an early stage of development; (3) economic development and the roles of actors and governments; (4) the vital role of learning in the dynamics of exchange; (5) the contemporary global financial crisis explored within the exchange-configuration approach; and (6) the differences between the exchange-configuration approach and the strict neoclassical framework and its potential contributions to the latter.

## NOTES

1. The UNDP Human Development Index is based on only three, broadly quantifiable variables, viz. income per head, education (as measured by enrolment and adult literacy) and life expectancy.

2. Commons, 1934.
3. Yet even such a basic concept as 'market' lacks a widely accepted definition. We return to this subject in Chapter 3.

# REFERENCES

Commons, J.R. (1934), *Institutional Economics: Its Place in Political Economy*, New York: Macmillan.
Knight, F.H. (1921), *Risk, Uncertainty and Profit*, Boston: Houghton Mifflin.
North, D.C. (1990), *Institutions, Institutional Change and Economics*, Cambridge, UK: Cambridge University Press.

# 2. The concept of exchange configuration

## 2.1 OVERVIEW

This chapter presents a general introduction to the exchange-configuration approach, an approach that is meant to explain how transactions come about and which underlying factors cause the immense variety of transactions that can be observed in the real world. It is a universal approach applying to transactions everywhere, even though in this book particular attention is paid to transactions occurring in developing countries and to the often significant differences between these transactions and those in developed countries. Further, this approach applies not only to market transactions but also to non-market transactions, namely intra-organizational and intra-family transactions.

The exchange-configuration approach is introduced at the outset in order to acquaint the reader with the central theme of the book. Hence, the presentation of background literature and the detailed description of the main terms and concepts to be used are postponed until the next and subsequent chapters.

The next section (2.2) is devoted to describing the three groups of elements of exchange which, in combination, determine the characteristics of transactions. A particular combination of exchange elements, the formation process of ensuing transactions and the characteristics of the transactions themselves form, what we call, an exchange configuration as represented graphically in Figure 2.1. Section 2.3 is concerned with the formation process of market and non-market transactions and pays special attention to the vital role actors play in the shaping of transactions. Section 2.4 is devoted to a discussion of the characteristics of transactions, expressed in terms of form and content, and how these characteristics derive from the elements of exchange and Section 2.5 discusses some differences between exchange configurations in developed and developing countries. Section 2.6 provides an overview of the interrelationship among exchange configurations at the macro-, meso- and micro-levels. Finally, Section 2.7 concludes the chapter by integrating the above material to capture the essence of the exchange-configuration approach.

## 2.2  INTRODUCTION TO THE EXCHANGE-CONFIGURATION CONCEPT

Economic activity is based and relies on transactions. The transaction is adopted here as the basic unit of analysis. Transactions can take any number of forms, within or outside markets. For example, the sale of an automobile by a dealer to an individual and the hiring of an employee by a firm are clearly market transactions. Each involves an explicit contract that the actors are free to enter into or to reject, and each involves a monetary exchange. On the other hand, a commitment within a farm household[1] by one family member to help cultivate the farm in exchange for food and shelter, and the delivery of an intermediate product by one department of a firm to another against some given accounting price, are normally considered to be non-market transactions. The latter transactions are implicit, open-ended and/or non-negotiable and the actors have a limited degree of freedom to enter into transactions with other actors. But, apart from the differences between the categories of market and non-market transactions, there are also major differences among transactions within these categories.

It is quite clear that the formation, form and content of transactions involving, say, a bottle of beer and a luxury liner differ vastly. In the first case, the item changing hands is one of a large number of identical items; it has a relatively low price and a short life span. That type of transaction is a rather casual event and settlement is almost immediate. In the second case, the item is extraordinarily valuable, has been made to order and has taken a considerable time to build, to mention only a few properties. As a result, the transaction is an elaborate affair taking a long time to negotiate and prepare – engaging specialists drawing up a complex, detailed and lengthy contract that aims to take account of a wide variety of eventualities and corresponding safeguards – and bringing along in its trail related transactions having to do with funding and insurance.

It is easy to see that these two sets of transactions differ and why this is so. The distinction is less clear when the items that are being traded are more similar, or even identical. Still, if one buys a bottle of beer in a bar, a club or a supermarket, the transactions tend to differ. Further, the age of the buyer is relevant here, as minors in most countries are not allowed to purchase alcoholic beverages and there are countries where consumption of alcohol is prohibited and the sale and purchase of beer are illegal acts. Apparently, other factors than the nature of the item that is being exchanged also have an impact on the nature of transactions.

Note that the examples discussed above all relate to market transactions.

But, as was emphasized above, transactions occur also in other contexts than the market, such as within the family or the firm. Since these non-market transactions are often used as alternatives to market transactions, they deserve to be considered and analyzed side by side.

What are the factors that shape the nature of market and non-market transactions and through which process do these factors make their impact felt? Answers to these questions are of fundamental importance for two reasons. First, since transactions are at the core of economic systems, a better understanding of their formation and of the underlying causes of their form, content and characteristics has considerable analytical value per se. But it can also enrich existing theories. For example, the literature on transaction cost economics – discussed in detail in Chapter 3 – explains why different categories of transactions occur under different governance structures (defined as that organizational framework that minimizes the transaction costs of exchange).[2] However, when the shaping process of transactions is better understood, it becomes possible to trace back the building blocks of transactions to their governance structures' roots.

Secondly, transactions are the target of a host of government policies. Take market transactions which can be affected by direct as well as indirect policies. Policy instruments such as price regulations and licensing systems have a direct bearing on the content of transactions. Other policy instruments – such as the formulation of contract law, protection of property rights, and investment in infrastructure – have an indirect influence by changing the conditions under which transactions take place. Both types of policies affect the pace of development and the distribution of income and wealth. But government policies are also directed at intra-organizational transactions, for example, in the form of safety regulations, and intra-family transactions regulating rights and duties of family members. In all these cases the effectiveness of policy measures can benefit from increased knowledge and understanding of the factors that promote or impede transactions and determine their shape and content.

There are several ways in which one may attempt to answer the general questions raised above. In this book we adopt a deductive approach by first reasoning out which general factors are likely to determine the decision-making process underlying the choice of transactions and their form and content, relying on available theories and intuition. On the basis of this approach we postulate that the decision-making process and the form and content of transactions, whatever their nature, derive from only three elements of exchange: (1) *the item, or items* exchanged in the transaction under investigation; (2) *the actors* engaged in decisions regarding this transaction; and (3) *the environment* pertinent to the transaction.

### 2.2.1   Elements of Exchange

That only three elements of exchange are needed to explain how all transactions with their enormous variety come about, may seem remarkable. But then it should be added that each of the three elements contains a considerable (and in some cases an innumerable) number of separate characteristics, dimensions, properties and attributes[3] that need to be considered. This subsection gives an overview by way of introduction; a more comprehensive discussion of elements of exchange is presented in Chapter 4.

It is quite obvious that the *item* exchanged is, in the majority of cases, the most powerful determinant of the formation of an exchange. For good reasons market transactions are often grouped according to this criterion, for example when we speak about the labour market, or the agricultural market. In our framework, depending on the transaction under scrutiny, the item can be one in a hierarchical tree of groups ranging from highly aggregate to highly specific. One step down from the all-encompassing group of 'items exchanged', a distinction can be made between goods and services and factors of production. Further, goods may be divided into consumer and investment goods, raw materials and semi-finished products. Still further down this hierarchical classification scheme, consumer goods can be subdivided into luxury goods, basic goods and so on. Careful specification and classification are of great importance for the understanding of any given exchange process and corresponding transaction. For example, when the item is a commodity, it makes a lot of difference if the commodity is or is not valuable, perishable, moveable or highly specific.

Further, in analyses of exchange account must be taken of the *environment* within which exchange processes take place. It should be noted that 'the environment' is a composite entity. Therefore, it cannot be broken down into a tree of groups, as can be done with 'item exchanged' and with 'actors'. Rather, the environment consists of various aspects which, combined, constitute the transactional environment. Each of these specific aspects, however, can be distinguished from others in an operationally meaningful way (for example, the physical, legal, cultural, technological and political aspects) and can be further decomposed. In connection with the physical environment, for example, it is often necessary to specify the rural–urban dichotomy or the specific location, the prevailing infrastructure, climate, and so on. In connection with the legal environment, not only is contract law relevant, but also the judicial system and still other aspects. It is much more difficult to specify the relevant aspects of the exchange environment than it is to indicate the characteristics of the item exchanged. In many cases, the specific nature of the exchange environment appears to be related to the item under consideration.

After having identified the relevant aspects of a given exchange environment the next step consists of the description of the specific characteristics of the sub-elements composing it. For example, important characteristics of the judicial system are its swiftness and fairness and when characterizing the infrastructure relevant for transactions in a village in a developing country, it makes a lot of difference whether the village is connected to main roads, and, if so, whether the connection is a hard surface road and wide enough for lorries to pass. Without preliminary experience, it is not always immediately clear which properties are worthwhile considering. In some instances a pilot study can be of great use.

The third and last element of exchange, consisting of the *actors*, stands out from the other two, because its impact on transactions is two-fold. First, as with the other elements, the characteristics of actors influence the form and content of transactions. Secondly, in an interactive process actors on different sides of a transaction can converge, agree and decide on a set of terms thereby activating the transaction. In that respect they are unique. We briefly consider both aspects.

Actors can be subdivided, as was the case with items exchanged, into various subgroups. The use that is being made of the item exchanged predetermines the relevant subgroups, such as consumers, employers, farmers, traders or investors. These subgroups can, if necessary, be divided still further, until one has reached the specific actor groups which are involved in the actual transactions under investigation.

The characteristics of these actors deserve careful consideration. One such characteristic, in the context of market transactions, is the number of actors within the groups as it is one of the main determinants of the degree of competition on the supply or demand side. Other examples are actors' legal status, material and financial wealth, preferences, level of information, moral standards, reputation, experience, skills and social capital. A specific transaction can undergo the influence not only of the actors directly engaged in this transaction, but also of other, potential transactors.

In terms of decision making we have already noted that only the actors have the capacity to consider the underlying conditions (that is the relevant characteristics of the various elements), to participate in negotiations and adapt the terms of transactions and to decide to proceed with it or not.

The unique and crucial role of actors in shaping and activating transactions will be discussed in more detail in Section 2.3.

Although there is a host of characteristics of exchange elements that can influence transactions in general, it will be shown that only a limited number of them is really needed to capture the essence of specific transactions. Hence, in practice, the number of characteristics to be considered remains manageable. The level of disaggregation of the transaction tends not to have any bearing on the number of characteristics required to explain it. For example, the number of dimensions of elements shaping transactions of marketed rice (the item) in an Indian village (the environment) and involving, say, small farmers and local shopkeepers (the actors) need not be larger than that required to capture world-market transactions of wheat. It is primarily the complexity of the exchange process that determines the number of characteristics that needs to be taken into account.[4]

### 2.2.2   Exchange Configurations

An entire constellation composed of a combination of characteristics of elements, the formation process of ensuing transactions and the resulting set of relatively homogeneous transactions, is termed here an exchange configuration.

The proposition that the formation of each transaction follows from a specific combination of the characteristics of the relevant exchange elements is expressed graphically in a preliminary way in Figure 2.1. In this figure, the ovals at the bottom contain the characteristics of the three elements of exchange that contribute to the shaping of the transaction under investigation. The role of actors in the process of shaping transactions and the relations between the characteristics of transactions and the elements of exchange are introduced in the next section. A more elaborate version will be presented at the end of this chapter.

At this stage the following two points must be emphasized. Firstly, we postulate that the concept underlying exchange configurations applies to market-related transactions as well as to non-market transactions, such as the transactions one finds within firms and within families.[5] The traditional economic literature tends to concentrate on the first-mentioned type. The rationale underlying non-market transactions is explained in the more recent literature on transaction costs and governance structures. This literature shows why, under certain conditions, non-market governance structures like the firm and the family provide attractive frameworks for the shaping of transactions.

Secondly, the relation between elements of exchange and the shaping of

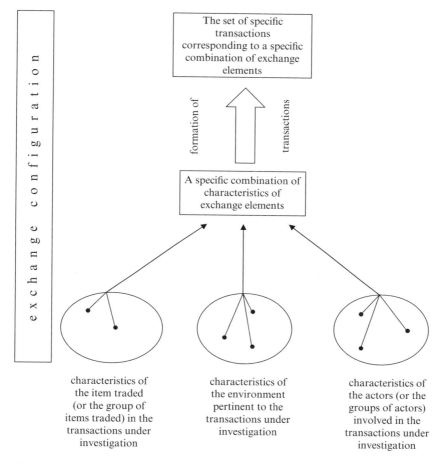

*Figure 2.1   A simple version of a stylized exchange configuration*

transactions is not a deterministic one.[6] As will be seen in the next section, there are several reasons for this. The most important reason has to do with the incomplete knowledge of actors – or, more generally, with their bounded rationality – affecting their decision processes. As discussed in the next section, adjustments to changed conditions may well be only tentative, delayed and incomplete, so the relation between cause and effect gets frayed. Obviously, the fact that exchange elements and transactions are not connected in a deterministic way complicates the testing of our main proposition. Therefore, the plausibility of our argument has to derive to a large extent from examination of case studies of real-world transactions.

## 2.3   THE FORMATION OF TRANSACTIONS

The economics literature contains a wide variety of studies analyzing the formation of specific types of transactions under particular conditions. The exchange-configuration approach, on the other hand, is a general conceptual framework within which all types of economic transactions can be analyzed. This section concentrates on the vital role of actors as decision makers in the formation process of transactions and then discusses the form and content of market, intra-organizational and intra-family transactions.[7]

### 2.3.1   The Role of Actors

According to the exchange-configuration approach the characteristics of the three elements of exchange in a transaction, the item(s) traded, the environment and the actors involved, can explain the properties of that transaction. But how does a combination of elements lead to a transaction? Unlike a cocktail, where it suffices to mix the ingredients, a transaction does not come about simply by the meeting of the relevant elements of exchange. A transaction is generated as a result of the actors' decision-making capacity which enables them to activate transactions. Compared with them, the two other elements are passive. In this respect the role of actors in transactions is the same as that of players in a game.

In short, the parties in a transaction consider, create, decide and execute. The parties, using their experience and knowledge derived from other more or less similar transactions and taking account of the prevailing properties of exchange elements, consider the terms of a possible transaction and adjust them where and whenever possible in their favour in negotiations with their counterparts. Next, they decide whether or not the expected outcome of the transaction is sufficiently attractive to go ahead with it or not. A transaction occurs only when the parties concerned have taken a positive decision, that is, when the actors' expected utility is higher than in the next best alternative. Finally, actors carry out and implement the agreed upon transaction. In case of conflict, still other actions may follow, such as bargaining for a settlement or presenting the case for judgment by others.

In the decision-making process, actors make use of their knowledge of past transactions. This knowledge (unequally distributed among actors) is extremely valuable; without it every transaction would have to be designed anew with all the transaction costs that experimentation necessarily entails. Undoubtedly, exchange would practically come to a standstill if actors were to become ignorant about previous exchanges and were unable to learn from them. In the following paragraphs the connection between past and present transactions will be elaborated, with the qualification that the discussion falls short of a dynamic analysis.[8]

While it is only natural that actors tend to copy major parts of earlier transactions when drawing up new transactions, this does not imply that actors mindlessly copy routines. It may be true that the majority of the actors tend to imitate and simply accept the prevailing forms as given, because they lack the willingness or ability to seek a superior alternative. But there are also actors who, even if they are not genuine utility maximizers, set themselves higher targets than others do. Therefore, a probing of alternative forms of transactions, with marginal changes being tested more often than wider ranging changes, is regularly undertaken by innovative individuals willing to risk undergoing higher transaction costs. Of course, the alternative forms will not always be implemented because, after serious consideration, they do not promise to be worthwhile, or because a counterpart party is unwilling to participate. Only when the experiment appears to provide a superior result by lowering transaction costs, is there reason to expect that the old transaction form will become less common and ultimately be abandoned.[9]

An important consequence of the large-scale copying of earlier transactions by actors is the remarkable continuity of (proto)types of transactions. In symbols this trend can be represented as follows:

$$T^*(\mathbf{M_t}) = f_t\left(I(\mathbf{X_t}), E(\mathbf{Y_t}), A(\mathbf{Z_t})\right) \tag{2.1}$$

$$T^A(m_{1,t}) = T^A(m_{1,t-1}) \text{ or } T^*(m_{1,t}) \text{ if } U(T^*(m_{1,t}))$$
$$> U(T^A(m_{1,t-1})) + C(T^*(m_{1,t}), T^A(m_{1,t-1})) \tag{2.2.1}$$

$$(\ldots)$$

$$T^A(m_{n,t}) = T^A(m_{n,t-1}) \text{ or } T^*(m_{n,t}) \text{ if } U(T^*(m_{n,t}))$$
$$> U(T^A(m_{n,t-1})) + C(T^*(m_{n,t}), T^A(m_{n,t-1})) \tag{2.2.n}$$

where subscript t indicates period t. $T^*(\mathbf{M})$ in Equation (2.1) indicates the make-up and conditions of a transaction represented by vector $\mathbf{M}$. The elements of this vector consist of the characteristics of a given, specific transaction such as quantity, quality, degree of standardization, price, delivery and payment conditions, and whether the transaction is legal or illegal, formal or informal, explicit or open-ended (these characteristics are described in detail in Section 2.4). The vector $\mathbf{M}$ is determined by $I(\mathbf{X})$, the characteristics of the item traded; E(**Y**), the characteristics of the exchange environment; and A(**Z**), the attributes of the actors (potentially) involved in T(**M**), ignoring the costs of adaptation. In reality, the actual form and content of a transaction, however, come about in a process in which the costs of adapting **M** are weighed against the benefits. This is expressed in the equations (2.2.1) to (2.2.n), each of which refers to an element of the vector **M**. The relations indicate that in the formation of the actual transaction $T^A(\mathbf{M}_t)$, actors use earlier transactions in a similar context as a point of departure, but adapt them to the extent that the improved expected utility derived from adjustments in any of the n elements m of vector **M** – that is $U(T^*(m_{i,t})) - U(T^A(m_{i,t-1}))$ – exceeds the cost of adaptation $C(T^*(m_{i,t}), T^A(m_{i,t-1}))$, where i=1. . . n. Since the latter costs are high for many of the n elements of M, the lagged variable tends to contribute most to the explanation of $T^A(\mathbf{M}_t)$. But price, for example, can be altered relatively easily and is therefore subject to frequent adaptation.

It is important to note here that actors are considered to be 'boundedly rational',[10] so they cannot be expected to know the optimal vector $T^O(\mathbf{M}_t)$, that is that specific type of transaction that minimizes the costs given the elements in $\mathbf{X}_t$, $\mathbf{Y}_t$ and $\mathbf{Z}_t$. As a result, adaptations in transactions in accordance with Equation (2.2) will mostly follow a trial-and-error process concentrating on only a few characteristics at a time. And when the search for improvement is successful, it will probably be so only to a limited extent, in the sense that the new transaction's form and content are likely to represent only a local optimum, still remote from the global optimum.

It follows from the above that changes in $T^A(\mathbf{M})$ over time can have different causes. For one thing, the form and content of transactions can change when the dimensions of the elements change, such as in the sale of agricultural produce when a newly constructed road connects a previously isolated community with commercial centres, or in the housing market when a new law thoroughly regulates property rights, or in a traditional industry when a newly developed production technique alters supply and demand patterns. It can safely be predicted that exogenous changes of this kind will have an impact on the form and content of transactions. Other changes result from experimentation within the existing dimensions of the elements of exchange represented by I(**X**), E(**Y**) and A(**Z**). In reality, the two types of changes may be hard to distinguish, for example, when an exogenous change that calls for an adaptation in $T^A(\mathbf{M})$ also triggers an existing, pent-up desire for innovation.

It stands to reason that with drastic shifts in the characteristics of the elements of exchange, such as occur when war breaks out, there is a strong incentive to alter transactions. The previously prevailing type of transaction for an item may then have lost its relevance. But the change in the transaction may be gradual. To use an example from an entirely different sphere: even after such a dramatic event as the introduction of the combustion engine, automobiles for some time looked like horseless carriages. A gradual change is even more likely when the shift is relatively minor. Therefore it is quite possible that, after such a shift, certain features of the original type of transaction can still be discerned in the new one. For example, in restaurants people often use credit cards to pay for their meal while leaving a tip in cash.

### 2.3.2 The Formation of Market Transactions

It needs to be re-emphasized that the shaping process of transactions as described above applies to market as well as non-market transactions. There are two layers to be considered in this regard. First, actors can choose between different governance structures – for example, markets, firms and families – as frameworks for the transactions they consider. Thus, a firm can decide to purchase legal advice and administrative services in the market, or to produce them internally. Similarly, a family can weigh the pros and cons of having its housekeeping tasks taken care of by its members or by a hired outsider. The actual decision depends on a comparison of the transaction costs in the different alternative governance structures. The second layer consists of the formation process of transactions within the selected governance structure. The remaining part of this section is devoted to the second layer of the shaping process. The formation of market transactions will be discussed in the following paragraphs and the formation of non-market transactions in the next subsections.

The variety of market transactions in the real world is bewildering. Hence, if we want to present a description of the formation of concrete market transactions after the general and abstract description in the foregoing pages, we have to be selective. For the present purpose, we concentrate on four cases describing different primary wheat-market transactions in the Punjab of Pakistan during the past decades. These cases are very typical of staple food markets in developing countries and have been chosen accordingly.[11] They will show how two groups of actors (small and large farmers in their role of wheat suppliers) operating in different physical environments (with and without a road connecting their village or fields to a trunk road) show varying decision-making behaviour. Small and large farmers will tend to do business with different groups of wheat buyers and conclude transactions that differ in terms of form and content.

Before we come to the description of the four cases a few introductory remarks are required. Firstly, the item traded (wheat) is the same for all cases discussed. As a result all configurations considered here have several properties in common, such as strong seasonality and bulky volumes. However, as will be seen below, one of its characteristics (the batch size) can differ considerably, with significant consequences for the resulting transactions. The second remark concerns the institutional environment. Wheat being the staple-food product in Pakistan, its economic and political importance is not easily overestimated. Even today wheat production alone contributes almost 6 per cent of GNP and wheat products are a vital part of the daily diet. A good wheat harvest is a boon for the nation as a whole and especially so for those living around subsistence level. Wheat is also much too important to be neglected by policy makers. In fact, the wheat market has been continuously dominated by the guaranteed minimum price offered at public procurement centres on the premise that without intervention private traders would exploit farmers and create artificial scarcity before the new harvest by manipulating the wheat stock. However, the fact that the procurement price was fixed systematically below the world market price indicated that the interests of urban consumers also figured as an important objective. The wheat-price policy had to be supported, of course, by a ban on private international wheat trade.

## Case 1
Small farmers/wheat suppliers living in villages away from the main road system faced some serious problems if, as was generally the case, they did not own camels or donkeys to move their marketable wheat to the nearest road for further transportation. In practice, this meant they had to turn to large landowners or village shopkeepers who would buy their batch before taking care of the transportation. Of course, limited competition among local wheat buyers depressed the price these small farmers obtained. But there were often other complicating factors at play. Many sharecroppers felt obliged to sell their batch to the landowner and, thus, were even more restricted than small landowners in the selection of their counterpart. Further, those farmers who had bought on credit at the local shop during the lean season had reason to sell directly to the shopkeeper.

The transactions in this case were of an informal nature characterized by oral agreement without paperwork. The prices that small farmers obtained were the lowest registered in this stage of the wheat-marketing chain for a number of reasons: limited competition among buyers, high transportation costs and small batch sizes. Payment partly took the form of settlement of a debt with the buyer. Other payment was obtained in cash, sometimes only after considerable time and effort.

**Case 2**

Predictably, compared with the above case, small farmers operating in villages enjoying a direct connection with main roads tended to be better off, because they obtained a higher price due to significantly lower transportation costs, and because they had a wider choice of wheat buyers. They could sell not only to the local shopkeepers and landlords, but, in principle, also to ambulant wheat buyers and a nearby state-procurement agent. In practice, however, the options were still restricted for sharecroppers and indebted suppliers for the reasons indicated above. Remarkably, state procurement was not particularly popular among small farmers for several reasons. Two of these reasons had to do with convenience: transportation had to be arranged for delivery of wheat batches at the procurement centre and revenue could only be cashed at a bank on presentation of a receipt obtained at the centre. The other reason was that the staff at some procurement centres reputedly failed to administer the correct weight of batches offered by small farmers. Ironically, the latter therefore often preferred to deal with the professional wheat buyers who were better trusted, collected batches from the field and paid on the spot.

Transactions in this case showed a somewhat greater variety of form and content than in Case 1, yet continued to involve large landowners and village shopkeepers as buyers. But in the present instance still other transactions of an informal nature were concluded with middlemen who, generally speaking, paid promptly, in addition to transactions with procurement agencies which had a more formal character as they were registered and as payment took the form of a bank claim.

**Case 3**

Even in poorly accessible areas, large farmers owning beasts of burden were clearly better off than their neighbours who depended on others for transportation. They had several options. The simplest option was to offer their own marketable wheat surplus together with the wheat batches they bought from local farmers for sale to professional middlemen. The latter required considerable commercial capital to operate and would therefore not be the same middlemen as those trading with small farmers. Farmers deciding in favour of this option only had to move their batch to the nearest road. The next option was to hire transportation to a procurement centre. It required more effort, but the revenue price would be better. Unlike small suppliers, large farmers, being influential persons, would not be treated unfairly. Finally, they could contact a commission agent and give their batch in consignment at the nearest commercial centre where wheat was collected for further processing – stocking, milling, distribution to bakeries – by private actors.

Large farmers in this configuration had a much better negotiating position than the small suppliers from the same villages. Not only did they have a greater choice of middlemen to trade with, they were also independent of others in order to get access to the market. With higher values at stake, the transactions tended to have a more formal character. Payment was settled frequently through bank transfers. On average, prices were higher in this configuration, if only because the batches were larger. Therefore, farmers who sold their own wheat together with the batches they had bought from small suppliers made a quick profit on their earlier purchases.

**Case 4**
Large farmers with direct access to roads were positioned most favourably compared to all other wheat suppliers considered in the present four cases. Their range of choice among wheat buyers, prices obtained and convenience of payment conditions would at least equal those of the farmers in Case 3. But their transportation costs were considerably less, so their net revenue was higher. Clearly these conditions had effects on the land (lease) market and on other configurations related to the local economy.

The above-described cases are representative of food crop market configurations in many developing countries. They illustrate how certain characteristics of exchange elements shape these configurations. It is particularly noteworthy that the number of characteristics required for an explanation of the differences between the configurations is very small.

**2.3.3    The Formation of Intra-organizational Transactions**

An organization can be seen as a structure allowing an aligning of views of the workers it employs and a focusing of their efforts toward certain goals. Organizations include economic, social, political, religious and educational bodies. Two groups of organizations stand out from the rest because of their overwhelming importance: firms, which are primarily profit-oriented and public institutions, which are meant to provide certain public services.

Organizations have a dual character. This duality is particularly prominent in the context of the exchange-configuration approach. Organizations are, first of all, actors capable of engaging in all sorts of economic activities, including market transactions. But they also provide a structure within which transactions take place which differ from market transactions. In fact, organizations exist precisely because they offer an alternative to market transactions yielding, according to the transaction-cost literature to be discussed in Section 3.3, lower transaction costs. In contrast with market transactions, where actors on either side of the transaction are legal equals, intra-organizational transactions involve actors arranged in hierarchical relations. Organizations are also free, within limits, to formulate their own rules for the formation and execution of their internal transactions.

*Intra-organizational transactions* concern mostly such matters as deliveries from one department (division) to another within the same firm; allocations of assets, benefits and burdens among departments and individual employees; provision of services (such as by the administration and marketing departments); and instructions to department units or individual workers. Also here the nature of the item exchanged (the goods, the benefits or the labour services) will impact on the shaping of the transactions. For example, it makes a difference whether or not the good concerned is valuable, or entails health risks during handling and whether the task is of a routine nature or carries great responsibility. The environment also matters. It is not only the external environment (for example, minimum wage and safety regulations and the impact of trade unions) that makes its influence felt, but also the internal environment, which depends on the rules formulated by the management (for example, the firm's organizational chart and specific rights and obligations of the employees) and on informal codes of conduct. Finally, the characteristics of the actors involved cannot fail to leave their mark on ensuing transactions. In this respect, such traits as skills, work attitude, numbers, experience and, of course, position in the hierarchy are of great importance. They determine who takes the initiative, gives instructions, ascertains results and so on.

For reasons indicated above, there is a strong tendency, also in organizations, to use past transactions as a blueprint for subsequent transactions. But we have to be aware of the fact that intra-organizational transactions, more than market transactions, are susceptible to idiosyncratic developments. One can see this illustrated, for example, when an individually owned firm incorporates, or even when a small firm hires an additional employee. But, next to limiting factors (see Box 2.1), there are other reasons why intra-firm transactions tend to change more frequently than market transactions. One of them is that the costs of adapting internal transactions to changed conditions are often lower than for market transactions. In markets a broad-based familiarity with accepted procedures facilitates exchange among unconnected actors, so changes in procedures cause resistance. This is compounded by the fact that the distribution of information about such changes among the relevant actors is far less easy than in firms. Another reason is that acceptance of tailor-made solutions comes more naturally within a firm whose workers share a certain common interest. Compare this with the shifting, loose relations among

---

## BOX 2.1 INTERNAL LABOUR 'MARKETS'

In their pioneering work, Doeringer and Piore (1971) introduced the concept of the internal labour 'market' as distinct from the external labour market. In the former, pricing and allocation of labour are governed by a set of administrative rules and procedures, whereas they are controlled by economic variables in the latter. The two are interconnected by so-called ports of entry and exit. Rules in the internal labour 'market' do not apply to outsiders. Criteria governing entry are fairly responsive to external market conditions, but lay-offs and promotion are determined by relatively fixed standards of seniority and ability often spelled out in management manuals.

The internal labour 'market' is an analytical construct deriving its utility from the fact that intra-organizational rules relating to allocation of labour, lay-off, hierarchical structure, wages, training, and advancement do not respond freely to variations in outside economic conditions. A change in rules disrupts workers' expectations and behaviour patterns that have developed in past practice and therefore may cause unrest on the work floor.

---

anonymous market actors with their conflicting interests. Consequently, it will be argued in the next section that the form and content of intra-organizational transactions differ from those of market transactions.

### 2.3.4 The Formation of Intra-family Transactions

In *intra-family transactions* the identities of the actors/family members and the durable relations among them make all the difference. The transactions are typically open-ended; they are characterized by give and take, where the benefits may tip to favour one side for extended periods and may, in fact, never be balanced. In other words, the giving and taking are often separated in time such as with the care parents and their children provide and receive during different stages of their lives. They are often also distributed unequally among family members depending on the latter's capacities and dispositions. Intra-family transactions centre around the distribution of domestic chores (for example, housekeeping, shopping, care, collecting firewood, administration) through which family members provide labour services to other members; the distribution among family members of consumption items such as food, lodging, clothing, health care, education and recreation; and the distribution of labour services and assets (for example, buildings, tools, machines, cattle, land) in production activities in or outside of the family.

The dominant item in many of these actions is labour services. Through the internal division of labour, the nature of these services (the physical strength, skill or experience required) often directly determines which family members are best equipped to undertake these tasks and how the transaction is shaped. Comparative advantage and returns to specialization appear to apply also in intra-family transactions.[12] The allocation of food, living quarters and clothes, items that are daily necessities, is largely a routine affair in the context of a family whose members care about each other's welfare and contribute according to their capabilities. This is not necessarily the case when other expenditures, such as on health and education, are allocated. These items are seen more as an investment in the recipient requiring a conscious weighing of the options.

Although the properties of the item exchanged in intra-family transactions play their role in the formation of these transactions, some specific aspects of the other two elements (the actors and the environment) tend to be much more influential. This is inherent to the nature of the family. Firstly, the ties that exist among family members (hard to attain for outsiders and difficult to shed for insiders) accentuate the importance of personal characteristics of the actors in intra-family transactions. Secondly, the family is the prime supporting unit and conduit of moral values across generations in society. As such it seeks to imprint a code of conduct on the young in accordance with the customs, habits and behavioural norms (that is, the informal institutions in North's terminology[13]) of its cultural environment. Clearly, transactions among family members are bound to reflect this influence. In Turkey, for example, many adult educated men hand over their salary to their fathers, who deduct some pocket money and dispose of the rest. Thus, especially in traditional societies, gender and age go a long way in establishing hierarchy, tasks, rights and obligations within the family, down to the way food is distributed among everyone's plates.

Yet, there are other relevant dimensions of elements of exchange that may soften the impact of the cultural environment on intra-family transactions. For example, the effect of wealth, income and education – when these are fairly evenly distributed – can be such that family members do not depend on each other economically and therefore are less stringently tied by mutual rights and obligations. This effect does not apply when only one member prospers and others feel they have a right to share in the benefits. But the most powerful force eroding the code of mutual support of family members derives from a public social-security system. Indeed, in countries where such a system does not (yet) exist, family relations tend to be more strictly embedded. Other environmental properties impacting on intra-family relations and transactions are the location, where especially urban and rural areas often make a great difference, and law, especially family law.

It is self-evident that in families where the behaviour of its members is largely guided by customs and codes of conduct, many transactions simply occur without being decided upon explicitly. Everyone performs the tasks expected of him or her. The shaping process of these transactions took place in the past, and present transactions are mostly determined by tradition. For instance, in many parts of rural Africa women are limited to cultivating domestic food crops and are not supposed to work on cash crops. Still, there are families where conscious, explicit decisions are made without regard for tradition and still more instances where the shaping of transactions is a mixture of these extremes. In the latter cases, generalizations about the formation process do not seem warranted. Depending on tradition and the characters of the participants, the decision-making process and resulting transactions may be anywhere between the extremes of unitary (dictatorial) and collective decision making, allowing different degrees of bargaining by household members. An exception can be made, however, for the important category of intra-family transactions between parents and their underage children in which parents tend to dominate.

## 2.4 CHARACTERISTICS OF TRANSACTIONS

After the brief discussion of the elements of exchange in Subsection 2.2.1 and the description of the formation of transactions in Section 2.3, we now turn to the third and last component of exchange configurations, namely the characteristics of transactions corresponding with $M$ in $T^A(M)$, the dependent variable in Equation (2.2).

The characteristics of transactions relate to form and content. Form has to do with the packaging of the exchange agreement. Content, on the other hand, encompasses in the case of market transactions for example, specifications regarding the item changing hands (type, quantity, quality and so forth) and the price, payment and delivery conditions of the transaction. This is what a large part of traditional microeconomics is concerned with. In the discussion below, the characteristics of transactions relating to content have been separated from those relating to form. But the dividing line between form and content cannot always be drawn very clearly.

It will be seen that many properties of transactions tend to display discontinuous, and sometimes even bimodal or binary distributions. For example, transactions rely on written or verbal contracts, are legal or illegal, are settled in kind or in money. In the following discussion, it will be indicated how various characteristics of contracts are connected with exchange elements. Market, intra-organizational and intra-family transactions will be discussed separately. The reason for this is that there are only few properties that apply to the same degree to all three types. Examples are properties relating to legality and morality. The other properties are prominent for only two types of transactions or are among the defining characteristics of only one type.

### 2.4.1  Market Transactions

The defining property of market transactions is that they are self-contained, that is the relation between the actors ends, in principle, when delivery and compensation have been completed (more on this in Subsection 3.2.1). Many characteristics of market transactions that have to do with content are very familiar. Examples mentioned already above are the quantity, quality, degree of standardization and the price of the item that have been agreed upon among the actors. These characteristics are all directly related to the item exchanged. Other well-known content-related characteristics are delivery and payment conditions. As regards the latter, it is useful to distinguish between payment in money and in kind. Although money is a most useful invention, market transactions that are settled in kind are fairly common when certain conditions prevail, for example, in a weak monetary environment where goods are scarcer than money, such as during periods of hyperinflation. Further, in rural areas of developing countries wages of seasonal agricultural workers are commonly paid in wheat or rice. The rationale in this case is that a large part of income of low-income households is spent on the local staple food. So, direct payment in kind economizes on trade margins. A more complex case of payment in kind is connected with sharecropping, a topic to be discussed at a later stage.

The value involved in a market transaction is an important property, because others often follow from it. One of these is that 'large' transactions are often expressed in elaborate, carefully worded, written contracts specifying courses of action in case of conflict, whereas 'small' transactions are mostly completed in a routine fashion. Thus we see that the content of a transaction can have consequences for its form. Written contracts are often preferred for transactions covering a considerable time span and/or involving uncertainty. The passage of time complicates transactions, but is often an unavoidable aspect of the item traded. This applies a fortiori to all credit transactions. But also with other items time may have to be considered, such as when delivery is inevitably lagged, or when the object must be hauled from a long distance. Uncertainty, another property of a transaction, may well be enhanced by the time aspect, but can also originate from the transactional environment as well as from the opportunistic behaviour of the actors themselves (see Subsection 3.3.1). Personal acquaintance with a potential counterpart can then act as a lubricant for a new market transaction. This attribute of actors is often a prerequisite in credit transactions when debtors cannot offer appropriate collateral. Information about someone's reputation and attitude can of course be gleaned from experience in earlier transactions. The term 'interlocking transactions' is reserved for such cases where an actor's reliability in an earlier transaction gives rise to a new transaction between the same actors. For example, an employer will more readily provide credit to workers who depend on him and whom he has come to know as reliable persons rather than to randomly selected individuals.

Further, a transaction may be legal or illegal, depending on its content. Illegal transactions are explicitly outside of the law and not condoned, and actors involved in them run the risk of being prosecuted. Another very important distinction, especially in the context of developing countries, is the one between formal and informal transactions. Formal transactions are in accordance with pertinent legislation; they are meant to be so designed. Informal transactions, on the other hand, are explicitly or implicitly exempted from a rigorous application of the law. Thus we see, for example, that indirect taxes are not collected on informal transactions, or that, in informal labour transactions, wages under the official minimum-wage level are condoned. The underlying arguments are that it is impossible to collect taxes from actors who are unable to keep books and that strict application of minimum-wage legislation (if at all feasible) would result in still higher unemployment. So informal transactions are mostly (but not exclusively) concentrated in the informal sector where firms are not officially registered, as such, and common accounting practices are unknown. Note, however, that the formal–informal dichotomy differs from the legal–illegal one. Thus, formal transactions can be illegal and informal transactions can be legal.

The last characteristic to be discussed refers to the question whether the transaction is explicit or open-ended with respect to the performances of the actors. A market transaction is typically explicit: the agreement defines the rights transferred and entails a full quid pro quo. But non-market transactions (see below) tend to be open-ended with undetermined aspects allowing adaptation of terms as events develop.

Now we come to the, much less varied, characteristics that relate to the form of market transactions. One such characteristic refers to the way in which the content is expressed: in written or oral form. As we have seen, this form depends often on other properties of transactions. But it should also be mentioned that written contracts require the ability to read and write and are therefore beyond the reach of illiterate actors. When confronted with written contracts drafted by others, illiterate actors often appear to be suspicious and to prefer an oral arrangement. Another characteristic has to do with the design: standard or tailor-made. Clearly, the choice depends on other properties of transactions, such as frequency and the amount involved.

### 2.4.2 Intra-organizational Transactions

Organizations can be private (for profit) firms and private and public non-profit institutions. They have much more flexibility in determining the form and content of internal transactions than if they were engaged in market transactions. In market transactions, individual firms have to accept the influence of their counterparts. But organizations are set up in an essentially hierarchical way, so the higher echelons can at the very least formulate the standards for intra-organizational transactions.

Assuming that organizations do indeed use this capacity in accordance with their individual needs and preferences, one can expect to find a bewildering variety of shapes of intra-organizational transactions. It is here that the exchange-configuration approach can help structure and categorize the specific chosen form and content of intra-organizational transactions. A few general examples are presented in the next paragraphs by way of illustration.

Many intra-organizational transactions, in contrast with market transactions, are characterized by their open-endedness. It applies, for example, to services performed by units such as administrative departments which are supposed to continue their work as before until further notice, or to simple jobs by individual workers who are to report back when the job is done. Organizations can afford to adopt this approach because, with their hierarchical set-up, they can reach an acceptable outcome through observation, correction and deliberation in a durable relation (another typical property of intra-organizational transactions) between principal and agent. The principle of 'learning-by-doing' is largely based on these processes. The advantage of open-ended transactions is that the transactions costs incurred by specifying performance and compensation are low. This is an important argument for those organizations in which many internal transactions are of the above-described nature.

While many task-related, open-ended transactions are formulated in a fairly informal and general way, this is not a general rule. Indeed, under certain conditions one can see that they are described in strictly formal and specific terms, for example, when considerations of hygiene or safety require special care, or when the task involves handling very valuable objects. In the latter cases, the required performance is specified explicitly, but the compensation is not. Note here that the nature of the task or the service (that is, the item exchanged) affects the content of the transaction. Organizations may consider it to be their own responsibility to shape and implement internal transactions that call for special care. But often such care is also required by the external environment, another exchange element, in the form of pertinent legislation.

Other reasons why intra-organizational transactions are drawn up in a formal way have to do with the internal environment, such as the size and nature of the organization. For large organizations, for example, writing out internal transactions is often the only way to keep track of what is going on inside and to make sure that instructions from above reach lower echelons without too much distortion.[14] There are also manufacturing firms that treat deliveries between units administratively much the same as market transactions. Price and other conditions are established through a process containing elements of negotiation and the results are laid down for future reference. Multinational firms may take this approach to considerable length such that the difference with genuine market transactions is hard to see. A different arrangement can sometimes be observed in international intra-firm transactions where internal (typically accounting or shadow) prices are determined hierarchically in such a way that profits are maximized in those countries where tax rates are most favourable. But especially in this case, transactions must be formally administered for subsequent scrutiny by the tax authorities.

Intra-organizational transactions, like market transactions, can be legal or illegal depending on their relation to the legal environment. An example of the latter are the transactions mentioned above where prices are manipulated to derive maximum benefit from international tax arbitration. Other intra-organizational transactions may directly violate regulations regarding waste emission or safety or they may incite illegal conduct. On the other hand, payment conditions will rarely be included in internal transactions and the same applies with even more force to arrangements for conflict resolution because one of the properties of organizations is precisely that conflicts are resolved ultimately by way of hierarchical decisions.

### 2.4.3   Intra-family Transactions

Written transactions among family members are mostly confined to occasions like marriage, divorce, inheritance and major donations. While the items exchanged differ substantially, the common element in these events is that they occur rarely in a lifetime, have a major impact on the lives of individual family members or change intra-family relations. Therefore, they are often drawn up in a formal way in accordance with relevant legislation, possibly sanctioned by the authorities, public or other. An informal, but written transaction other than the ones mentioned above may take the form of a letter in which, for example, a relatively well-off member of the family agrees to lodge, feed and clothe a distant cousin and pay his enrolment fees for the duration of his education.

But the great majority of intra-family transactions is based on a verbal exchange (explicit or implicit) or even on a tacit understanding. This has to do with the items exchanged in these transactions, with the relations among the actors and with the environment within which the transactions take place. Many of the tasks distributed among family members – doing the dishes, walking the dog, mending appliances – are relatively minor and of a routine nature. The transactions connected with such tasks are often open-ended. The same principle also applies to transactions among family members working on a family farm, a subject discussed in more detail especially in Subsection 6.3.2.

When the distribution of tasks has been settled, they form, over time, streams of individual transactions, which are only rarely interrupted or discussed. But even in these simple transactions, the relation among family members may also play a role. Intra-family transactions differ from other transactions, because the family is meant to be concerned with joint welfare, and because the wellbeing of one member affects the wellbeing of the others. In such a context – with lasting relations among a limited number of persons, considerable common objectives, limited conflicting interests and no dissenters – many transactions tend to become implicit. When mutual trust prevails, it is not necessary to write down the content of minor transactions, a consideration that can also apply to more substantial transactions, such as contributing to and spending household income.

Clearly, many families do not conform to this rosy picture. First of all, when family members apply different standards of performance, conflicts can arise. Moreover, family members may doubt the good will of others. Even then, they may engage in transactions with each other without explicit conditions, because doing otherwise would demonstrate a lack of trust with serious repercussions. Not only is the family reputation at stake here; a demonstration of distrust can develop into an open internal conflict and may, at some point, threaten to disrupt family ties. Developments like these are taken seriously in any cultural environment and often trigger off efforts of mediation inside and outside the family.

The misuse of power relations between certain family members – such as among parents and their children and, in some regions, between parents and their daughters-in-law – can result in mental and physical abuse or exploitation. The transactions related to such activities are obviously immoral. Intra-family transactions can be despicable in much the same way as certain market transactions (see Box 4.2). In these cases, family dependency and the protection of family reputation that convention requires tend to contribute to, rather than solve, the problem. Finally, when formal rules are violated, intra-family transactions become illegal.

## 2.5 DIFFERENCES BETWEEN EXCHANGE CONFIGURATIONS IN DEVELOPED AND DEVELOPING COUNTRIES

The structural differences between developed and less developed countries are reflected in the characteristics of exchange elements as they can be observed in these two groups of countries. From this it follows that exchange configurations also display characteristic differences. In this section we discuss a few selected differences for market, intra-organizational and intra-family transactions.

### 2.5.1  Market Transactions

Observation suggests that the degree of competition in markets of manu-factured products is, in general, likely to be lower in developing than in developed countries. Competition can be curtailed by a number of conditions that often prevail in developing countries: a poor physical infrastructure, small markets relative to the optimal scale of production, protective policy measures that seal off domestic markets against foreign competition, discriminating policies favouring certain groups (families, clans) of actors, and unequal access to capital, education and information. It appears that these conditions cannot easily be changed.

On the other hand, competition is fierce in those markets in develop-ing countries where access is easy and potential supply abundant relative to demand. Such conditions typically apply in such important markets as those for unskilled labour and traditionally produced commodities. In other words, the degree of competition in market configurations in developing countries tends to show much greater variation than in developed countries.

Further, markets in developing countries often display considerable frag-mentation, which relates to the occurrence in the same country of distinct exchange configurations for relatively homogeneous items. Various elements of exchange are responsible for this phenomenon. Thus, due to high transportation costs as a result of a poor infrastructure, markets for the same staple food in different areas may be separated. This case occurs, for example, when inhabitants of the port town on the coast are supplied by the world market, whereas the rural population depends on local supply. Also credit markets can be separated, but for an entirely different reason: users of credit without a dependable source of income or material wealth cannot access the formal credit market and must turn to informal lenders, such as professional money lenders, employers, shopkeepers, friends and family members. Finally, direct market-intervention measures, such as price ceilings and demand restrictions, tend to prevent clearance of the official markets concerned such that black markets arise. In developing countries such conditions still apply in significant numbers of markets, especially of foreign exchange, despite liberalization programmes in the past decade.

### 2.5.2  Intra-organizational Transactions

Firms in many developing countries can be divided into different groups according to the type of technology and form of organization (modern vs. traditional) they apply. The latter category, consisting of firms relying on traditional technology and informal forms of organization, abounds in developing countries, whereas it is practically extinct in developed countries. The transactions of firms in this category will be discussed in detail in subsequent chapters; here we only mention some typical traits of their internal transactions. Owners/managers of traditional firms do not keep books. In the majority of cases they are unable to do so, but in other cases they pretend ignorance. So one important characteristic of internal (as well as external) transactions in which traditional firms engage is that they are not recorded. Further, workers' tasks are rarely defined clearly; their content tends to emerge over time. This condition applies especially when the employees are family members who work as apprentices. Finally, since official regulations do not apply, the safety conditions for the workers are often poor and working hours, which tend to vary strongly over time, can regularly exceed the legal maximum by far.

### 2.5.3  Intra-family Transactions

In developing countries certain intra-family transactions are much more prominent than they are in developed countries. One such type of transaction derives from the fact that public social-security systems protecting against loss of income due to illness, old age and so forth, if they exist at all, are not accessible to the majority of the population. The family is the most important alternative insurance arrangement meant to provide a certain degree of protection. Thus, family members are under a strong moral obligation to help their needy, even distant, relatives. At the same time they can turn to their relatives, if the need arises. The give-and-take in the transactions on which this arrangement is based may, of course, be very uneven when comparing individual family members, but for the family as a whole it is perfectly balanced.

Further, compared with developed countries, members of families in developing countries are much more frequently engaged in production-related transactions with other members, especially in agriculture. Capital being very scarce in the developing world, the labour-to-land ratio in agricultural production is relatively high there. Land-owning families can hire labour in the rural labour markets or they can use family labour. But hired workers must be monitored more closely than family members who have a direct interest in farm output, so farming families display a strong preference for family labour.

## 2.6   INTERRELATIONS AMONG EXCHANGE CONFIGURATIONS

Exchange configurations are interconnected in a number of ways. On the macroeconomic level, factor (labour, land and intermediate inputs) market transactions are interrelated with product market transactions through the circular flow of income. Firstly, the demand for factors is directly derived from the demand for products. Secondly, the factorial income distribution generates a household income distribution which, in turn, determines the demand for products. The first link, from products to factors, can be readily identified and empirically described. The second link, however, is more diffused, working itself through the whole economic system often via a large number of different market and non-market exchange configurations, which jointly affect the factorial and household income distributions, and, through them, the demand for products.

A useful conceptual and data system to help capture these and other interrelationships of an economy-wide nature is the Social Accounting System (SAM). The SAM is a comprehensive, disaggregated and consistent system that incorporates a wide variety of transactions among actors. Of special relevance in the present context is that the classification scheme used in the SAM can take account of many of the important dimensions of exchange elements, that is, characteristics of the factor or product exchanged, of the environment and of socio-economic attributes of the actors. The various socio-economic groups appearing in the SAM can be broken down according to different indicators, yielding relatively homogeneous groups of actors (for a detailed discussion of the SAM concept see Pyatt and Thorbecke, 1976).

The SAM can also be very helpful in bringing out the segmentation resulting from the prevailing dualism in many developing countries. Thus, for example, it can be examined whether the mapping of value added generated by production activities to production factors takes a block-diagonal form. Such a form will materialize when particular production activities – say, traditional agriculture and modern manufacturing – stand out as users of particular production factors – say, unskilled and skilled labour, respectively. It should also be noted that, to some extent, the mapping from the factorial to the household income distribution in developing countries may display a similar block-diagonal pattern as certain socio-economic groups rely on specific factorial sources of income.

Note that in the above-mentioned cases the links between exchange configurations are established by the aggregate flows of goods and factors of production circulating in an economy and by the economic exchanges between nations. But it is important to realize that behind these volumes are the decisions by actor groups operating in different configurations in different capacities. For example, actors who are producers/sellers in one configuration exert demand for labour, credit, imported raw materials and so on in other configurations. In these ways levels of activity and such qualitative factors as the prevailing views and expectations of actors are transmitted among configurations at the macro-level.

In addition to the structural, macroeconomic links among exchange configurations there are other links on a lower level of aggregation. Meso-level links exist, for example, between market transactions of similar, respectively, complementary items. The sign and magnitude of the cross elasticity of demand for pairs of goods indicate the type and degree of interconnection among products. For example, the area of land allocated to the production of an agricultural product – and, thereby, its volume of production – may well be affected by the price of another product.

Links of another nature can even exist between transactions involving identical goods that nevertheless belong in different configurations. Such cases can arise when markets are not allowed to clear, for example, when the distribution among users is based on a licensing (rationing) scheme rather than on the equilibrium price to be paid. Users unable to satisfy their demand in the official, licensed market and willing to pay a higher price may attempt to find additional supply elsewhere in what necessarily is an illegal or black market. The item traded in these markets is the same, but the legal environments obviously differ, so we have different configurations. But supply and demand in the two configurations are closely interconnected. Supply in the black market will be larger, the more attractive it is in comparison with the conditions in the official market, but the flow thus diverted is at the expense of supply in the official market. Further, demand in the black market depends on the unsatisfied, or excess demand prevailing in the official market. Even the volume of demand in the official market, constrained as it is by the volume of official supply, is indirectly connected with conditions prevailing in the illegal market.

Connections between market configurations such as those mentioned above tend to be well studied, more so than connections between market and non-market configurations. The latter type is especially important for developing countries. For example, intra-family transactions of cereals, so important on small family farms in these countries, are linked with the nearby cereal markets. Decisions by farm households regarding the quantity to produce and the allocation of total output between own consumption and marketable surplus take into account the market conditions. The marketed surplus, in turn, becomes a part of supply flowing into the food market.

The connection between so-called interlocked transactions is established even on the micro-level. The connecting exchange element in this case is the identity of individual actors, which is of special relevance in credit transactions where the debtor cannot provide other collateral than his reputation. Thus it can be observed that an actor who has established his reliability in one or more non-credit transactions is accepted more readily as a borrower in a credit transaction. In fact, share tenancy contracts[15] can be particularly strong catalysts for subsequent credit transactions, because sharecroppers have an incentive to remain on the site at least until the harvest has been reaped. Further, if the credit is provided by the landowner, the latter can rather easily secure repayment, when the harvest is divided between owner and tenant.

## 2.7   AN EXTENDED SYSTEM

Following the above discussion, we have a reached a stage where a bird's eye view can be presented of the approach proposed in this book. The point of departure for this exercise is the graphical representation of a simple version of an exchange configuration, as given in Figure 2.1. The extensions are summarized in Figure 2.2.

Obviously, the core of our argument – which is that the form and content of transactions are shaped by the underlying characteristics of exchange elements – is unchanged. But, firstly, it must now be underlined that many of the characteristics of elements of exchange are interconnected. As will be seen subsequently this consideration simplifies the analysis. In Figure 2.2, the interconnections have been represented by the arrows between the three ovals containing the exchange elements. For example, certain products, such as agricultural and mining products, are directly connected with the physical environment. Such a direct link also exists between labour as the item traded and the actors offering their labour services. Still other links occur between the environment and actors, for example through culture, or, vice versa, through the impact of actors' behaviour on the quality of soil, water and air. More examples are given in the detailed discussion of exchange elements in Chapter 4.

Secondly, we draw attention to the influence that actors' experience with past transactions has on the formation of new transactions. Past transactions have obtained their form in past configurations, but they have a forward effect because, as postulated in Subsection 2.3.1, they are a valuable part of the stock of experience of present-day actors. Past transactions act as a drift anchor for new transactions and facilitate the latter's formation immensely. The arrows connecting past with present transactions and present with future transactions in Figure 2.2 express the strong link between them. It must be emphasized that, despite the introduction of different time periods, the argument, at this stage, is still essentially of a static nature. A dynamic version and extension of the exchange-configuration approach, discussing the various dynamic forces that move exchange configurations from one state to the next, will be presented in Chapter 7.

The third extension concerns the unique and fundamental role that actors play as decision makers in the formation of transactions as described in Subsection 2.3.1. Actors, when considering the form and content of new transactions, take into account the relevant properties of exchange elements and, thus, establish the link between elements of exchange on the one hand and the shape of transactions on the other. It is only appropriate that the description of the role of actors/decision makers occupies the central position in Figure 2.2.

Fourthly, the box that has been drawn in Figure 2.2 on the left-hand side of the bold vertical boundary line indicates the 'other exchange configurations' that make their influence felt on the exchange configuration considered here. Of course, the latter may in its turn have a similar influence on these other configurations. This extension reflects the discussion in Section 2.6.

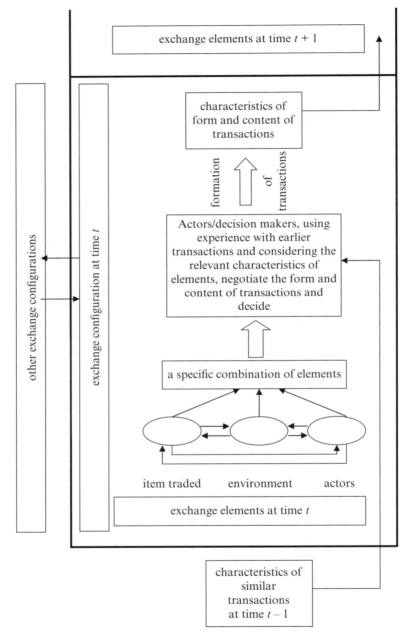

*Figure 2.2    An extended version of a stylized exchange configuration*

# NOTES

1. In developing countries, in particular, the farm household is typically a producing and consuming unit within which many virtual transactions occur.
2. Markets, firms and family enterprises and farms are examples of alternative governance structures.
3. We use the terms dimensions and properties as synonyms to characteristics throughout the book.
4. Readers familiar with the sociological literature will note a superficial similarity between the exchange-configuration approach and Boudon's theory of social change (Boudon, 1981). According to the latter theory social change can be explained on the basis of three groups of elements. The central element is the system of social interaction (or the interdependent system) consisting of categories of actors characterized by individual and relational variables. The second element is the environment including institutional, economic and historic variables. The third element consists of outcomes, such as events and distributions. The feedback from the outcomes on the environment and/or the system of interaction leads to different types of social change as Boudon illustrates with various empirical developments. But social change can derive also from exogenous developments, such as technological innovation. Some of the terms used in the two approaches – 'elements', 'actors', 'environment' – are indeed identical. But the concepts, arguments, relations and purpose clearly differ.
5. The question of whether still other types of transactions, such as political transactions, can also be explained by the exchange-configuration approach has not been considered in this book.
6. In Elster's terminology the exchange-configuration approach can therefore be seen as a 'method', that is '[a] frequently occurring and easily recognizable causal pattern [. . .] that [is] triggered under generally unknown conditions or with indeterminate consequences' (Elster, 2009, p. 23).
7. The rationales for market and non-market transactions will be discussed in Chapter 3. The following quote from Newbury (1989) serves as an introduction:

   An organized market is a particular type of institution for facilitating the exchange of goods and services via a medium of exchange (money). [. . .] In reality, [. . .] the potential gains from trade on a particular market may not be large enough to justify the emergence of an organized market. Even when the gains are sufficient, it may not be possible for the marketing agent to capture a sufficient fraction to cover his operating costs, and again the market will fail to emerge. In such cases alternative arrangements may be able to provide similar services at lower cost. A restaurant is a market for meals, but a family may be able to provide similar services with lower transaction costs.

8. A full discussion of the dynamics of exchange configurations specifying the various dynamic forces that move exchange configurations from one state to another will be presented in Chapter 7.
9. The strength of market transactions is precisely that such information will spread quickly and widely, especially when the transactions concerned are characterized by a high frequency.
10. For a discussion of bounded rationality, see Subsection 3.2.2.
11. The cases are based on Cornelisse, 1984 and Cornelisse and Naqvi, 1987, 1989.
12. See Fafchamps and Quisumbing, 2003.
13. For example in North, 1990.
14. But it should be added that the inclination for or against a formal approach can also be strongly influenced by elements of national culture, as Hofstede's well-known studies have shown. See Hofstede, 1980.
15. Sharecropping is discussed in Box 4.7.

# REFERENCES

Boudon, R. (1981), *The Logic of Social Action: An Introduction to Social Analysis*, London: Routledge.

Cornelisse, P.A. (1984), 'Wheat market flows in the Punjab', *The Pakistan Development Review*, **23** (1), 65–79.

Cornelisse, P.A. and S.N.H. Naqvi (1987), *The Wheat-Marketing Activity in Pakistan*, Islamabad: P.I.D.E.

Cornelisse, P.A. and S.N.H. Naqvi (1989), 'An appraisal of wheat-market policy in Pakistan', *World Development*, **17** (3), 409–419.

Doeringer, P.B. and M.J. Piore (1971), *Internal Labor Markets and Manpower Analysis*, Lexington, MA: Heath.

Elster, J. (2009), 'Excessive ambitions', *Capitalism and Society*, **4** (2), 1–30.

Fafchamps, M. and A.R. Quisumbing (2003), 'Social roles, human capital and the intra-household division of labor: evidence from Pakistan', *Oxford Economic Papers*, **55** (1), 36–80.

Hofstede, G. (1980), *Culture's Consequences: International Differences in Work-related Values*, London: Russell Sage.

Newbery, D.M. (1989), 'Agricultural institutions for insurance and stabilization', Chapter 14 in P. Bardhan (ed.) *The Economic Theory of Agrarian Institutions*, Oxford: Clarendon Press, pp. 267–296.

North, D.C. (1990), *Institutions, Institutional Change and Economic Performance*, Cambridge, MA: Cambridge University Press.

Pyatt, G. and E. Thorbecke (1976), *Planning Techniques for a Better Future*, Geneva: International Labour Office.

# 3. Terms and concepts for an analysis of exchange

## 3.1 OVERVIEW

As indicated in Chapter 2, this book revolves around the proposition that the characteristics of any transaction are rooted in only three groups of basic elements. These groups consist of the *item* that is being exchanged, the *environment* in which the transaction occurs and the *actors* involved in the transaction, respectively. The purpose of the present chapter is to indicate how this approach to transactions is connected with the existing literature. It describes the concepts developed by other authors that will be used here. It also reviews the meaning attached to terms like exchange, transactions and markets that are continuously used in this study.

Section 3.2 provides a discussion of a variety of terms and concepts derived from the body of literature that has become known as the new institutional economics (NIE). Section 3.3 contains a selective outline of transaction cost economics (TCE), a rapidly expanding branch of NIE. TCE argues that transactions with different characteristics are placed under different governance structures in order to economize on transaction costs. In more than one respect TCE complements our own approach as outlined in Chapter 2. Where TCE is concerned with the justification of the main governance structures within which transactions occur – such as markets, firms, families and public bureaus – our approach goes further in aiming to identify the specific exchange configuration and resulting transactions that obtain given the specific nature of the elements that prevail in the setting under consideration. Further, in order to set the stage for evaluating the performance of exchange configurations, concepts from the structure–conduct–performance literature are reviewed in Section 3.4. Finally, Section 3.5 discusses individual and organizational learning processes, without which exchange and development cannot proceed.

## 3.2   TERMS AND CONCEPTS DERIVED FROM INSTITUTIONAL ECONOMICS

As the name suggests, NIE is concerned with the role of institutions in society. It defines the nature of institutions and attempts to unveil the latters' effects on individual and group behaviour, especially on their economic dimension. It also pays explicit attention to the nature of transactions and to economic decision making by imperfectly informed actors with cognitive limitations.

The NIE literature has contributed much to an understanding of the impact of the (institutional) environment and of (actors') economic decision-making processes on real-world transactions. It has done so by incorporating important facts of life, such as decision making under uncertainty and bounded rationality, which had long been ignored in other branches of the economics literature.

Several terms and concepts used in our work originate from the NIE literature. The NIE is based, among others, on the assumption of methodological individualism and as such complements and enriches the neoclassical paradigm. Some recent additions to mainstream economics, such as game theory and the theories of collective action and of behaviour under asymmetric information, reject the assumption of perfect information that is characteristic of neoclassical economics. As a result, it can be argued that big chunks of NIE have become an integral part of mainstream economics.

### 3.2.1   The Process of Exchange

**Exchange**
Exchange is a prerequisite for economic development. It promotes productivity improvements, directly, by allowing specialization, the exploitation of comparative advantages and the reaping of economies of scale and, indirectly, by making available for use in production a wide range of inputs and tools produced elsewhere, technologies designed elsewhere and assets owned by others. Obviously, the process of exchange itself has been furthered immensely by the invention of money.

The term exchange has several meanings, some of which are very remote from the meaning attached to it by economists. Here we concentrate on the kind of exchange where something of value (that is, a scarce item) is exchanged for another scarce item. Items in economic exchange are used for a variety of economic purposes such as consumption, investment and production or the generation of income. So, apart from some brief remarks in Section 6.2, we shall ignore the exchange of 'gifts' (a subject dear to the heart of cultural anthropologists) even though the gifts concerned may be valuable and gift-giving may help in building a social network. Neither do we incorporate political transactions – in which, for example, votes are exchanged for political favors – in the exchange-configuration approach.

The term 'exchange' is used in this volume as an umbrella term encompassing all sorts of transactions (see below). While it is a useful concept for analysis at an aggregate level, it is necessary to move to a more disaggregated level of analysis to see how exchange is carried on in the real world and to understand the reasons why there is need for specificity. Following Commons, the basic unit of analysis or the ultimate unit of activity adopted in this book is a transaction (Commons, 1934, p. 58).

### Transactions and transaction activities

Since Commons' early writings on institutional economics the view that transactions are essentially concerned with the transfer of rights of ownership has become widely accepted. Therefore, legal and cultural aspects of transactions are considered increasingly in the economic literature in addition to purely economic aspects. The term 'transactions' will be used in this book in a general sense to indicate various forms of agreements among willing owners in which ownership rights are transferred. In turn, the term 'contract' is used to cover transactions based on explicit agreements as discussed below.

Further, we use the term 'transaction activities' to indicate such activities as the search process (for information, potential counterparts and so forth), the negotiations, the formulation of the terms and the selection of the form of the agreement, the execution of the agreement and the handling of possible differences between transacting parties. This approach is prompted by our proposition that all the above-mentioned transaction activities undergo the influence of the three groups of elements of exchange.

Commons distinguished three different types of transactions, namely bargaining, managerial and rationing transactions.[1] In bargaining transactions rights of ownership are transferred against payments or future performances on mutually agreed upon terms by legal, but not necessarily economic, equals. A more common term for this group of transactions is 'market transactions' (see below). A managerial transaction, on the other hand, grows out of a relation between a legal superior – who may be an individual, or a hierarchy of individuals – and a legal inferior, such as exists in labour relations in firms and in government organizations. A relationship of command and obedience in an employment relation must be preceded by a bargaining transaction between the same actors in which they are legal equals. But within the ensuing employment relation (the actual managerial transaction), the employee transfers his right to determine where and how to apply his efforts. Finally, rationing transactions are the result of negotiations among several participants who have the authority to apportion the benefits and burdens to members of a joint enterprise. Commons reserved the term for such decisions as boards of directors take when determining their corporations' dividend policy.

When we deal in this book with bargaining transactions – or, our preferred term, market transactions – we concentrate on transactions between individual actors and between individual actors and firms. Bargaining transactions among firms are not considered in much detail here in order to limit the scope of the study. Managerial transactions are discussed among others in connection with TCE (in Subsection 3.3.2) and with intra-organizational transactions in the formal and informal sectors. Rationing transactions share some common properties with transactions in the context of the family as a governance structure. But, although Commons suggested that the three general types he distinguished are all-encompassing we will argue that the type of transactions one finds within families does not fit well into his taxonomy and that, therefore, family transactions warrant a class of their own.

Market transactions can differ enormously in terms of content and form. They include the simple everyday transactions that everyone is familiar with as well as the complex transactions involving the future transfer of highly valuable assets from one enterprise to another. They are concerned with the transfer of property rights, that is the alienable rights to use, to appropriate returns and to change the form or substance, where it must be underlined that the transfer is made voluntarily between partners of legally equal status. Of course their economic status and therefore their bargaining power may differ greatly with the result that the benefits of transactions may be distributed very unevenly and possibly, depending on the criterion one applies, even unjustly. Still, since actors decide voluntarily and have the opportunity to forego the transaction, they must expect that the transactions they engage in are superior to the next best alternatives.

It is clear that the ease with which market transactions can be concluded depends to a great extent on how property rights are defined and protected and how their transfer is arranged. Transactors have conflicting interests: both want as much as possible in return for as little as possible. Thus, in an environment of insecure property rights, transactors have an additional reason to beware of unwanted actions by their counterparts. Matters like trust, confidence, credibility, identity and safeguards become all the more important under these conditions.[2] One way to limit uncertainty in transactions is to do business with people who are considered trustworthy, such as relatives, friends and clansmen. It also follows that in a cultural environment where reliability is highly valued and promoted, and where deviations from the norm bring considerable social cost to the violator, transactions can be set up at lower cost than in a different environment. Norms of behaviour are included among the group of elements of exchange we call 'environment'.

In addition to the possible security derived from societal norms of behaviour, transactors can profit from another element of 'environment', that is the laws defining among others property rights and their transfer. The advantage of the formal protection of property rights from the point of view of an injured party is that it is less noncommittal and more binding than norms of behaviour and that transgression can be corrected in court through legal recourse. Still, as will be seen, the protection provided by legal structures has several limitations that have to do not only with their formulation and enforcement, but also with the various costs of having to rely on legality.

**Contracts**
The terms 'contracts' and 'transactions' are sometimes used interchangeably, but this custom will not be adopted here. Specifically, contracts are considered to stipulate which rights are transferred under which terms. The term will be reserved for a sub-group of transactions consisting of explicit agreements about the rights and obligations involved, in contrast to transactions which may also have an open-ended nature.

Contracts provide an additional way to limit the risk and uncertainty involved in transactions by specifying the terms of the agreement. They may do so in two ways. Firstly, the clearer and the more comprehensive the contents (or the conditions) of a contract are, the more security they provide to the parties about the mutual obligations in the transaction. Secondly, the form (or the make-up) of a contract is relevant in this respect. For obvious reasons, a written contract is more secure than an oral contract, and the more so when ambiguities about the legal interpretation are prevented by using appropriate constructions and formulations.

For a long time economists have been interested primarily in a very limited part of the content of contracts: price and quantity only. In reality, of course, contracts often contain information about the item exchanged and the concomitant ownership transferred such as the obligations of each party, the payment conditions, and how eventual conflicts would be resolved. Indeed, the prices and quantities of economic textbooks are highly stylized and incomplete representations of the contents of real contracts.

Contracts can come in many forms. As mentioned above, a contract can be settled in oral or written terms, but under certain conditions even a nod, a wink or a gesture suffices. An oral contract can be satisfactory for simple transactions involving relatively small amounts. But, in communities where few people can read or write, oral contracts dominate by necessity. For more complex transactions spanning considerable time periods, written contracts are preferred. However, except perhaps for simple transactions, it is practically impossible to draft at reasonable cost complete contracts (sometimes also called classical contracts) that take account of all eventualities. For one thing, this has to do with the efforts and costs involved in describing all relevant eventualities and formulating the required responses of the contractors to each of these. For another, and more importantly, due to their bounded rationality[3] actors are unable to foresee all eventualities. Thus, when actors are boundedly rational (as will be assumed here), contracts cannot be fully contingent in the Arrow-Debreu sense.

This limited capacity to foresee can have a major impact on the outcome of a transaction. Still, even if an unforeseen eventuality occurs, it is quite conceivable that the parties to the contract subsequently work out a fair adaptation that takes account of the new situation. In that case the fact that a contract is incomplete is not very serious. On the contrary, it is then entirely rational in terms of cost-efficiency not to deal in advance with all contingencies, but to tackle them if and when they materialize.

But contractors can afford to adopt such an easygoing attitude only if, at the time of signing the contract, it is certain that both sides will be prepared to cooperate in an eventual modification even if it means that some of the parties are thereby made worse off. Generally speaking, this is an unrealistic assumption. Thus the incompleteness of contracts is to be taken seriously after all. Stronger still, contractors have to consider the possibility that the other parties are not trustworthy right from the start. Or, in Williamson's terminology, they have to beware of opportunistic behaviour.[4]

Under certain conditions opportunism can indeed be a severely complicating factor in negotiations. Fortunately, such conditions are not the rule. As experiments by Axelrod and others have shown, a cooperative attitude towards other transactors may well develop and eventually come to dominate simply because this appears to be a successful strategy (Axelrod, 1984). For such a situation to come about, it is important that contacts between actors not be limited to a definite number and that retaliation follows provocation.

Finally, it should be noted that even high-quality judicial systems can rarely pronounce judgment swiftly and at low costs to the contractors in case of disagreements about the execution of contracts. Therefore contracts, in addition to specifying the terms of the actual transfer, may include descriptions and conditions of arbitration procedures aiming at settling possible disagreements.

## Markets

If there is one fundamental concept that is continuously used in the economic literature and still is relatively underdeveloped theoretically and rarely defined when applied, it is probably 'markets'. For example, Tirole having noted in a leading textbook on industrial organization that 'the notion of a market is by no means simple' concludes after a discussion of different market definitions: 'For the purposes of this book the empirical difficulty of defining a market will be ignored. It will be assumed that the market is well defined' (Tirole, 1988). Box 3.1 gives an impression of the general and often vaguely formulated properties of markets mentioned in the literature. In most publications dealing with markets, no effort is even made to explicitly indicate the meaning attached to the term. Hence, there is a special need to clarify how we look at markets in this book. Specifically, the relation between market and non-market transactions will be outlined as well as the criteria by which one market is distinguished from another.

In this book market transactions are defined as bargaining transactions (see above) that possess a few additional properties. One of these properties is that each 'transaction entails a full quid pro quo, and there is no left-over business or outstanding balance' (Ben-Porath, 1980, p. 4). This implies that each market transaction is self-contained. Even when the execution of the transaction spans a period of time, such as in a loan transaction, the terms cover all obligations required of the transacting parties. This is not the case in non-market transactions, such as those within firms and families where transactions are more open-ended, allowing adaptation of terms in the course of time.

Apart from being bargaining transactions with full quid pro quo, market transactions, in our view, must also have properties connected with frequency of occurrence and spillover of information. In definitions of markets in the literature these properties are mentioned only rarely. But an essential property of markets is that the transactions they encompass undergo the influence of other transactions as information about the latter's form and content is used in subsequent negotiations among transacting parties. This requires that some minimum of information about transactions in a market must permeate to other agents and that transactions must be concluded with some minimum frequency.

Further, we distinguish one market from another by requiring that the transactions that are grouped in one market show a certain degree of similarity. This is a purposely unrefined and even imprecise formulation.

## BOX 3.1   MARKETS GALORE

When going through the literature we found over a hundred definitions of markets. Examples of properties (re)appearing in definitions are:

- a place (not necessarily physical) where buyers are in contact with sellers;
- any context/area in which exchange takes place;
- a place/aggregate/organization where prices are formed;
- a place where goods are exchanged for money;
- a place where buying and selling occurs;
- a group of buyers and sellers affecting the terms of one another's transactions;
- a process actuated by the interplay of various individuals;
- a set of transactions;
- a place where the fundamental forces of supply and demand meet;
- a social institution which facilitates exchange.

Different definitions of markets emphasize different aspects, as the above list illustrates. Indeed, the variety of interpretations derives to a large extent from the fact that most authors consider only a few specific aspects of markets and adjust their interpretation of the term accordingly. Therefore, one definition is not always superior to another. In general parlance the market often refers to the physical market place where goods are actually bought and sold. In textbooks, on the other hand, students are introduced to the abstract interpretation of the meeting of demand and supply. Further, legal approaches often concentrate on aspects that express market power and the possible misuse of it. Marketing experts are concerned only with the very specific markets where their products and those of their competitors are bought and sold. And, finally, policy analysts are concerned mostly with rather broadly defined markets, as they consider the impact of policy instruments that may improve the functioning of these markets. For each of these uses one interpretation is often quite appropriate, while it may not be suitable in another context.

It is deliberately imprecise in order to allow a variable degree of precision and a variable set of criteria, tailored to the specific market context under investigation (see Box 3.1). In any case, the item traded (say, labour or automobiles in studies of aggregate goods or factors, or university-trained technical labour or convertibles in more disaggregated studies) and the specific region under consideration will appear among the determining criteria identifying a given market.

### 3.2.2 The Decision-making Process

It is generally agreed that uncertainty is an undesirable phenomenon. As a result all societies have made attempts at containing it by establishing layers of ordering, often called institutions (to be discussed briefly in the next subsection). Still, even though many of these institutions are highly effective, in the real world uncertainty can never be eliminated even under the best of circumstances. Thus, it is a fact of life that decisions – including decisions regarding transactions – must be taken under uncertainty.

It follows that institutions are an important aspect of the exchange environment, one of the three elements of exchange. Institutions influence transactions in two ways. Firstly, the rules embodied in institutions have a direct impact on the behaviour of actors and on the shape of transactions. And, secondly, the extent and effectiveness of the rules determine, together with other factors, the remaining uncertainty that actors still have to cope with.

Several approaches to uncertainty have been developed in the past century.[5] Here we shall use the view developed by Knight (1921) that distinguishes between uncertainty and risk. Knight defines risk as a situation where the result of an action is not known, but where the probability distribution of outcomes is known, such that the expected outcome can be calculated. Uncertainty, on the other hand, applies when the probability distribution is not known, so expected outcomes cannot be calculated. This type of uncertainty is called genuine, fundamental or Knightian uncertainty.

Uncertainty can have different causes. One has to do with states-of-the-world that cannot be predicted, such as with political developments and military and other conflicts. An extreme form of such uncertainty occurred in transition economies directly after the collapse of communism, when the old political, economic and legal order had been destroyed, but when it was still unclear how this void was going to be filled (van de Mortel, 2000, p. 16). Another cause relates to the impossibility of knowing the plans and strategies of other decision makers. This type of uncertainty derives not only from limited communication and information. There is also a prickly edge to it, because decision makers must take account of the fact that they may be consciously misled by competing decision makers and by their counterparts in mutual transactions (the consequences of this 'opportunistic behaviour' are discussed in more detail in Subsection 3.3.1).

Since risk in the Knightian sense is calculable, it is less of a concern than uncertainty. One can, in principle, obtain protection against risk from insurance companies[6] or through various self-help arrangements. Therefore Knight claimed that risk, unlike uncertainty, offers no opportunities for profit-making. This is indeed true if all actors are risk-neutral. But in reality some are risk averters in the sense that they prefer to obtain a payment of a certain amount over a drawing right on a probability distribution that yields an expected payment of the same magnitude. Risk lovers (who have the opposite preference) and risk-neutral persons can enter into profitable transactions with them. Clearly, the attitude towards risk is a relevant trait of the group of elements of exchange labelled 'actors'.

Now suppose for a moment that we live in a vastly simplified world subject to risk, but not to uncertainty. Even then it cannot be realistically assumed that decision makers are able to assess exactly the probability distribution of outcomes of their actions and compute correctly the expected outcome of their actions because of the limitations of the human mind. In this connection, Simon introduced the term 'bounded rationality', that is the inability to process all relevant information due to 'the cognitive limitations of the decision maker – limitations of both knowledge and computational capacity' (Simon, 1987, p. 266). Since there are strong indications that bounded rationality is an important factor in economic decisions we incorporate this concept in the exchange-configuration approach.[7]

Obviously, if we allow for uncertainty the problems that decision makers actually face are even more complex. This fact of life has important consequences for the outcomes of economic decisions, for, as Tintner (1941) demonstrated, achieving maximum profits or utility under uncertainty is not possible except by accident.

North argues that, in order to cope with a world of Knightian uncertainty, people rely on a tool, called mental models. These mental models are systems structuring the available information, thereby helping to interpret the surrounding world. Depending on the amount of information available, a model may deviate more or less from what goes on in the real world. In this regard, learning[8] is seen as the processing of new information that conforms to the mental model. In other words, mental models filter the information derived from experiences (North, 1994, p. 364).

Furthermore decision makers often use simple shortcuts to arrive at decisions in a complex environment. For example, people may apply rules of thumb that have led to reasonably satisfactory outcomes in the past, or they may follow the example of other decision makers who have some authority and credibility because of successful decisions made on earlier occasions. When decision makers search for better outcomes, they will often proceed by way of trial and error where expected benefits and costs will determine the extent of the search. When the costs are considerable, the range of considerations they can investigate is bound to be limited. In that case, when a superior outcome is found, it is likely to be a local rather than a global optimum. In turn, when a local optimum is adopted and used as a starting point for subsequent investigations of a limited number of considerations, the optimal solution may well be overlooked. It also follows that such heuristic dynamic processes are characterized by path dependence.[9]

Another key question is what decision makers aim for. The position taken in this book is that not all decision makers are totally selfish, but that they care to different degrees for the welfare of others. In other words, the goals of decisions extend beyond the narrow utility of the decision maker alone. Therefore, they weigh the impact their decisions have on others. This consideration is of particular importance in our discussion of transactions within a family-type exchange configuration such as the family farm.

The upshot of this brief discussion is the following: When considering the behavior of actors deciding on transactions there are good reasons to step away from the highly restrictive neoclassical assumptions regarding the behavior of *Homo economicus*. Instead we recognize that actors' decisions are necessarily flawed due to human limitations and uncertainty and we allow for considerations that transcend purely individual utility and individual transactions.

Uncertainty and bounded rationality, each by itself, prohibit the reaching of unique, optimal results. Therefore this conclusion must hold even more strongly in the real world where both occur simultaneously. This explains why decision makers show 'satisficing' rather than optimizing behaviour in the sense that they accept outcomes that at least meet certain minimum thresholds.

### 3.2.3   Institutions

Several authors, among them Adam Smith, have recognized that a long process of disciplining preceded the rise of markets.[10] In this connection, Hodgson, discussing the precedence of norms and rules, states that 'Markets are not an institution-free beginning' (Hodgson, 1998, p. 182). North emphasizes the importance of institutions as a reaction to uncertainty, thereby facilitating exchange. Institutions structure human behaviour by providing a framework for cooperation and, thus, reduce uncertainty. This is reflected in his definition of institutions as any form of constraint that human beings devise to shape human interaction. Two types of institutions are distinguished, that is formal and informal institutions.

Political and economic rules are examples of formal institutions:

> Political rules broadly define the hierarchical structure of the polity, its basic decision structure, and the explicit characteristics of agenda control. Economic rules define property rights, that is the bundle of rights over the use and the income to be derived from property and the ability to alienate an asset or a resource. (North, 1990, p. 47)

These institutions are the result of a political bargaining process in which various parties participate. Understandably, they reflect the views and the relative bargaining strength of these parties.

It should be clear that compliance with these rules is not to be taken for granted. After all, formal institutions constrain human behaviour. Most people would agree that full compliance with the rules is entirely desirable because it makes other people's behaviour more predictable and thus limits uncertainty and even physical danger. At the same time individuals regularly make exceptions if it benefits them. Hence, enforcement of formal rules is required; without it the rules become ineffective. Because of the strong external effects involved in rule-abiding behaviour, enforcement is typically a public sector's task.

North insists that institutions may be inefficient and still persist (ibid. p. 93). One reason is that it may be in the interest of decision-making groups to maintain the status quo, regardless of the ensuing inefficiency. So, as long as they are able to prolong this situation, an adaptation will be avoided. Further, due to Knightian uncertainty, it may be unclear if or why inefficiency exists. Until relevant information is forthcoming, corrective measures cannot be undertaken. A third reason has to do with what is called 'lock-in'. The decisions that individuals reach will be influenced by the prevailing institutional framework, as will decisions regarding innovations and learning processes. In fact, once these decisions are made, it is in the interest of the actors concerned that the institutions be maintained.

Informal institutions also constrain human behaviour, but, unlike formal institutions as defined above, they are normally not shaped and enforced by public authorities. Customs, conventions and traditions that influence and guide individual behaviour, belong to informal institutions and so do collectively held norms and values. The latter are part of what we call culture. Williamson refers to informal institutions as the social-embeddedness level.

---

### BOX 3.2   INSTITUTIONS AND NEOCLASSICAL THEORY

Formal and informal institutions provide numerous layers of ordering and thereby create a world in which uncertainty is significantly muted as compared with a world without institutions. Ironically, the existence of institutions, ignored by neoclassical economists, allows them to disregard uncertainty and still make sense.

---

Formal and informal institutions are often closely interconnected. In a democratic society formal institutions are created by representatives of the people whose norms and values they supposedly share and reflect. Hence, one would expect the two types of institutions to be in harmony with each other. Such a situation has a number of advantages. One of them is that enforcement of formal rules is much facilitated. But such an outcome is not guaranteed. Different susceptibility to change – formal institutions can change more rapidly than informal institutions – may be a cause for disharmony. The norms and values of a society tend to be very stable. This relative constancy contributes to a degree of continuity in history, linking the past with the present and the future, and 'provides us with a key to explaining the path of historical change' (North, 1990, p. 6).

When examining an economic phenomenon, it is often helpful to consider the conditions in the past and their influence on developments that have led to the present situation. The term development path summarizes this idea that the present is shaped by the past. From this is derived the term path dependence which describes the notion that processes of economic decision making are linked through time. Still, we should be aware that development paths cannot be predicted with precision and that path dependence is not a deterministic concept. In North's words, the past does not neatly predict the future.

Institutions clearly follow a dynamic of their own. Applying game theory and using evidence from historical cases, Greif (2006) presents a system in which institutions[11] evolve in reaction to internal and external forces. We recognize the impact of changing institutions on the shape and content of transactions. However, we mostly treat changes in institutions as given exogenously in the exchange-configuration approach.

Finally, we draw attention to the kind of rules that apply within organizations, such as those discussed in Subsection 2.3.3 on the formation of intra-organizational transactions, and in markets and families. Also these rules are meant to structure human behaviour, but they differ in a number of ways from the institutions defined by North (1990). Public authorities are not involved in their formulation and enforcement, so they do not belong to the category of formal institutions. But neither are they tantamount to informal institutions like conventions and customs and values. So, in order to distinguish them from North's institutions, they are referred to in the literature as institutional arrangements.[12] The impact of these rules on transactions can be very strong. There is more about these arrangements in Subsection 3.3.2.

## 3.3    TRANSACTION COST ECONOMICS

### 3.3.1    Introduction

TCE is a branch of NIE inspired by an observation by Coase (1937) and others that markets and firms should be considered as alternative modes for organizing transactions. A relevant question then is according to which criterion one such mode is adopted rather than the other. Coase suggested that transaction costs play a decisive role in the selection process.

But it was mostly Williamson who, in a series of publications, developed a coherent theory of TCE (Williamson, 1975, 1979, 1985, 1996, 2000). He identified the properties of transactions that complicate the negotiation process and that, thereby, determine which problem-solving organizational mode (governance structure) is selected. He also provided the analytical connection between specific combinations of these properties and the preferred mode. This matching procedure lies at the heart of TCE. The theory has contributed much to an understanding of different types of transactions and of the governance structure (market, firm or other) within which decision makers position their transactions. It has also shown that the firm should not be seen merely as a production function, but especially as an organizational mode selected to minimize transaction costs that arise in certain contractual situations.

It should be underlined that TCE, by its nature, is mostly concerned with relatively complex transactions generating considerable transaction costs. These are transactions that often cannot easily come about in a market setting and therefore lead to the use of alternative modes of governance, such as firms, hybrids and families. The following discussion of TCE is a selective one.

Economic man in NIE, and therefore also in TCE, differs from his colleague in neoclassical economics in that his rationality is bounded. In

## BOX 3.3   TRANSACTION COSTS

Transaction costs in TCE are defined primarily with a view to explaining the use of different modes of contractual governance. They include '. . . the ex ante costs of drafting, negotiating and safeguarding an agreement and, more especially, the ex post costs of maladaptation and adjustment that arise when contract execution is misaligned as a result of gaps, errors, omissions and unanticipated disturbances' (Williamson, 1996, p. 379).

Simon's words, he is intendedly rational, but only limitedly so (Simon, 1957, p. xxiv). His cognitive ability is restricted, so he cannot know all the facts, and his limited computational ability does not allow him to figure out all relevant outcomes. Further, even apart from his own limitations, he lives in a world of uncertainty.

But Williamson introduced into TCE an additional complication relating to human behaviour, namely opportunism, or self-interest-seeking with guile. It implies that economic man in TCE (in contrast to economic man in neoclassical economics and in NIE) has explicitly lost his virginity. The neoclassical *Homo economicus* will not lie, because in a world where everyone is fully informed that does not pay off. To economic man in NIE, on the other hand, lying may pay off, because his boundedly rational fellowmen may well be deceived. But it is in TCE that such opportunistic behaviour is explicitly recognized as an important part of human nature that needs to be incorporated in an analytical framework. The reason is that opportunism is considered to be an essential factor contributing to transaction costs.

More specifically 'opportunism refers to the incomplete or distorted disclosure of information, especially to calculated efforts to mislead, distort, disguise, obfuscate, or otherwise confuse' (Williamson, 1985, p. 47). In other words, opportunistic behaviour drastically extends the nature of uncertainty. Without it, boundedly rational economic man already faces grave decision problems due to his limited abilities and the uncertain states of the world. But being aware of opportunism, he must also take account of the possibility that the information he has obtained may be contaminated through conscious manipulation and strategic behaviour by the people he is dealing with. Such a situation corresponds with the well-known concept of asymmetric information.

This *uncertainty* is one of the three characteristics of transactions giving rise to the contractual problems that, according to the theory of TCE, can explain why transactions occur in different organizational settings. The other two are *asset specificity* and *frequency* of transactions.

*Asset specificity* has to do with the investments underlying a transaction. It refers to 'durable investments that are undertaken in support of particular transactions, the opportunity cost of which investments is much lower in best alternative uses or by alternative users should the transaction be prematurely terminated' (Williamson, 1985, p. 55). The specificity can refer to customized physical assets, but, for example, also to human assets in the form of specialized training, or to assets installed at a specific site (Williamson, 1996, pp. 59 and 105). The impact of transaction-specific assets on a transaction is not hard to see: in such situations the parties in the transaction are virtually bound together. As soon as the specific investments are made the parties concerned are locked in and lose easy exit opportunities. Obviously, it is in the interest of the supplier to complete the transaction, because by definition the investments already made have the best chances of coming to fruition within this particular contract. But the buyer is also bound. First of all, he stands to profit from the specific investment and, further, when he turns his back on the other party in a transaction characterized by asset specificity, his reputation will be tainted, such that new negotiations with other suppliers will be especially costly.

Thus, with asset specificity, a mutual dependency arises. But, in a situation of dependency opportunistic behaviour pays off, so both parties may end up haggling continuously over the execution of the transaction. Therefore, transaction costs can become a major concern under these conditions, to such an extent that a specialized governance arrangement, such as a firm, becomes attractive.

*Frequency* is the third characteristic to be mentioned here. By itself it does not create transactional problems. On the contrary, frequent transactions generate much and widespread information on market conditions and allow regular adaptation to changed circumstances. A high frequency, however, is problematic in the presence of the other two problem-causing characteristics (uncertainty and asset specificity). In that case it exacerbates the existing high transaction costs and strengthens the desire to avert it.

### 3.3.2 Governance Structures

**The basic concept**
TCE is concerned with the problem of high transaction costs that arise from complicating characteristics of transactions, namely uncertainty, asset specificity and frequency, in combination with certain characteristics

of human beings, namely bounded rationality and opportunistic behaviour. The central thesis of TCE is that decision makers attempt to reduce these transaction costs by bringing transactions within appropriate organizational frameworks. In other words, the latter, called governance structures, are selected on the basis of their problem-solving capacity, while keeping in mind the costs they involve. They are defined as frameworks 'within which the integrity of a contractual relation is decided' (Williamson, 1985, p. 41) and they are the result of 'an effort to craft order, thereby to mitigate conflict and realize mutual gains' (Williamson, 2000, p. 599). Various types of governance structures, namely markets, firms, hybrids, public bureaus and families, are distinguished.[13] They are briefly outlined below.

*Markets*   Markets are the organizational mode within which relatively simple transactions take place. These are the transactions scoring low on asset specificity and uncertainty. They are often based on past experience of the transacting parties themselves and require only standardized arrangements. They may or may not use written contracts, but even in the latter case the contracts are non-specific and settlement is either practically instantaneous or strictly regulated. Their relative simplicity allows the typical quid pro quo character of market transactions (see the text on markets in Subsection 3.2.1).

The ordering in markets derives in the first instance from competition which creates an incentive for parties to behave responsibly, the more so when the conditions fostering cooperative behaviour apply. Further, market contracts have a short-term nature and this limits the number of potential complications during the lifetime of these contracts. Of course, enduring relations may develop between market parties, but they are based on successive short-term transactions. Changing conditions can be incorporated relatively easily in subsequent contracts, so procedures for adjustments to such changes are not required. Still, when a conflict arises, the market as such does not provide means for settlement, so the only recourse left is court ordering outside the market. This is another important characteristic of markets as a mode of governance.

*Firms*   But suppose now that a transaction scores high on asset specificity. This characteristic, in combination with bounded rationality and opportunism, gives rise to the complications described in Subsection 3.3.1. In the first instance, market parties may try to tackle the problem by drafting a comprehensive contract. But the contract is bound to be incomplete as the contractors are constrained by their bounded rationality and uncertainty. So there tends to be room for different interpretations of the contract, which is all the more harmful when it is used opportunistically. Market governance is not likely to be able to defuse such conflicts satisfactorily. A settlement can only be reached through courts of justice which are not well-informed on product technicalities and branch customs, and may therefore come up with unexpected outcomes for both sides. These may be reasons for the parties concerned to look out for an alternative governance structure. The direction they take will depend largely on the frequency of the transaction.

As indicated above, the contractual problem caused by uncertainty and asset specificity is acute and needs to be settled urgently when transactions are characterized by high frequency. An obvious option is to bring the transaction under a firm, thus providing a hierarchical governance within which disputes can be solved by a person who derives the necessary authority from his position in the firm.[14] This is why labour is often employed and why machines and equipment are often purchased by a firm rather than hired from outside. Such solutions provide considerable flexibility as all foreseeable eventualities do not have to be described precisely and hedged against. Moreover, when dealing with unforeseen complications, there is room for sequential adaptations. But this solution does not come without costs, for firms must be administered and employees be monitored and bureaucratic structures have limitations of their own. Obviously, these costs must be weighed against the benefits.

*Hybrids*  On the other hand, when frequency is low, the problem of high transaction costs is less pressing. The chances are that the costs of a specialized governance structure cannot be recouped. So, under these conditions the decision regarding the governance structure will rarely be radical and far-reaching. It may consist of adding to the contract a clause arranging for arbitration in case of a conflict. In addition parties may have recourse to so-called safeguards so as to signal a willingness to cooperate (a credible commitment prior to the transaction), such as the promise of early payment when the order is confirmed and therefore before the delivery is made. But penalties may also be specified. Such governance arrangements – introducing their own conflict-solving approach of arbitration strengthened by commitments and threats, but stopping short of hierarchical solutions – are called hybrids (Williamson, 1998, pp. 38 and 39 and Speklé, 2001).

*Public Bureaus*  Public bureaus are seen as 'the organization form of the last resort' when 'for probity or political reasons the government chooses to manage the transaction itself' (Williamson, 2000, pp. 603 and 604). This governance structure is a rather special one, restricted as it is to particular

transactions involving a government. It will only be used when even regulations do not provide a satisfactory solution.

*Families*   Families have also been recognized as a governance structure. They have been brought forward as such in a systematic way by
Ben-Porath and Pollak (see Ben-Porath, 1980, Pollak, 1985), but in the
transaction costs literature much less attention has been paid to them
than to other governance structures, like markets, firms and hybrids
(see Williamson, 1992). However, we discuss families in their capacity of
governance structures in some detail below because of their special significance in developing countries.

The family in its role as a governance structure is characterized by the
fact that identity matters and relations are often durable. Family members
know each other's strengths and weaknesses and take an interest in each
other's wellbeing, so activities undertaken in the context of a family can
profit from reduced transaction costs connected with incentives, monitoring, altruism and loyalty. These are the reasons why the family has been so
successful in this role for such a long time and under such widely differing
conditions. But it also has some disadvantages. These relate to conflicts
that may extend from the emotional to the economic sphere and vice
versa, a permissive attitude towards slack performance, an inadequate
match between capacities of family members and requirements and size
limitations.[15] Families can operate as governance structure in developed
as well as in developing countries, but they are clearly more important
in developing countries for reasons to be indicated below. But first the
concept of transactions within a family must be clarified.

Many transactions among family members take the form of what
Commons called rationing transactions. These are the transactions with
which parents (as a collective of legal superiors) apportion benefits and
burdens among their underage children (the legal inferiors). Other transactions between family members may well be called managerial transactions when, for example in a family firm, they are based on employment
relations in which one person is the legal superior and his relative the legal
inferior. Even though, within families, both types of transactions are often
coloured by affective relations, the classification still applies.

This is not the case however with respect to transactions among
members of a family who are legal equals. These are the transactions in
which members of a family (or an extended family) offer their land, funds
or labour services in a joint production, or share in the joint provision
or consumption of services, food and lodging. To bring these transactions under Commons' bargaining transactions would require excessive

stretching of the definition. The main reason is that, what we call, family transactions are in most cases about intentions and therefore tend to be implicit (that is, without an outspoken agreement), imprecise and open-ended.

Family members can afford to accept this vagueness of terms because they are part of a select group with special interpersonal relations based on affection and intimate knowledge of personal characteristics. The interpersonal relations form a first layer of ordering for intra-family trans-actions. Another layer consists of the customary rights and obligations prevailing among members of a family and the awareness of the costs of non-compliance with these informal rules. If parties acknowledge and accept the informal rules there is less need for transactions to be precise. For example, children may take care of their elderly parents while living in the parental house and expecting to inherit it, perhaps without ever having discussed the agreement.

A related argument why (intra-)family transactions deserve to be distinguished from market transactions is the following. Unlike market transactions, the potential number of counterparts in family transactions is very limited. As families go, neither entry nor exit is easy. So there is little or no room for competition between suppliers and users in family transactions and the same applies for bargaining.

### The family as a governance structure in the developing world

The TCE literature has very little to say about the family as a governance structure. On the other hand, in the development economics literature the family has been studied in great detail given the enormous importance of small and subsistence farmers in the developing world. Hence, the first set of intra-family transactions to be discussed here are those within the family farm, easily the main mode of organization of production in agriculture worldwide.[16] Two aspects are considered: the reasons why the family mode of organization tends to dominate other modes, and the nature of the transactions that occur within that mode.

In many farming tasks the skill, effort or care applied have a significant bearing on the size and quality of the harvest and the quality of the land. A similar argument applies to the treatment of cattle, draft animals and so on. But it is very difficult and costly, except, for example, in harvesting, to monitor the efforts of individual hired workers, so there is considerable advantage in using instead the labour of family members who have incentives to perform well. The incentives may be intangible, such as loyalty towards relatives or establishing a favourable reputation in family circles, or other, such as a share in current output or in the accumulated wealth.

The items supplied in these transactions are primarily labour services, land and the use of draft animals or implements. The rewards are characteristically much less clear, although family workers may be paid the going wage rate. But in the other cases, compensation can take the form of food and lodging and care when sick, promises of a counterpart share in output or accumulated wealth or the expectation that the favour will be returned at some future date. Obviously, the flexibility of these compensation arrangements, possible only among persons who trust each other, is another advantage of intra-family transactions.

**The family as a provider of social security**
Especially in low-income countries, the family also plays a major role in countering the risks of missing income due to unemployment, illness and disability. These are the types of risks that cannot be insured with private insurance companies (see Box 3.4). In high-income countries the problem of missing insurance markets is met through various forms of public intervention. The expenditures involved in these schemes reach levels between

---

## BOX 3.4   MISSING INSURANCE MARKETS

Individuals who estimate that they are prone to the risk of losing income due to, for example, unemployment and disability are likely to opt for an insurance policy, while others who do not expect to run much risk will be less eager to do so. Therefore, insurance companies that base their premium calculations on the average risk for the entire population will not be profitable. But when they use a higher risk profile and fix the price of insurance policies accordingly, individuals with 'good risks' will become even more reluctant to buy a policy. This is the adverse selection argument. But there is also the moral hazard problem. Thus, individuals protected by an insurance policy against, for example, unemployment may feel less pressed to find a new source of income when they lose their job than if they had no such insurance. This behavioural change induced by the insurance also necessitates a rise in the premium level with, again, the danger that those who are less likely to react in this way will not insure themselves. Such problems can be avoided if insurance companies can discriminate between the good and the bad risks and fix their premiums accordingly. But opportunistic behaviour of the insured prevents such a simple solution. Private insurance companies will not provide coverage against these risks.

10 and 20 per cent of GDP illustrating the immense importance attached to the insurance against these risks. In low-income countries, however, the tax-raising and administrative capacity of the public sector is too limited to allow such elaborate schemes. The result is that, for lack of alternatives, the risks concerned have to be absorbed mostly within families by providing support to those relatives who lack other means. This type of support has a nearly obligatory nature, embedded as it is in cultural norms that are strictly imposed as they form the basis of the (private) social-security system. It may well extend to relatives in the third and fourth degree. Possible conflicts in the family governance may be resolved by elders or by other members occupying a position of authority.

The family has several advantages with respect to these transactions in terms of transaction costs. One is that insiders facing relatively small risks cannot escape and outsiders facing relatively large risks cannot join, so the adverse selection problem is mitigated. Another advantage is that the moral hazard problem can be contained, because the behaviour of family members can be closely monitored such that possible profiteering can be observed and countered. But there are also some structural disadvantages for the family as a provider of insurance. The first is that the size may well be too small for a balanced distribution of risk. As a result, those family members with a relatively high absorptive capacity may suffer severe losses of disposable income and privacy. In fact, this prospect may be a reason for them to forgo opportunities for material improvement. Secondly, blatant misuse of the system may have to be accepted to avoid tension among relatives.

While it is clear that pure intra-family transactions (open-ended transactions between legal equals) differ from pure market transactions, there is a grey area where the two overlap. These are the transactions in which the actors are all connected to each other by family ties, but the terms are fairly well-defined and take account of the going market conditions. The difference with market transactions, however, lies in the softness of the terms or in the reaction of the injured party when the execution is incomplete. Loans afforded to relatives are such an example. There may be a gift element in the terms of the loan, an expression of the (expected) loyalty or affection among family members. Or the creditor may not insist on full and punctual repayment in accordance with the agreement, again as a gift, or because the promise of future repayment by a trusted relative is accepted. It is this softness and somewhat open-ended nature of the transaction, rather than the debtor's reputation that characterizes the difference with market transactions.

### 3.3.3 Governance Structures in Relation to Exchange Configurations

Following the above discussion of governance structures for transactions, there is a need to outline the relation with the exchange-configurations concept we introduced in Chapter 2. The present subsection briefly expounds the connections and differences between the two concepts.

First recall that governance structures are organizational frameworks 'within which the integrity of a contractual relation is decided' and which are the result of 'an effort to craft order, thereby to mitigate conflict and realize mutual gains'. Therefore governance structures act as ordering regimes for transactions; potential transactors, when deciding on the shape of transactions, choose between the alternative regimes with a view to minimizing transaction costs. As Williamson puts it: 'transactions are aligned with governance structures' (Williamson, 2000, p. 599). Two conclusions follow from this description. The first is that governance structures are typically institutional arrangements, that is they are meant to structure human behaviour (see Subsection 3.2.3). The second is that governance structures are among the crucial characteristics of the exchange environment, one of the elements of exchange which, according to our proposition, contribute to the shaping of transactions.

In contrast, an exchange configuration was described in Subsection 2.2.2 as the entire constellation composed of (1) a particular combination of characteristics of elements of exchange, (2) the formation process of transactions emanating from these characteristics and, (3) the resulting set of homogeneous transactions. So exchange configurations are analytical tools that are meant to be operationally useful in capturing distinct real-life exchange settings.

But governance structures and exchange configurations also differ in scope. Governance structures relate to a relatively small number of major regimes for ordering transactions, where each contains particular rules of behaviour within which vast numbers of transactions are executed. From the perspective of the transaction-cost literature, the transactions under a given governance structure are, of course, homogeneous. But they are not so from the point of view of exchange configurations. Under the umbrella of one governance structure – say, markets – figure large numbers of very different exchange configurations. Furthermore, governance structures are relatively fixed, consisting of a few well-established entities, namely markets, firms, hybrids, public bureaus and families. Exchange configurations, on the other hand, range from highly aggregated to highly detailed constellations where their delimitation typically depends on the context.

## 3.4 INDUSTRIAL ORGANIZATION

As will be shown in Chapter 7, dissatisfaction with the results of prevailing transactions is among the strongest forces of change in exchange configurations. In this connection the extensive literature on industrial organization (IO) can provide useful insights, despite some limitations, when used in connection with the exchange-configuration approach. The limitations relate to the fact that the IO literature focuses on the tactical and strategic moves that firms make under various market conditions. In other words, the behaviour of actors other than firms and the performance of transactions other than market transactions are ignored. Still, given that firms as a group are the most active and influential actors in market economies, there are good reasons to examine their conduct and the instruments they apply when attempting to maintain or improve outcomes of transactions. This is indeed how this literature is used in the dynamic setting of Chapter 7.

The backbone of industrial organization is the structure–conduct–performance (SCP) paradigm. As the name suggests, the basic argument of this approach asserts that a given market structure (described by an array of variables and parameters) gives rise to certain forms of conduct (the tactical and strategic decisions that firms make) which lead, in turn, to certain outcomes. Figure 3.1 presents a schematic overview. The figure shows that efforts have also been made to explain how market structure derives from basic supply and demand conditions. Further, account is taken of the impact of public policy measures on structure and conduct.

Early contributions to the SCP approach were of an empirical nature offering descriptions of observed combinations of market conditions and, coupled with them, various types of conduct. Together they provide a rich source of information on firm behaviour apart from valuable insights into the multiple relations between structure and conduct in practice. Later on, with the introduction of game theory, the nature of studies took a new turn in form and content as practical observation and verbal description made room for theoretical argument and mathematical tools. Not surprisingly, the new contributions concentrated on market conditions characterized by the interplay of oligopolistic, mostly non-cooperative competitors. They clearly demonstrated the overwhelming importance of one or only a few specific properties of market structure (the assumed 'context') and conjectures concerning reactive behaviour of competitors.

As can be gleaned from Figure 3.1 'performance' in the SCP approach derives directly – and, according to some authors such as Spanos and Lioukas (2001), exclusively – from 'conduct' which consists of the acts of those who decide on firms' strategies, tactics and transactions. The literature shows how evaluation of performance leads firms to reformulate their

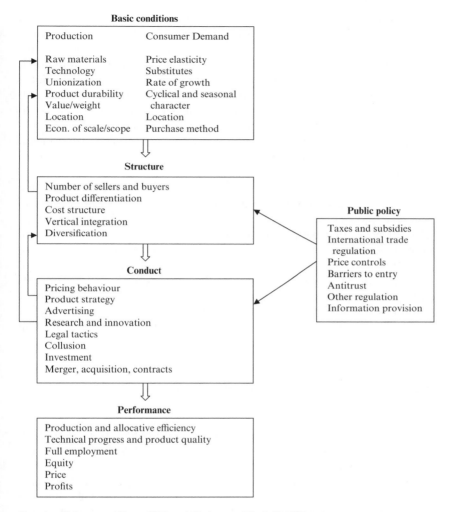

*Source:*   Scherer and Ross, 1990 and Carlton and Perloff, 2005.

*Figure 3.1   The structure–conduct–performance paradigm*

strategies and tactics with the aim of altering structure and/or conduct so as to improve their future performance. Thus we see that analyses that emphasize performance naturally develop into a normative approach. In fact, Barney (1997, p. 32) defines a firm's performance directly in normative terms by relating performance to the question of 'whether the firm is able to generate the expected value'.

It should also be noted here that the criteria applied in establishing performance can vary strongly with the viewpoint of the judging parties. Two strands of the SCP literature illustrate the wide difference in this regard between a socio-economic and a business-economic evaluation. In a socio-economic evaluation such criteria as production and allocative efficiency, equity, full employment and progress may be applied.[17] In this view, abundant profits are a sign of inefficiency and an invitation to identify and eliminate their cause. But the alternative view takes the perspective of the business sector. From that viewpoint profits are considered favourably and any developments that may reduce profits are seen as 'threats'.[18]

Nevertheless, even if different judges apply different criteria, when the outcome of the transactions they are considering is unsatisfactory they will often try to take measures in order to improve results. The measures they may consider differ with the nature of the judging party, for example, an individual actor, a firm or a public policy-maker. It will appear in Chapter 7 that many of these measures imply a change in one or more elements of exchange. In other words, in addition to the relation that runs from elements of exchange to certain characteristics of transactions (the 'regular' relation in the exchange-configuration approach), there is also an effect from certain characteristics of transactions (unsatisfactory outcomes) on elements of exchange.

## 3.5 INDIVIDUAL AND ORGANIZATIONAL LEARNING

Even in the simple, static version of the exchange-configuration approach as presented in Chapter 2 actors are engaged in various learning processes: they accumulate experience derived from past transactions, observe actions by other actors and absorb information about changing elements of exchange in order to prepare themselves for decisions regarding the form and content of new transactions. But in a dynamic setting learning plays a still more prominent role. For example, each of the various pivotal acts by firms considered in the SCP approach – namely collecting information on performance, evaluating performance, and designing tactical and strategic moves – involves learning processes. In Chapter 7 it will be shown that learning processes can initiate changes in exchange elements with major consequences for ensuing transactions. In fact, it is not an exaggeration to say that exchange and development cannot do without learning. This section introduces terms and concepts connected with learning processes by individual actors and organizations.

Learning is described by some authors as the process of acquiring new knowledge and behaviour.[19] In this connection knowledge relates to the content of information stored in one's memory and in other accessible sources for, one hopes, future recall. Note that in this view understanding adds a dimension; it gives meaning and significance to knowledge within a cognitive structure. Other authors do not distinguish between learning and understanding.[20]

As everyone knows, learning is not always easy. The capacity to learn depends on one's absorptive capacity which is a function of innate capabilities and prior knowledge. Prior knowledge helps because the difficulty of absorbing new knowledge increases with what is called cognitive distance. The latter concept refers to the difference between one's existing knowledge and the content of new knowledge. The greater the distance to be bridged the harder it is to absorb newly offered information. From this it follows that learning is facilitated by previous learning and that, to a greater or lesser extent, learning is path dependent.[21]

The literature distinguishes two main approaches to learning.[22] Behavioural approaches do not allow – or, at most, minimize allowance – for conscious thought or decision processes and choice.[23] Learning is mechanistic and involuntary resulting from reactions to performance feedback: in case of success the action tends to recur whereas in case of failure it tends to fade out. Learners in these approaches are mostly passive. Feedback is generated by what happens in the world around them and learners pick up stimuli that feed their response. Thus, work, behaviour and management routines develop, spread and disappear in reaction to positive and negative outcomes. The great advantage of these views is that they can explain how actors can learn despite their frequently observed lack of understanding of causal relations, their perceptual errors and faulty judgments. This is the type of learning a curio seller, for example, goes through when he notices by accident that his business improves if his shop window is less cluttered. He is without a clue why he sells more when he displays fewer articles, but he does not miss the point and develops a new routine.

Cognitive approaches, on the other hand, see learners as being able to perceive, analyze, plan and choose. Their strength lies in the ability to explain how learners (people and organizations) can suddenly embark upon novel directions. Here learning underlies analysis, and analysis guides action. Clearly, the success of actions in cognitive views depends on realistic assessments by learners of the world around them. This is the type of learning that leads to reasoned innovations and discoveries such as those propelling technological progress. Cognitive learning has far-reaching consequences for exchange configurations as a result of the wide variety of shifts in properties of elements of exchange it brings about.

Especially when considering the transfer of knowledge, it is necessary to recognize that some forms of knowledge are more difficult to acquire than others. Complexity is, of course, one factor restricting accessibility, but here we concentrate on another factor, namely openness to new learners. To begin with, there is the so-called tacit, or internal or embedded knowledge. This is the knowledge acquired through experience and on-the-job training in activities ranging from administration, management, sales and finance to designing, engineering and testing. It is the kind of knowledge that is stored in people's heads or that has materialized in machines and tools, so it can rather easily be kept private. In the absence of other sources, outsiders can obtain this knowledge only from the persons who possess it or, indirectly, from the tools and machines in which it is embodied. On the other hand, explicit or disembedded knowledge has been laid down in writing, formulas and manuals. Still, this form of knowledge is not necessarily accessible to everyone as the owners may carefully protect it as valuable, private property. Disembedded knowledge is a free good (is in the public domain) only when presented in open publications.

We now turn to the subject of organizational learning. The latter term may, at first sight, seem to be a misnomer since only individuals are capable of learning. However, as the rapidly growing literature on the subject shows,[24] there are good reasons to examine organizational, in addition to individual, learning processes.

In terms of knowledge, a static concept, there is no essential difference between individuals and organizations. The knowledge of an organization can be seen as the sum of the knowledge of its members. This view corresponds with an influential organizational school of thought that regards organizations as repositories of knowledge or competences and other resources. Note, however, that much of this knowledge is tacit. As result, for example, imitation of the procedures, production processes or products of one organization by another is not always as simple as it seems and may, in fact, appear to be costly. In any case, the copier must acquire information – therefore, must learn – about the things he wishes to imitate. Even if the information should be complete, the fact that it is applied in a different organization – with different ways, prior knowledge and other resources – means that the outcome will differ from the original. But in reality the information is rarely complete. Most copiers have to do additional, now original, learning to fill the information gap with sometimes novel results.

There are, however, two very important differences between individual and organizational learning. The first has to do with the ways in which organizations can facilitate and stimulate learning by its members, ways that are rarely available to individual learners. Take for example the equipment one finds in laboratories and the materials that are required for experimentation and testing. The fixed and current expenditures that must be made for such activities are beyond the reach of individual actors. Further, organizations act as platforms for social interaction among their members. As sociological theories emphasize and as everyone with practical experience can testify, participation in social activities is a remarkably effective force in the exchange and creation of knowledge and ideas. So the interaction of workers by itself can contribute to the learning process within an organization. Moreover, in various ways (by imbuing workers with a common purpose, by arranging courses, and so on) the management can try to stimulate and direct internal learning in the interest of the organization.

The second type of difference with individual learning has to do with externally oriented activities of organizations, such as employing new members and buying new machines. When an organization engages a new employee with knowledge that differs from what is internally available, its knowledge base changes. Note that the change occurs even though the knowledge of old and new members remains the same, at least in the first instance. But the interesting part of the new situation from the point of view of the organization resides, of course, in the opportunity it provides to increase the level of knowledge of old and new members by stimulating interaction. This learning process can be especially useful if valuable tacit knowledge is imported with the new employees. Similarly, organizations can derive additional tacit knowledge from the new tools, machines and equipment it acquires.

Having come to this point, we can make an important observation. In the exchange-configuration approach it is argued that transactions derive from exchange elements, one of which consists of actors. But in the above paragraphs we have seen that actors (organizations especially) can change their profile significantly by engaging in certain transactions. We have here another example of a number of two-way relations between actors and transactions which derive their importance from the dynamic loops they can produce. We return to this matter in Chapter 7 where we discuss the dynamics of exchange configurations.

# NOTES

1. Commons, 1934, especially pp. 55–69.
2. These considerations have a fairly long history; see Bowles, 1998, p. 87.
3. This concept will be discussed in some more detail in the next subsection.
4. The phenomenon of opportunism is an essential part of TCE and will be discussed in Subsection 3.3.1.

5.  See, for example, the entry on Uncertainty in Hodgson et al., 1994.
6.  In certain cases insurance companies do not provide such protection. See Box 3.4.
7.  See Conlisk, 1996.
8.  Learning within a dynamic framework is discussed in more detail in Chapter 7 which deals with the dynamics of exchange configurations.
9.  The theory of the evolution of complex systems has made much progress in the formalization of search processes. See for example Kauffman et al., 2000.
10. See DiMaggio 1994, p. 37.
11. Greif's definition of institutions is wider than North's as it also encompasses organizations; see Greif, 2006, p. 30.
12. See Nooteboom, 2000, p. 93.
13. Note that governance structures are institutional arrangements as described in Subsection 3.2.3.
14. In Commons' terminology these are managerial transactions; see Subsection 3.2.1.
15. For more comprehensive discussions, see Ben-Porath, 1980 and Pollak, 1985.
16. A very important subset of family farms, especially in developing countries, consists of family farms producing at least partially for own consumption. The transactions within the latter type of farms will be discussed in more detail in Subsection 6.3.2.
17. See, for example, Scherer and Ross, 1990, p. 5.
18. For a discussion, see Barney, 1997, p. 68.
19. Maier et al., 2003.
20. See Rizzello, 2003.
21. Nooteboom, 2000, p. 71.
22. See, for example, Starbuck and Hedberg, 2003, p. 330 ff.
23. This is the kind of learning referred to in the field of social economics emphasizing the link between individual behaviour and group outcomes through the influence that other people's choices have on individuals' decisions. See, for example, Schelling, 1978.
24. For an illustration, see the various contributions in Dierkes et al., 2003.

# REFERENCES

Axelrod, R.M. (1984), *The Evolution of Cooperation*, New York: Basic Books.

Barney, J.B. (1997), *Gaining and Sustaining Competitive Advantage*, Reading, MA: Addison-Wesley.

Ben-Porath, B. (1980), 'The F-connection: families, friends and firms and the organization of exchange', *Population and Development Review*, **6** (1), 1–30.

Bowles, S. (1998), 'Endogenous preferences: the cultural consequences of markets and other economic institutions', *Journal of Economic Literature*, **36** (1), 75–111.

Carlton, D.W. and J.M. Perloff (2005), *Modern Industrial Organization*, 4th edn, Boston: Pearson/Addison-Wesley.

Coase, R.H. (1937), 'The Nature of the Firm', *Economica*, NS, **4** (16), 386–405, reprinted in G.J. Stigler and K.E. Boulding (eds.) (1952), *Readings in Price Theory*, Homewood, IL: Irwin.

Commons, J.R. (1934), *Institutional Economics: Its Place in Political Economy*, New York: Macmillan.

Conlisk, J. (1996), 'Why bounded rationality?', *Journal of Economic Literature*, **34** (2), 669–701.

Dierkes, M., A.B. Antal, J. Child and I. Nonaka (eds.) (2003), *Handbook of Organizational Learning and Knowledge*, Oxford, UK: Oxford University Press.

DiMaggio, P. (1994), 'Culture and economy', in N.J. Smelser and R. Swedberg (eds.), *The Handbook of Economic Sociology*, Princeton, NJ: Princeton University Press and New York/Russell Sage Foundation.

Greif, A. (2006), *Institutions and the Path to the Modern Economy: Lessons from Medieval Trade*, Cambridge, UK: Cambridge University Press.

Hodgson, G.M. (1998), 'The approach of institutional economics', *Journal of Economic Literature*, **36** (2), 166–192.

Hodgson, G.M., W.J. Samuels and M.R. Tool (1994), *The Elgar Companion to Institutional and Evolutionary Economics*, Aldershot, UK: Edward Elgar.

Kaufmann, S.A, J. Lobo and W.G. Macready (2000), 'Optimal search on a technology landscape', *Journal of Economic Behavior & Organization*, **43** (2), 141–166.

Knight, F.H. (1921), *Risk, Uncertainty and Profit*, Boston: Houghton Mifflin.

Maier, G.W, C. Prange and L. von Rosenstiel, (2003), 'Psychological perspectives of organizational learning', Chapter 1 in M. Dierkes, A. Berthoin Antal, J. Child and I. Nonaka (eds.), *Handbook of Organizational Learning and Knowledge*, Oxford, UK: Oxford University Press.

van de Mortel, E.G. (2000), *An Institutional Approach to Transition Processes*, Aldershot, UK: Ashgate.

Nooteboom, B. (2000), *Learning and Innovation in Organizations and Economics*, Oxford, UK: Oxford University Press.

North, D.C. (1990), *Institutions, Institutional Change and Economic Performance*, Cambridge, UK: Cambridge University Press.

North, D.C. (1994), 'Economic performance through time', *American Economic Review*, **84** (3), 359–368.

Pollak, R.A. (1985), 'A transaction cost approach to families and households', *Journal of Economic Literature*, **23** (3), 581–608.

Rizzello, S. (2003), 'Introduction', in S. Rizzello (ed.), *Cognitive Developments in Economics*, London: Routledge.

Schelling, T.C. (1978), *Micromotives and Macrobehavior*, New York: Norton & Company.

Scherer, F.M and D. Ross (1990), *Industrial Market Structure and Economic Performance*, (3rd edn.), Boston: Houghton Mifflin.

Simon, H.A. (1957), *Models of Man*, New York: John Wiley & Sons.

Simon, H.A. (1987), 'Behavioral economics', in J. Eatwell, M. Milgate and P. Newman (eds.), *The New Palgrave Dictionary of Economics*, New York: W.W. Norton.

Spanos, Y.E and S. Lioukas (2001), 'An examination into the causal logic of rent generation: contrasting Porter's competitive strategy framework and the resource-based perspective', *Strategic Management Journal*, **22**, 535–574.

Speklé, R.F. (2001), *Beyond Generics: A Closer Look at Hybrid and Hierarchical Governance*, Rotterdam, NL: ERIM.

Starbuck, W.H and B. Hedberg (2003), 'How organizations learn from success and failure', Chapter 14 in M. Dierkes, A. Berthoin Antal, J. Child and I. Nonaka (eds), *Handbook of Organizational Learning and Knowledge*, Oxford, UK: Oxford University Press.

Tintner, G. (1941), 'The theory of choice under subjective risk and uncertainty', *Econometrica*, **9**, 298–304.

Tirole, J. (1988), *The Theory of Industrial Organization*, Cambridge, MA: MIT Press.

Williamson, O.E. (1975), *Markets and Hierarchies: Analysis and Antitrust Implications*, New York: The Free Press.

Williamson, O.E. (1979), 'Transaction costs economics: the governance of contractual relations', *Journal of Law and Economics*, **22** (2), 233–261.

Williamson, O.E. (1985), *The Economic Institutions of Capitalism*, New York: The Free Press.

Williamson, O.E. (1992), 'Transaction cost economics', Chapter 3 in R. Schmalensee and R.D. Willig (eds.), *Handbook of Industrial Organization*, Amsterdam: North-Holland.

Williamson, O.E. (1996), *The Mechanisms of Governance*, New York: Oxford University Press.

Williamson, O.E. (1998), 'Transaction cost economics: how it works; where it is headed', *De Economist*, **146** (1), 23–58.

Williamson, O.E. (2000), 'The new institutional economics: taking stock, looking ahead', *Journal of Economic Literature*, **38** (3), 595–613.

# 4.  Elements of exchange

## 4.1  OVERVIEW

The primary aim of this chapter is to describe the fundamental elements of exchange *items, actors* and *environment*, which are the three pillars underlying the exchange-configuration approach. Depending on the transactions to be analyzed, the elements have to be subdivided or decomposed into more specific categories and subgroups. This chapter will indicate the major subgroups and components to be distinguished as well as those characteristics that appear to be the most powerful and discriminating determinants of the shape and content of transactions.

The nature of the three elements and the major differences between them are taken up in Section 4.2, which also contains operationally useful taxonomies and sub-divisions for each of the three elements. The exchange elements are then discussed in more detail in the subsequent sections. Subsection 4.3.2 focuses on factors of production (a subgroup of the exchange element item exchanged), and describes explicitly the ways in which the most relevant properties of exchange elements impact on the formation, form and content of market transactions relating to credit, foreign exchange and land respectively. Space limitations prohibit similarly detailed descriptions for other transactions. But, throughout the chapter, brief indications are presented of the impact that certain dimensions of elements have on the make-up of ensuing transactions.

Many aspects of elements of exchange needed to define an exchange configuration such as the incomes of the consumers and the number of actors on both sides of a transaction are easy to quantify. Other aspects of elements, however, cannot readily be expressed in quantitative terms. It is important to categorize the state or content of each of these aspects. This can be done by way of scales or scores, or in some limiting instances, through qualitative values or a binary classification (for example, rural vs. urban location, modern vs. traditional technology, and skilled vs. unskilled workers). Since a given exchange configuration has to be defined by the most discriminating characteristics of the elements constituting it, this can be done by way of a profile of the latter where some characteristics are expressed quantitatively and others more qualitatively or even in binary terms. It will be shown subsequently that, in general, only a relatively small and manageable number of properties (the profile) are required to delineate a specific configuration.

Certain characteristics are highly interrelated and form clusters. For example, actors endowed with a high/low level of schooling tend to have high/low incomes and are relatively well/poorly nourished. Such clusters of correlated characteristics can be large as the discussion of credit market transactions in Subsection 4.3.2 will show. Where these clusters occur, the discriminating effect of one or more characteristics is often amplified by others such that the form and content of the ensuing transactions show clearly distinct properties.

## 4.2 THE NATURE OF THE THREE ELEMENTS OF EXCHANGE

Elements of exchange are unlike elements in chemistry. Among others, the latter have a unique interpretation independent of the settings in which they occur. Elements of exchange, on the other hand, have a variable nature. They typically vary with the type of exchange that is being analyzed and, therefore, can assume different identities in different settings. Thus, in a setting of highly aggregated, stylized transactions, the elements are equally aggregated. For example, in an analysis preparatory to the formulation of a national employment policy, the element 'item exchanged' may be as general as 'unskilled-labour services' in the country concerned. However, in specific market analyses, which are often concerned with highly specific transactions, the elements conform to real-life items, actors and exchange environments. For example, the 'item exchanged' in a market study could be as specific as 'olive-oil enriched margarine'.

There is an inherent difference between items and actors on the one hand, and exchange environments on the other. Items and actors form two main sets each consisting of innumerable members which can be classified according to different criteria. Starting at the highest level of aggregation (the all-encompassing group of 'items exchanged' as well as the comparable group of 'actors') one can disaggregate further and further into subgroups until one reaches the level of the individual items and actors corresponding to a real world situation. Each subgroup is relatively homogeneous in terms of the criteria applied and can be singled out to fulfill the role of element of exchange. Thus, one may wish to concentrate on an actor group like 'consumers' or 'consumers under thirty', for example.

The 'exchange environment', in contrast to the other two elements, is a composite. It can be decomposed into different parts or components, such as pertinent legislation, culture and infrastructure. Indeed, for a better understanding of an exchange environment, it is very useful to distinguish between these parts and consider them separately, in the same way as one can usefully distinguish between a heart and a liver and between bones and muscle tissue in the study of the human anatomy. But the point is that only combinations of components can form a genuine exchange environment. A single environmental component cannot sensibly figure as an element of exchange.

In practice, it appears easy to identify the element 'item(s) exchanged', as it is in most cases the object of the exchange under study. And when the item has been identified, the relevant 'actor groups' suggest themselves as a matter of course. But this is not a general rule. In some cases, it is also necessary to consider actors who are not directly engaged in the exchange under investigation, but who are potential participants and, thereby, influence the exchange indirectly. The theory of contestable markets focuses precisely on this consideration. In still other cases, interest in and focus on a specific actor group is the reason why an exchange analysis is undertaken, such as in studies of the access of low-income groups to medical services, or the housing market. Obviously, part of the problem of identifying the relevant actors' set is then solved from the outset.

It is more cumbersome to identify the relevant 'exchange environment', that is to specify which components of the environment need to be taken into consideration in a specific analysis of exchange. Therefore, it may be necessary to undertake a pilot study to identify the major components of the exchange environment before delineating a real life configuration.

In a study of a certain set of transactions the first task is to identify and capture the main characteristics of elements defining the corresponding exchange configuration. Thereafter the characteristics (or properties or dimensions) must be described in quantitative or qualitative terms. The first task might appear extremely difficult, given that the number of potential characteristics of elements of exchange that may conceivably be relevant in identifying any exchange configuration is nearly endless. The list of characteristics of exchange elements presented in Box 4.1 below provides a brief example of the range that could be considered. But in practice it turns out that often relatively small sets of characteristics suffice for a satisfactory delineation of specific exchange configurations. Recall, for example, the four cases presented in Subsection 2.3.2 relating to the Pakistani wheat market, where only a few characteristics were needed to describe and discriminate between various market-exchange configurations. This remarkable reduction in numbers when moving from the general to the particular will be discussed fully in the next chapter.

## BOX 4.1   ELEMENTS OF EXCHANGE AND THEIR MAJOR CHARACTERISTICS

The present list of exchange elements and their characteristics is far from exhaustive. It is primarily meant to illustrate how exchange elements can be subdivided/decomposed and to summarize some of the more important characteristics. Characteristics of environmental components are not given here; many of them are discussed in the following pages.

### 1. ITEM EXCHANGED
**Product/service**
   Final good
      Consumer good
         Luxury good
         Necessary good
      Investment good
      Export product
   Intermediate good
   Raw material
*Characteristics*:
-Intrinsic characteristics, e.g. weight; volume; quality; production costs; degree of homogeneity; storability; perishability; exhaustibility; tradability; transportability
-Other characteristics: type of use; degree and extent of substitutability (on the demand and supply sides); specificity of assets used in production; volatility of supply/demand; construction time

**Labour services**
   Self-employed
   Wage-employed
   Family labour
*Characteristics:*
-Intrinsic characteristics connected with the task to be performed requiring different combinations of skills
-Other characteristics: major source of income; context of use

## Credit
Often subdivided according to its characteristics (see below)
*Characteristics:*
-Intrinsic characteristics: provides a time bridge and allows transformation by the borrower
-Other characteristics: duration (from long to short term); form (money or kind); purpose (e.g. for consumption or production); security (personal or collateral-based)

## Land
Often subdivided according to its characteristics (see below)
*Characteristics:*
-Intrinsic characteristics: in fixed supply; immovable; comprises agricultural soil and mineral deposits and serves as a base for construction works
-Other characteristics: fertility; location; accessibility; solidity; elevation and levelness; minability

## Foreign Exchange
*Characteristics:*
-Intrinsic characteristic: a stock or flow of foreign currency
-Other characteristic: degree of convertibility

## 2. ACTORS
Often subdivided according to their nature (individuals, firms, families, public and other organizations) and by economic activity (employers, workers, farmers, consumers, investors etc.)
*Characteristics:*
-Intrinsic characteristics: consider, activate and implement exchanges; initiate tactical and strategic action (see Chapter 7)
-Other characteristics: number and density; nature of legal status; economic activity; personal characteristics (age, sex, character, preferences, innate skills); income; assets; level and type of education; objectives; power; experience; information; network

---

**3. EXCHANGE ENVIRONMENT**
Often decomposed into:
the cultural component
the political component
the legal component
the physical component
the technological component
the socio-economic component

---

The second task requires a quantitative or qualitative description of the relevant characteristics identified in the first stage. The complexity of this task varies with the nature of the respective characteristics. Some properties – such as a commodity's physical characteristics like weight and volume, or a worker's years of schooling – can fairly easily be quantified. But other properties needed to define an exchange configuration do not lend themselves to ready quantification. This is particularly true of some of the categorical dimensions of the exchange environment such as the underlying cultural aspects, the policy and legal framework and the socio-economic structure. When faced with essentially qualitative and categorical characteristics, it is important to indicate their state or content by way of scales or scores. For example, the quality of a road system can be described by the number of lanes, their width, surface material, congestion and density. Even the cultural environment can be described adequately by the scores of a limited number of well-defined aspects. In other cases a binary classification can be useful (for example, rural vs. urban location, modern vs. traditional technology, skilled vs. unskilled workers). In fact, it will be argued in Chapter 5 that many characteristics which are used for taxonomic purposes, when expressed in quantitative or qualitative terms, follow binary distributions.

## 4.3   ITEM EXCHANGED

The economics literature shows that the properties of the item that is being exchanged are a very powerful determinant of the nature of the exchange process. This is so obvious that it may even be overlooked. In fact, major fields of economic analysis are identified simply on the basis of the item traded. Examples are agricultural economics, labour economics and finance. Also market transactions are distinguished along these lines. In the economic literature, economists can simply refer to, say, the labour market and thereby conjure up for the reader a fairly comprehensive picture based on the specific characteristics of labour services, the specific users and suppliers they involve, the rules that apply and the consequences these aspects have for the transactions in that market. And, for the same reason, the labour market can be distinguished usefully from, say, the credit or the steel market or the market for television sets. Similarly, production is often broken down into sectors according to the goods that are being produced.

Items exchanged can be classified according to different criteria. The first operationally useful distinction is between products (including services) and factors of production. At the macroeconomic level this distinction is reasonably clear. The demand for factors is directly derived from the demand for products through the production process, which relates the two in the circular flow of income. In transactions, production factors generate income to their suppliers in the form of wages, salaries, rent, interest and profits. Factors of production, as the term suggests, are mostly used as inputs by producers, although there are exceptions: labour may be consumed directly in the form of domestic services and also land and credit may be used for consumption purposes. On the other hand, products are used by consumers (as finished products) as well as by producers (as raw materials, inputs and semi-finished products).

### 4.3.1 Characteristics of products and services

With regard to products (excluding services), such physical characteristics as weight, volume, storability, perishability, tradability and transportability are important determinants of a given exchange configuration. These characteristics can directly influence transportation costs, required speed of handling and the potential size of the market, and also the organization of market activities. For example, it is not accidental that auction halls are often situated close to production sites of vegetables. Products can, of course, also be differentiated according to their uses – consumption, investment or current production – especially because they involve different user groups. Sometimes a finer distinction is desirable, such as between luxury consumer goods and basic necessities because they face different demand patterns or are subject to different government policies (a component of the exchange environment). Other examples of product characteristics that impact directly on the corresponding exchange configurations are the extent of supply volatility (agricultural products) and the required construction/production time. In the latter case the so-called hold-up problem can arise because delivery of the product is by necessity delayed and the suppliers' reliability can become a burdening issue in such commodities as new ships and buildings.

The main characteristic of services is that they are strictly non-storable, so they cannot be produced ahead of demand. This characteristic in combination with the uneven distribution of demand over time can easily result in queuing (for example, restaurants) although this can sometimes be mitigated through time-differentiated pricing (for example, early-bird specials offered by some restaurants, special rates in rail transport and telephone services). Some services are also non-transportable, such as personal services and services supplied by repair shops and hotels and restaurants, so the buyer must travel to the source. In such cases the ratio of transportation costs to purchase price rises rapidly with distance thereby severely limiting the geographical span of suppliers. But the non-transportability characteristic is not necessarily fixed and constant. New developments in communication technology have greatly enhanced the transportability of such important services as banking and insurance, and even retail trade on the internet, with major consequences for the orientation and degree of competition in these sectors.

As indicated above, the item traded has such a strong impact on the nature of market exchange that it is used to differentiate between markets on an aggregate level. At a more disaggregated level elasticities of demand can be used to break down items in finer categories. Economic theory suggests that it is useful to define an industry (or a market) as embracing those firms producing close substitutes, as measured by the cross elasticities of demand between two goods. Somewhat analogously, producers can be grouped together using some measure of substitutability on the supply side (for example, the cross elasticity of supply) which is simply a method of discovering the degree to which producers are affected by each other's pricing behaviour in their production decisions. Thus, up to a point, the boundaries of a product market exchange configuration can be drawn on the basis of these cross elasticities. Still another characteristic of products relates to the degree of homogeneity of their quality. Products which vary significantly in terms of quality, and where knowledge and information of their true quality are not shared evenly among users and suppliers, may belong to different exchange configurations and follow different rules and adjustment mechanisms than products of more homogeneous quality.

### 4.3.2  Characteristics of factors of production

Next we turn to the major distinguishing characteristics of factors of production, that is, of labour, credit, foreign exchange and land.

**Labour**

One of the most important characteristics of labour is that it gives rise to the predominant source of income for most households, whether it comes in the form of imputed labour income or as wages or salaries. Precisely because of this important role, workers can find themselves in a position of dependence towards those offering remuneration for their services. Under such conditions workers may even have to tolerate serious harm to their physical and mental integrity. In many countries these considerations have resulted in legislation of greatly varying detail and intensity to protect workers against exploitation, dismissal and hazardous work conditions. Thus, labour exchange elicits by its nature a body of pertinent legislation which must be taken into account as a part of its environment. Nevertheless severe violations of formal rules can be widely observed (see Box 4.2).

Labour services are closely connected with their suppliers, providing a direct link with another element of exchange, namely actors (labour is embodied in the seller). This link gets stronger as the degree of specialization increases. Whereas such diverse characteristics as dexterity,

---

## BOX 4.2   OBNOXIOUS TRANSACTIONS

Some types of market transactions, such as those where child labour or body parts are traded, fill the observer with repugnance. What makes these transactions so abhorrent? Kanbur offers three explanations: extremity of outcomes in the negative direction and/ or weak agency (in the sense that the actor does not clearly see the consequences or does not bear the consequences) and /or inequality in market relations (where the terms of the transaction are an expression of the actor's desperation) (Kanbur, 2003).

We may add that reasons why certain market transactions are obnoxious are directly connected to elements of exchange. Thus, in transactions involving child labour or body parts, what drives our judgment is the combination of (1) the nature of the items traded, (2) the weak and unequally distributed attributes of actors, and, (3) moral standards which are part of the exchange environment. And it may also be pointed out that non-market transactions can be equally obnoxious. For example, the market transaction with which a parent pledges the labour of a child against a loan is preceded by an intra-family implicit and uneven transaction between parent and child concerning the latter's labour.

decisiveness, vigilance, physical strength, good taste, level and type of education, reliability, experience and social skills are appreciated in all workers, for highly specialized activities good scores on only two or three characteristics are often enough to qualify as a skilled worker.

Since a good match between job requirements and workers' talents is in the interest of users and suppliers of labour, the connection between the two in production activities tends to be strong. Reciprocal commitments pay off. It explains why labour-market transactions are mostly concluded for indefinite periods of time and where the day-to-day specification of tasks is relegated to intra-firm transactions. In contrast, financial funds rarely bear the supplier's stamp and can be made to suit widely different uses. As a result, suppliers of funds are much less closely tied to the activities they help to finance than workers are to the job they perform.

Another important issue regarding labour has to do with the principal-agent problem. Employers, supervisors, or, more generally, principals on the one hand, and workers on the other often have conflicting interests. Principals want diligent, flexible, loyal workers at relatively low cost, whereas workers have other preferences, such as high remuneration, a steady employment, safe, pleasant, easygoing work conditions, independence and prestige. Workers, who are often much better informed about the details of their work than the principals, can rather easily cover up any discrepancy between the target work load set for them by their principals and their actual performance. This problem, related to the phenomena of asymmetric information and opportunism, has given rise to a whole body of literature. It has also generated a variety of (non-market) intra-organizational exchange configurations to reduce transaction costs. It is worth noting that the family is generally less susceptible to the problem caused by the need to monitor closely the performance of workers (see Subsection 3.3.2).

### Credit[1]

The pivotal characteristics of credit are that: (1) it provides a time bridge, in the sense that whatever is supplied by the lender is to be repaid in some form by the borrower at a later date, and (2) the borrower is free to transform and convert whatever is provided in loan by the lender. Both characteristics create considerable risk to potential lenders, so it is only natural that the latter will seek security from potential borrowers.[2] These properties of credit dominate the nature of credit transactions because of the far-reaching consequences they have for users and suppliers. In the following we shall discuss this matter in some detail for the case of credit-market transactions as they occur in developing countries and demonstrate how and why the characteristics of the item (credit) and the risk they entail mesh with certain characteristics of the actors (users and suppliers of credit). The discussion will also provide another opportunity to illustrate the impact of elements of exchange on the formation, form and content of these transactions. Box 4.3 presents a summary of the main conclusions.

The security that lenders demand from borrowers takes two main forms. The first form of security consists of valuable transferable assets, satisfactory cash flows and/or of reliable flows of income to which lenders may lay claim when borrowers fail to fulfil their obligations. Especially in developing countries many people are unable to provide such security. The second source derives from borrowers' identities and reputations and relations with their lenders. This case applies when the lender knows the borrower so he can judge the borrower's character beforehand and monitor his actions after the loan has been extended. Clearly, this type of loan is feasible only within relatively small communities. Thus we see that the security aspect in credit transactions creates roughly two categories of borrowers, those who can provide material collateral and those who cannot.

Collateral in the form of income or assets can be assessed objectively by people with no inside knowledge of the borrower as a person. This type of appraisal lends itself to a formal, administrative approach by bureaucratic institutions like banks. The other type of security, consisting of reputation, can be properly appraised only by insiders with personal knowledge of the borrowers, like shopkeepers, employers, landlords and professional moneylenders.[3] In other words, the nature of the security offered in credit transactions tends to differentiate between two categories of lenders organizing lending operations in different ways. Further, the form of collateral determines the scale of operations of credit suppliers. When the security derives from the borrower's identity and reputation even professional moneylenders can oversee at most a few hundred clients and that only if they can rely on assistants. On the other hand, when material collateral is offered the lender's scale of operation is constrained only by management limitations.

Having come to this conclusion, the argument can be carried still further, because the amount of loans lenders can manage has direct repercussions for their interest in financial intermediation. Consider the situation in which moneylenders find themselves. Their professional reach is limited geographically and socially to the people they know, as money lenders often claim. For most of them, this is the binding constraint for lending rather than the amount of funds they can obtain from other lenders. For institutions like banks the situation is entirely different. Their capacity to make loans stretches far beyond the amount of own capital. In fact, they generate income precisely by intermediating between lenders

### BOX 4.3    FORMAL AND INFORMAL CREDIT-MARKET CONFIGURATIONS

| **Formal credit** | **Informal credit** |
|---|---|

*Main Characteristics of Elements of Exchange*

| *Item* | *Item* |
|---|---|
| Credit: in the form of money; time bridge; transformation permitted; thus involves severe risk for lenders | Credit: often in kind; other characteristics idem |

| *Actors* | *Actors* |
|---|---|
| Borrowers: can provide material collateral | Borrowers: cannot provide material collateral (in most cases) |
| Lenders: bureaucratic institutions; large scale of operation; financial intermediaries; sophisticated system of administration | Lenders: e.g. employers, shopkeepers, professional moneylenders; scale of operation restricted by circle of known persons; casual records at best |

| *Environment* | *Environment* |
|---|---|
| Actors are target of directive (and sometimes invasive) government policies; registered, regulated and monitored by monetary authorities | Often hostile environment due to high loan rates; actors outside realm of monetary authorities |

*Main Characteristics of Transactions*

| *Formation* | *Formation* |
|---|---|
| Initiative by borrower; purpose and collateral verified and evaluated; approved along hierarchical lines; time-consuming process; haggling, when concessional rates are at stake | Initiative by borrower; very short decision process; little or no haggling |

| *Form* | *Form* |
|---|---|
| Formal contract recording parties/signatories, conditions (price, duration, instalments), security, penalties, pertinent law, action in case of conflict | Informal record specifying borrower, date, amount |
| *Content* | *Content* |
| (Also see Form); loans mostly meant for productive purposes; amounts relatively large; longer duration; loan rates relatively low | Loans mostly for consumption; amounts often very small; short duration; moneylenders' rates extremely high, other unofficial rates less extreme to low |

and borrowers, that is, by transforming the size and conditions of funds they solicit from external sources in accordance with the requirements of users of funds.

As follows from the central tenet of the exchange-configuration approach, having identified two clearly separable groups of borrowers (with opposite scores in terms of material collateral) and two groups of lenders (catering to the needs of one or the other group of borrowers), the form and content of the emerging loan transactions must also be different. This matter will be taken up below, but first attention must be given to another important aspect (and a characteristic of the exchange environment), namely the influence of governments and monetary authorities. The interest authorities have in credit operations has several causes, one of which has to do with financial intermediation. Where intermediaries collect funds from other actors on a large scale, there are reasons to impose rules of financial prudence, because default by one intermediary may well have negative external effects by creating a confidence crisis affecting financial and economic development. Therefore, financial intermediaries must nearly always be officially registered and licensed as such and be subjected to supervision by monetary authorities. The rules not only limit their freedom of action; accountability also requires a sophisticated system of administration. Secondly, money-creating intermediaries can influence the money supply and thereby the general price level, another external effect warranting supervision. Thirdly, credit markets have attracted a good deal of policy intervention especially in developing countries for a combination of reasons; credit markets are considered a prime conduit of resources towards productive uses as well as a victim to structural failures. In reaction, many governments in developing countries have stepped in by setting up government-owned financial institutions, by instructing private banks to direct funds to particular sectors or socio-economic groups often at artificially low interest rates and by combating moneylenders. In the course of time, it has become clear that these strong measures rarely have the desired effect and often have undesirable side-effects. Since the 1980s a reversal of policies can therefore be observed, but remnants of the old measures are still in place in various parts of the developing world.

We are now ready to examine how the different scores of the characteristics of exchange elements discussed above give rise to different credit-market configurations. At the most aggregate level only two configurations are distinguished in what follows. Subsequently we show how a more refined analysis of rural credit yields five operationally distinct rural informal credit-exchange configurations.

*Formal vs. informal credit configurations*   At first sight it may appear surprising that credit exchange can be captured by only two configurations, considering the multitude of dimensions relevant to the item credit. But closer inspection reveals that the scores of some dimensions are interconnected in clusters. For example, it has been noted that creditors doing business with debtors offering material collateral can achieve high levels of activity which allows them to engage in financial intermediation which invites monetary supervision and which makes them an easy target for government policy. In other words, a particular score in one dimension leads to particular scores in others thereby strengthening the discriminatory effect of the first. This phenomenon is not confined to credit-market configurations; it appears to apply in many other cases such that the number of dimensions that need to be distinguished in the majority of analyses of exchange is often remarkably small (for a more elaborate discussion see Chapter 5). With reference to the differences in status of the lenders, we have labelled the two configurations in the present case as the formal (official) and the informal (unofficial) credit-market configurations. Box 4.3, which presents a summary of the main properties, deserves special attention.

   The formation processes of transactions in the two configurations usually start similarly with an application by the borrowers, but diverge directly thereafter. In the formal market, forms must be filled out specifying the purpose of the loan and the collateral offered after which the collateral is verified. In the informal market, on the other hand, a decision can be taken quickly. A moneylender, for example, has, in principle, all the necessary information available and can decide immediately. Because of the simplicity of the process, he has a cost advantage in the formation stage compared with formal lenders.

Predictably, the form of transactions in the official credit market is strictly formal with contracts specifying the rights and obligations of the signatories in legal language. Borrowers and lenders keep copies. The contrast with the form of unofficial transactions cannot be greater. If records are kept, they mostly take the form of a chit that is filed or pinned to the wall giving the name of the borrower, the date and the amount. Moneylenders often use a self-devised script to maximize discretion. Borrowers rarely obtain a copy. In some cases transactions are confirmed in the presence of a person of authority.

Several aspects of the content of official and unofficial credit-market transactions have been mentioned in the above paragraphs and in the box. Here we concentrate on the foremost aspect, the interest rate and, in particular, on the striking difference between the rates in the two markets. As is well-known, rates charged by moneylenders and shopkeepers are often over 100 per cent on an annual basis, whereas bank loan rates are much lower even when there are no official price ceilings so loan rates can approximate the scarcity price. One explanation for the difference lies in the cost composition. In general, the following relation between price and costs holds in the absence of inflation and assuming continuous employment of funds:

$$r(1 - p)L \geq (i + a + p)L, \text{ or } r \geq (i + a + p) / (1 - p) \qquad (4.1)$$

where $L$ = loan amount; $r$ = loan rate; $p$ = risk of default; $i$ = opportunity cost or credit rate; $a$ = costs of administration and monitoring. It is likely that banks have an advantage in nearly all cost components. Further, banks operate mainly in urban areas where seasonal fluctuations in economic activities are much less extreme than in rural areas, so funds will not remain idle for extended periods. In other words, cost considerations can help to explain a sizable part of the difference between lending rates in formal and informal markets. But, considering the very unequal bargaining positions of parties on either side of informal credit transactions, it is hard to avoid suspecting that lenders appropriate considerable monopoly rents.

As the terms of loans from official lenders are much more favourable than those of loans from unofficial lenders, potential borrowers possessing adequate material collateral have a very strong incentive to turn to the official credit market. This is indeed the argument underlying the division applied in the above discussion: borrowers with material collateral do business in another configuration than those without. But it must be added for the sake of completeness that the separation is not airtight; exceptions occur. For example, a trader may need commercial credit on shorter notice than banks can deliver. Or, credit may be needed for consumption purposes, like wedding expenses, that banks are unwilling to finance. Or, the loan is meant to finance an illegal or other type of activity that demands utmost discretion. In such extreme cases borrowers with potential access to the official credit market can be seen crossing over to unofficial lenders.

*A more disaggregated breakdown of rural informal credit-exchange configurations* At least five distinct rural informal credit configurations can be identified, each focused on a particular lender group.[4] The first of these configurations consists of *friends and family*. In general, loans from friends, relatives and neighbours are given for a short period of time, interest free and with no collateral. These transactions are entered in on the basis of the principle of reciprocity. Loans are informal, typically with no witnesses or written records. Furthermore the lack of an explicit interest rate and repayment date is rather common.

However, there exist mechanisms to enforce the implicit obligations. Typically defaulters are penalized by being barred from future borrowing. Alternatively, lenders can resort to community authorities to enforce obligations. If need be, lenders can negotiate with the borrower's family members, the village head or the religious authority. Given the relevance of reputation in the village context, the disapproval of the authority may be enough of an incentive to meet the obligation. Generally, information tends to flow freely within villages and small communities. Information asymmetries are relevant only when a participant in the transaction is not a community member. These information flows enhance mechanisms to monitor and enforce contracts at the village level. Loans from friends and family protect borrowers against idiosyncratic household specific risks but not against events affecting the whole community such as the possibility of drought.

The second configuration consists of *Rotating Savings and Credit Associations* (ROSCAs). ROSCAs tend to operate in a systematic and well known manner. The ($N$) members contribute a pre-specified sum ($S$) to a cash pool ($NS$) at regular intervals, which is then allocated to each member in turn until all have received the pool (Christensen, 1993). ROSCAs are widespread all over the developing world and are particularly relevant in the African context. The explicit function of ROSCAs is to pool savings and tie loans to deposits. In this way, incentives to participate are a more disciplined approach to savings and the possibility to acquire capital faster than by saving in autarky. The major problem is represented by default risk. This is initially reduced by the social sanctions that would be imposed on defaulters by the community. The wide popularity of ROSCAs across different countries reflects the flexibility of this form of organization, able to adapt to different cultural environments. Although widely used by relatively poor individuals, this institution can also be found in urban areas bringing together better-off households.

*Pseudo-Grameen* schemes represent a third type of informal rural credit configuration. The Grameen Bank in Bangladesh has proven to be extremely successful in channelling credit to very poor informal borrowers (predominantly women). Because of its very success, pseudo-Grameen schemes have mushroomed in many parts of the world – developing as well as developed – with somewhat mixed results. Since under the right set of conditions this institution can play a major role in intermediating funds from the formal to the informal sector, its main characteristics are described next.

The scheme works as follows: groups of, say, five perspective borrowers are formed spontaneously through a self-selection process. In the first stage, only two members of a group receive a loan. Only if the original loan is repaid with interest in time do the other members of the group become eligible for a loan. Strong incentives are built in for group pressure and group monitoring. In this sense, the joint liability and collective responsibility of the group substitutes as the collateral on the loan.

The average size of the loan is low with a maximum of approximately US$75. The loans have to be repaid in one year in weekly instalments. The interest rate is 20 per cent per year and significantly lower than that charged by moneylenders. A savings obligation by the members is tacked on to the loan. The borrowers are poorly educated, if at all. Most of them are illiterate. The Grameen Bank therefore provides them with the training needed to deal with the bank in a week-long training programme. This training, together with the strict supervision of the loan repayment, teaches them the difference between a grant and a loan.

The actors group in the fourth configuration includes *traders* and small farmers. In many settings traders, shopkeepers and merchants play a crucial role in providing credit to informal borrowers and in acting as intermediaries between the formal and informal credit sectors. The typical pattern is for traders to purchase the output of small farmers and extend credit before the harvest, and to pay for the goods purchased (net of interest and principal on the loan) after the harvest upon delivery of the products. Thus, the typical contract interlinks output and credit. Because of the various links involving traders, their potential intermediation role as channellers of formal credit to informal borrowers can be capitalized on and significantly strengthened. In particular, one extremely important advantage that groups (associations) of traders organized across different regions and climatic zones possess is the ability to insure borrowers against village or zone-specific risks.

The final configuration consists of *moneylenders*. In contrast to groups or networks of traders, moneylenders operate in a very specific and limited regional area (typically a village and surrounding farming area). They can insure informal borrowers at best only partially against household-specific idiosyncratic risks. Their potential role as channellers and retailers of formal credit is much more circumscribed. Moneylenders rely mostly on their own equity capital; but, in some instances, can borrow from banks, urban savers or from traders.

### Foreign exchange

Foreign exchange is a financial asset denominated in foreign currency and is therefore, strictly speaking, not a separate factor of production. But it is often treated as such because, especially in developing countries, the transformation from domestic into foreign currency and vice versa requires an additional, often complicated transaction. Still, the purchasing power embodied in foreign exchange can be directly employed only if held in the form of directly convertible – also, hard or strong – currencies. Hence, in transactions of an item like foreign exchange, a distinction must be made between strong and weak currencies. Below we describe two foreign-exchange configurations: the official and black market ones.

In developing countries markets of foreign exchange have for a long time been subject to government intervention meant to stabilize inherently volatile exchange rates as well as to channel the available foreign exchange towards favoured uses (often below the scarcity price) and away from certain other uses. Various forms of exchange-rate regimes have been established – floating rate, flexible peg, fixed peg with or without rate differentiation – supported by elaborate systems of import duties, quantitative restrictions on imports of luxury goods, restrictions on export of funds (capital flight) and so forth. Black markets sprang up where demand for foreign exchange was frustrated by these measures. Since the 1980s, foreign-exchange regimes (much like credit-market regimes) have become far less restrictive although excess demand in some official markets is still large enough to maintain parallel black markets. But, generally speaking, the black-market premium, the difference between black and official rate, has fallen considerably.

Black markets are of special relevance in the context of the exchange-configuration approach. They illustrate how strongly actors/decision makers can react to policy measures (a component of the exchange environment) resulting in widely diverging, though closely connected configurations. Limiting ourselves to the supply side, the connections reside, for example, in the difference between black and official rate as a determinant of supply in the black market and in the appearance in black markets of foreign exchange collected by under-invoicing exports in official markets.[5]

## Land

Because land cannot be moved, its location is an essential characteristic, often connected with its use, another aspect. In urban centres land is mostly used to support houses, shops and offices. Other aspects render land more or less appropriate for other uses. Thus, the availability of valuable mineral deposits provides opportunities for mining as does high fertility in combination with the availability of surface water for agriculture. Land being immovable, its value depends also on its connections and accessibility. Therefore, in exchange configurations involving land there are strong links with infrastructure, a component of the exchange environment. Further, the fact that land is, generally speaking, in fixed supply deserves to be taken into account as it has implications for price formation. It also means that, when more land is needed for a certain purpose, it must go at the expense of another use. Thus, forests may be turned into agricultural land and agricultural land into residential areas with major consequences for the corresponding exchange configurations. The fixed supply of land has further inspired the application of 'land augmenting' agricultural technologies, another component of the exchange environment.

Land other than lots in residential areas is rarely sold. It changes hands mostly through inheritance and is therefore often part of a family tradition defining people's roots. As an old African chief testifying before a British Land Commission at the beginning of the twentieth century said, 'land belongs to a large family of which many are dead, a few are living and countless numbers are still unborn'. Further, in many developing countries the ownership rights of land have not been well established, mostly because an up-to-date, undisputed and efficient land registry system does not exist.[6] For these and other reasons (such as prestige and assured income derived from land owned) landowners are reluctant to sell, so land-sale configurations tend to show low levels of activity.

On the other hand, land-rental markets – especially in agricultural areas, the case on which we concentrate here – brim with activity. It is easy to see why: land-rental markets provide an opportunity to adjust the size of land holdings towards the desired farm size despite fixed landownership. An important additional reason derives from imperfections in other markets, particularly in the agricultural labour market.[7] First, consider the position of a family owning more land than it can cultivate. It can of course hire labour to achieve an efficient labour/land ratio, but this solution creates new problems. One problem is that production cycles on farms in the same area tend to coincide causing synchronicity of demand for labour, such that landowners cannot be sure they can hire enough workers when they need them. Another problem has to do with the cost of supervising day-labourers who may not have a strong incentive to work diligently. Both problems can be overcome by leasing out land. Now consider the position of a family owning less land than it can cultivate. When members of such a family seek employment as wage labourers, they obtain a wage reflecting average labour productivity. But as tenants they have the revenue of their labour in their own hands. In other words, actors with opposite scores of labour/land ratios living in the same area can profit from transactions in the land-rental market. Also note that, because actors can switch from the land-rental to the labour market and back again, we have here another example of two closely connected configurations.

Next, we come to the question of the content of rental contracts: fixed or share rent. This matter has attracted the attention of economists who have for a long time been baffled by the continuous and widespread existence of share-rent contracts. Fixed-rent contracts have always been accepted as efficient arrangements of agricultural production; under neoclassical assumptions (which ignore the problem of asymmetric information in the labour market referred to above) it can be demonstrated that tenants are as productive as landowners under owner-cultivation. Share-rent contracts, however, would not live up to this standard. Marshall showed that share-croppers, if 'left to their own devices', will apply inputs only in proportion to their share of the marginal value output, a demonstrably suboptimal situation.[8] So why would landowners enter into share-rent transactions? Part of the answer lies in the fact that there are various practical ways in which landlords can persuade share tenants to apply the desired amount of labour.[9] One such solution is to share non-labour costs of cultivation in the same proportion as the output.

Each of the three alternative land-use arrangements we considered – owner-cultivation, fixed-rent tenancy and sharecropping – corresponds with a certain type of contract and corresponding configuration. According to the exchange-configuration approach, the contract actually selected by the actors concerned depends on the relevant exchange elements. In this case actors' attributes appear to play the leading role. First consider agricultural workers and landowning families with a low land-to-labour ratio. It stands to reason that individual actors in this group will score differently in terms of managerial skills, capacity for work and of assets like draft animals and agricultural machinery. Those with high scores on each of these attributes will prefer a fixed-rent contract, those with low scores are likely to opt for a wage-labour contract and the others will aim for share tenancy. But landowners with high land-to-labour ratios will also show different scores of attributes and, accordingly, will prefer different contracts. Precisely the different contents of the contracts allow accommodation of actors' capacities and preferences.

## 4.4  EXCHANGE ENVIRONMENT

As indicated in Section 4.1, an exchange environment typically is a composite consisting of various components or parts. The scores of environmental components and subcomponents in different geographical areas are never exactly the same. So, by comparing the scores in different locations, economic actors often have an opportunity to select a suitable environment for their activities and transactions.[10] Thus, a multinational firm can select one particular city for its headquarters on the basis of attractive scores regarding the local fiscal, legal, political and cultural components of the environment. Similarly, workers discriminate between employers, among others, by taking account of commuting time and atmosphere at work. But the most significant illustration of actors reacting to differences in exchange environments relates to the millions of migrants per year accepting inconvenience, hardship and danger when moving to a different location. Policy makers, realizing that their decisions can affect settlement choice, sometimes manipulate components of the exchange environment in order to attract or discourage particular actor groups. Thus in the former case, they may create special trade zones, or offer tax facilities. As will be seen, the selection of specific combinations of environmental components by specific actor groups can lead to remarkable clusters of special types of transactions. An example in point is the formal/informal sector dichotomy discussed in Subsection 4.4.2 and in Chapter 5.

In order to facilitate the discussion, exchange components have been grouped into three sets: (1) cultural, political and legal components; (2) physical and technological components; and (3) the socio-economic component. They will be discussed briefly in this order in the following subsections.

### 4.4.1  The Cultural, Political and Legal Environment

The environmental aspects to be discussed under this heading are directly connected with the formal and informal institutions[11] discussed in Subsection 3.2.3. Recall that institutions are the constraints devised to order human behaviour. Formal institutions are enforced by public authorities, whereas informal institutions – such as customs, traditions and norms and values – are not.

**Culture**
Culture, in the sense of collectively held norms and values, influences people's behaviour, including economic behaviour. First of all, it is worthwhile noting that norms and values, while collectively held, express themselves in the behaviour of individuals, such as economic actors, which provides another example of a connection between one element of exchange and another. Understandably, norms and values have their greatest impact in circumstances where people interact frequently and intensively, such as within families and firms. Intra-family transactions are strongly influenced by cultural aspects, for example in connection with gender-related division of labour and position in the family.

---

### BOX 4.4   ATTEMPTS AT IDENTIFYING PROMINENT CULTURAL VALUES

In his well-known study, McClelland (1961) analyzed 1300 children's stories and, on this basis, established a score of the need for achievement in 30 mostly developed and semi-developed countries. Comparison of these scores with economic growth performances suggested a positive relation; similar exercises for the concern for affiliation and power did not produce a consistent pattern. In a more recent study comprising 40 developed and less developed countries, Hofstede (1980) identified dimensions of values shared by workers in a formal business environment. He distinguished four such dimensions: (1) power distance, expressing inequality in power, prestige and wealth; (2) uncertainty avoidance, indicating lack of tolerance for various kinds of uncertainties, regarding physical environment, relations with other people and human fate in life and afterlife; (3) individualism, considered a virtue in some countries and a dangerous, alienating property in others; (4) masculinity, comprising, among other things, the concern for advancement, the preference of earnings over service and the desire to dominate. Different countries tend to score differently on these dimensions (for example, masculinity scored high in the US and low in the Netherlands) thereby reflecting the great variety among nations' cultural profiles.

---

The cultural component tends to play a particularly significant role in low-income communities where interpersonal relations are designed to steer the decisions that individuals make toward common goals of survival. In more affluent communities, the higher levels of income and resource endowment and access to public social-security systems free people from a survival strategy and permit them a much higher degree of independence and individuality in their actions. Further, developing countries tend to be characterized by higher degrees of cultural variation,[12] which can have important implications for the analysis of economic behaviour. Thus, in analyses of exchange configurations, a finer degree of disaggregation by regions and/or socio-economic groups may be required in developing than in more industrialized countries, in order to capture their distinct characteristics.

Some cultural aspects have economic foundations, or, at least, can be rationalized on economic grounds. They can relate to the intra-family allocation of food and of labour, care and other tasks among men and women, boys and girls, old and young, to the rights of the first-born son and other children and so on. In the wider context of tribe or clan they often concern rights to the use of communal land.

Other cultural aspects, such as religious beliefs, clearly have extra-economic foundations. While they are exogenous to economists, this group of cultural aspects can have an enormous influence on transactions. An example in point is the Islamic banking system which, in accordance with the Koranic prohibition of interest, has devised a separate set of financial instruments.

The importance of collectively held norms and values for transactions in general derives from the fact that they steer human interaction, including in matters related to exchange. In an environment where honesty and fairness in dealing with other people are firmly embedded, transactions come about more easily if only because transaction costs are lower. Clearly also the form and content of transactions will be influenced. These insights have been elaborated in the rapidly expanding literature on social capital (see Box 4.5), which also underlines the self-reinforcing effects of an environment characterized by trust and cooperation. There are three factors at work here: (1) the intrinsic motivation by individual actors whose attitude towards others reflects the cultural environment, (2) the external social control, and (3) the tendency among actors to reciprocate in a way similar to how they were approached (the golden rule). The collective variant of social capital discussed here has been variously described as trust congealed, as a lubricant of societal relations and as the ligaments in the invisible hand.

---

## BOX 4.5   SOCIAL CAPITAL

The concept of social capital originated in sociology, while gaining much attention in political science and especially in economics. Unfortunately, the term has been subject to different interpretations so that it has become necessary to indicate which meaning is attached to the term. We mention here only two, influential, views.

According to Putnam social capital consists of those aspects of social organizations – like trust, norms and networks – that can improve social efficiency by allowing coordinated action (Putnam et al., 1993), or of social networks and the norms of reciprocity and trustworthiness that arise from them (Putnam, 2000). The latter definition asserts that norms and trust derive from networks. Other authors, however, propose a different ordering. On the other hand, Bourdieu uses social capital in a much more limited sense, namely as the potential resources stored in networks of relations (Bourdieu, 1986). The first view emphasizes the collective side of social capital, whereas the second focuses on the advantages that individual actors derive from it. This is why we discuss social capital here under the heading of Culture in the present subsection as well as under the heading of (actors') Assets in Subsection 4.5.2.

---

For the above reasons, a (positive) relation between social capital and economic growth strongly appeals to intuition, but it has appeared very hard to find empirical support for such a relation. This is partly due to the problems one encounters when attempting to measure items as trust, norms and networks. Empirical tests have concentrated on trust which, while still treacherous, is considered the simplest one to quantify. Knack and Keefer, using data for 29 developed countries (Knack and Keefer, 1997), and Zak and Knack, having added 12 less developed countries (Zak and Knack, 2001), present such tests. After rigorously testing for robustness, it has been found in another study that trust affects growth significantly only when the level of development and the quality of institutions are low.[13]

### Political factors
Markets tend to be more imperfect and market failures tend to occur more often in developing than in developed countries. This is largely due to such structural problems as poor infrastructure (resulting in monopolistic

## BOX 4.6   MARKET IMPERFECTIONS

In market economies public intervention in economic affairs may be justified when market imperfections occur. This is a necessary, but not a sufficient condition, for the public sector may also fail in its attempts at correction. In other words, the expected net welfare gain must be weighed against the actual welfare loss resulting from a market imperfection when deciding for or against intervention

Three main groups of market imperfections are traditionally distinguished (see the classic Musgrave and Musgrave, 1973). The first one relates to imperfect allocation, mostly caused by external effects, asymmetric information and excessive market power. Secondly, imperfect distribution has to do with society's preference for other distributions of wealth and income than markets generate. And thirdly, imperfect stabilization refers to the inability of markets to bring about full employment, price stability and other macroeconomic objectives.

competition and extremely high transportation costs), unequal access to credit markets, unequal distribution of education and information and virtually absent insurance markets. Market imperfections contribute to the segmentation of exchange configurations and vice versa in an interdependent and reinforcing way.

Up to the 1990s the belief in benevolent, omnipotent government in combination with the realization that the performance of markets in developing countries tends to suffer from inherent weaknesses, resulted in particularly strong interventionist policies. Rather than eliminating causes of market imperfections, policies aimed at steering actors' behaviour with strong instruments like direct price intervention – particularly in agricultural, credit and foreign exchange markets – and the discretionary distribution of permits and licenses. Understandably, this strong intervention generated equally strong reactions. While some actors conformed mostly to the rules, others defied them and often bribed officials in order to reduce the chance of getting caught, or, at best, engaged in unproductive rent seeking. Where they were in force, these policy measures became a very powerful component of the exchange environment, giving rise to the development of distinct exchange configurations, one consisting of official markets and another of unofficial, or illegal, or black markets.

Although the interventionist stance of governments in developing countries has softened, the tendency to intervene in imperfect markets, rather than to create conditions for an improved functioning of such markets, has not disappeared. Even worse, many governments may be remiss in performing even such primary public tasks as providing good quality legislation, efficient administration, a fair judicial system, a sustainable public budget and an acceptable level of inflation. The quality of a country's governance is nowadays seen as an important factor for the prospects of its exchange system.

The political arena is populated by such diverse groups as politicians (executives and parliamentarians at various levels of government), civil servants, pressure groups, voters, political parties and advisory committees, each with different motives and instruments. Their interaction, obviously strongly influenced by the prevailing distribution of power, results in the formulation of formal rules (that is the legislation to be discussed below) that restrain human behaviour in addition to the informal rules discussed above. The public-choice literature aims to describe and analyze this process of interaction and its outcomes.

Political decision making undergoes the influence of the norms and values embraced by the society concerned. There are several reasons for this: the decision makers themselves are part of society; they are regularly lectured by others who claim to represent segments of society; and they will gain more electoral support when their standpoints reflect widely held views. Thus, especially in democratic settings, public action taken tends to reflect societal preferences as expressed in the relative size of the various categories of public revenues and outlays and the attitude towards the private sector.

In the development literature, the objectives, motivations and acts of the state (that is the institutions consisting of the government and the administrative machinery available to execute the measures issued by the government) have often been idealized.[14] The government is viewed as the caretaker of the common good whose decisions are punctually executed. The foremost, and certainly most influential, proponent of this early approach to planning is Tinbergen (1956), who developed a complete theory of quantitative economic policy based on the assumption that governments, or policy makers, possess clear-cut objectives. Policy models can then be solved for the quantitative values of specific policy measures or instruments which fulfil the predetermined values of the desired targets. But, in developing countries, as well as elsewhere, reality is more complex and cannot be captured fully by planning models, however sophisticated they might be.[15]

Politicians and civil servants are not only less than perfectly competent but they also use part of the power vested in them to promote their own interests and to follow a course that suits their own preferences. The bureaucracy is itself one of the most powerful groups in society; it has a vested interest in the promotion and interpretation of measures which work in their advantage in terms of employment, career opportunities, prestige or even income through bribes and other forms of corruption. This means, among other things, that official policy objectives and intentions may, at least partially, reflect the desires of the government and the bureaucracy, as power groups in society, rather than the broader national interests. Also significant differences may exist between the policy intentions, as such, and the actual policy measures which ultimately reach and affect actors in markets and other exchange configurations.[16]

Pressures are continuously exerted on the government. They can be internal, in that they originate with certain segments of the government (a typical example would be when a coalition is in power), or from the bureaucracy itself. Alternatively, pressures can be external and be exerted by foreign and organized domestic groups.[17] These external pressures are likely to influence the policy makers and elicit a response which renders the political and the socio-economic systems interdependent.

The public choice and collective action literature has analyzed how interest groups can gain access to the state and impose regulations which benefit those groups. In those instances where the state and its agents are not neutral and passive, but tend to pursue their own selfish objectives the positive theory of 'rent-seeking' applies.[18] Groups which control (influence) the government can capture 'contrived rents' which are 'artificial transfers in the sense that they result from government restrictions, such as the granting of monopoly positions, protection or any other kind of regulation or rule' (Nabli and Nugent, 1989, p.102).

It can be argued that the environment within which policy makers reach decisions in developing countries is more fluid and volatile than in more developed countries.[19] Decisions are often made on an ad hoc and relatively arbitrary basis, and different policy measures may lack in internal consistency. The fluidity and volatility of the political environment is influenced by a number of forces. Firstly, social and economic tensions caused by skewed income and wealth distributions and differences of religion, caste and tribe membership, language, education and regional origin tend to be significant and act as major obstacles to converging on an acceptable consensus. Secondly, developing countries are often in transition from one type of societal and economic organization to another, with inevitable frictions and crises. Thirdly, institutions and the legal foundations tend to be weaker than in more developed countries. The relative youth of institutions in newly independent developing world countries, combined (in some cases) with an absence, or lack of experience with democratic traditions, impedes further the peaceful resolution of conflicts and adds to the overall uncertainty in the general environment within which markets have to operate.

These reasons may explain the relatively higher frequency of totalitarian and centralized regimes in developing countries on either the left or the right wing of the political spectrum. One important implication of the existence of such regimes is that they tend to either (1) interfere with the operation of markets and, at the limit, replace markets with centralized planning and inflexible regulations; or (2) adopt a more laissez faire approach to markets which might, in itself, reinforce the impact of the spontaneous distortions and market imperfections.

Furthermore, politicians and civil servants in developing countries are subjected to a two-fold bias which can have key implications on the shaping of exchange configurations and their operation. One has to do with the administrative convenience of steering protective measures (such as import licences and subsidized credit) in the direction of the modern sector of the economy where firms are easier to reach. Modern firms, in comparison with firms in the traditional sector, are larger but fewer in number and better administered. The second bias derives from the inclination of bureaucrats to avoid the antagonism of powerful groups. The combination of these two biases may lead to actions favouring the modern sector of the economy and the urban areas. Conversely, it is likely that the traditional sector and the rural areas may be negatively affected. The above behaviour will tend to polarize the economy along dual–dual lines as indicated previously and reinforce the 'urban bias'.

**Law, the judiciary and law enforcement**
The relevance of an efficient legal system for exchange relations and especially for market transactions has already been underlined in Chapter 3. The way in which property rights are defined and protected and, in the case of ownership of land, administered, as well as the speed and fairness of operation of the judicial branch and the effectiveness of law enforcement are among the most important aspects of the exchange environment. They determine the size of transaction costs, define the playing field on which exchange takes place and, thereby, impact on the frequency, form and content of transactions. Hall and Jones suggest that countries with a long-standing tradition of careful attention for these aspects of the exchange environment produce significantly higher output per worker (Hall and Jones, 1999). As indicated, the purpose of these formal institutions is to

reduce uncertainty and, thus, facilitate exchange. Unfortunately, however, it can be observed that, compared with developed countries, the effectiveness of formal institutions in developing countries still lags far behind. An illustration in point is provided by the empirical analysis of the protection of property rights in various developing countries as carried out by De Soto and his team. According to their findings, property rights in the various countries examined are poorly defined[20] such that they cannot readily be used as collateral with serious consequences for economic development (De Soto, 2000). In a similar exercise Djankov et al. suggest that it takes vastly more time and effort to formally start up a business in developing than in developed countries (Djankov et al., 2002).

Formal rules are formulated and implemented by people who may have their own interest at heart rather than the social wellbeing. North puts it very strongly as follows: 'if the institutional framework rewards piracy then piratical organizations will come into existence' (North, 1994, p. 361). Considerations like these have led to the development of an economic theory of predation.[21] Under conditions of predation – that is, extortion, appropriation, theft – property rights are insecure, so to unprotected actors it does not make sense to invest in productive assets or in education as it is unlikely that they will be able to reap the rewards of their efforts. The consequences of such situations for economic growth are easy to predict.

### 4.4.2    The Physical and Technological Environment

**The physical environment**
A number of characteristics directly related to location and space have a bearing on the functioning of exchange configurations. The first and foremost dichotomy is between rural and urban areas. Especially in developing countries one can, without much exaggeration, often describe the prevailing situation as one of regional dualism. The higher population density and concomitant centralized availability of services, communications and information in urban areas lead to larger, more integrated market-based exchange configurations than develop in rural areas. As a result the division of labour is much greater and the use of money more frequent in urban activities. The more pervasive presence of government in cities, combined with a higher population density, encourages the organization of a variety of pressure groups such as industrialists and labour unions that can have a major effect on policy formulation. One notorious effect is the urban bias one can observe in policy orientation in a number of developing countries turning the internal terms of trade against agriculture and in favour of urban producers and consumers.

Another difference between rural and urban areas affecting exchange configurations derives from the highly seasonal and annual periodicity and synchronicity characterizing agricultural production and income variables. Agricultural production follows a clear-cut seasonal pattern that influences product and factor exchanges. The regularity of the various agricultural tasks from planting to harvesting generates periods of peak demand for labour (at planting and harvest time) and credit (before planting and before the harvest for consumption purposes) followed by periods during which demand is limited. In addition, there is the risk of crop failure due to vagaries of the weather or to pests and diseases. Moreover, when there is a crop failure, entire regional economic activities (including exchange) are often simultaneously and negatively affected. Due to this simultaneity, the risk of crop failure is normally not insurable. In urban areas where the economic base is more diversified, negative developments in one sector may be compensated by positive developments elsewhere, such that the general level of activity tends to show less volatility.

The importance of infrastructure as a lubricant to the exchange process in reducing transaction costs and expanding market-transaction opportunities has been illustrated in the Pakistani wheat-market cases of Subsection 2.3.2. Roads and bridges figure predominantly in this respect. Precisely in developing countries where roads do not yet form an intricate and dependable, all-weather network and where many villages are not connected to trunk roads, the effects on exchange can be widely observed in the form of highly segmented and often monopolistic and monopsonistic markets. Under these conditions the beneficial effect of a new road cannot easily be overestimated.

Other components of infrastructure, such as irrigation systems, help to regulate the availability of surface water which depends on the climate, another component of the physical environment. Irrigation systems can reduce the variability of an uncontrolled water supply. One aspect of risk for agricultural activities can thus be limited. Another category of infrastructure consists of information and communication systems providing access to radio, telephone, internet and other facilities. The impact on the exchange of services and products that do not travel well may be limited, but these facilities can enlarge the reach of actors enormously in other exchanges.

### The technological environment
Over the centuries, technological development has been the most important vehicle of structural economic change. Hence, the impact of technology and technological change must be taken into account when

considering the evolution of exchange configurations over time, as will be done in Chapter 7.

It has been argued that demographic development promotes technological progress, because larger numbers of interconnected people can make more discoveries.[22] Diamond's view on the millennia-long evolution of human civilization extends this argument.[23] He argues that in early stages of civilization landmasses with long distances along the East–West axis are conducive to the development and diffusion of agricultural products and production processes and to the domestication of wider ranges of animals. On the same latitude, climates are mostly similar, so useful findings can find wide application and can be further perfected. According to Diamond this is one of the major reasons why the Eurasian continent obtained the head start which eventually led to its dominating position.

Technological development, including the introduction of new products and production and other techniques, has had a profound and diverse impact on exchange configurations through its influence on the level of income, the environment, the organization of production, the demand for factors of production and material and immaterial inputs, the supply of new items, and, thus on the form and content of a great variety of transactions. Roughly since 1750, the rate of technological change has vastly increased. Before then, technological development depended mostly on serendipity and gradual improvements introduced by artisans.[24] Thereafter, it rapidly became the result of targeted efforts employing accumulated scientific knowledge. A well-known illustration of this phenomenon is the graph presented by Fogel that shows how the world population, growing slowly over a period of some ten thousand years, rockets up together with technological development during the last two centuries.[25] The Oglethorpe Crypt of Civilization, sealed in 1940, provides another illustration. The crypt contains records and objects meant to provide 'an encyclopedic inventory of life and customs up until 1940'. The crypt will be opened in the year 8113, but already now, only a few decades after having been sealed, its contents seem strangely dated as references to such familiar present-day phenomena as fast-food restaurants, e-mail communication, mobile phones and personal computers are missing.

Technological progress is driven by research which can usefully be separated in two entirely different categories: scientific and applied research.[26] The results of scientific research are presented in open publications, so they are non-excludable. Since they are also non-rival – the use by one user does not preclude the use by others – it follows that basic research produces a public good which justifies subsidization by the public sector. Institutions such as universities receive earmarked subsidies on the condition that they produce a stream of scientific publications of a certain minimum quality. This transaction is followed up by intra-organizational transactions in research institutions employing researchers appointed on the basis of foregoing market transactions. In other words, the measure of success in basic research activities depends on a string of transactions.

Applied research is an instrument, in contrast to scientific research the results of which are an end product. Firms financing applied research intend to use its results to improve their performance in terms of profitability, market share and consumer satisfaction. It is clear, however, that these benefits can be reaped only if competitors can be excluded from application of the innovations. Secrecy provides exclusivity for some time; patent registration can extend the period of exclusive exploitation of innovations. Also in the case of applied research success depends on the researchers employed by means of labour-market transactions and on the way they are managed in intra-firm transactions. But the ultimate test of success lies, of course, in the market transactions through which the products embodying the innovations find their way to the users. So also in the case of applied research, outcomes depend on a variety of transactions.

While new technologies create new opportunities, they require certain conditions to be fulfilled in order to take root. For example, the attractiveness of many modern production technologies resides in the economies of scale they offer. But scale economies can be reaped only when the market is large enough to absorb the vast quantities produced and when the marketing skill is present to actually sell the products. Further, even relatively unsophisticated production techniques can be used only if the technical skill to install, run and, especially, to maintain and repair the accompanying tools and machines is locally available. Finally, sufficiently large financial funds must be available for the major investments that new technologies often entail, which implies in practice involvement of a venture capital market.

The above paragraph illustrates how the technological component of the exchange environment is intertwined with certain exchange configurations and with certain characteristics of other exchange elements. But it also shows that – even if they can be seen as public goods, in the sense that they are in principle available to all – modern technologies will settle in those places where the accommodating conditions are satisfied. Developing countries can offer these conditions only in certain sections of their economies at best. The result is that their technological environment differs from that in other countries with corresponding consequences for the shape of transactions. Yet the tentacles of the information (internet) super-highway are reaching further and further – even into the most remote areas of the globe.

The limited capacity of developing countries to absorb modern production technologies leads to a situation where more or less isolated pockets of production activities applying state-of-the-art technologies co-exist with sectors consisting of production units using traditional technologies. But this dichotomy between modern and traditional production sectors in developing countries is not based on the employed technology alone; it possesses additional dimensions. To the extent that modern technology is indeed applied in large-scale, internationally oriented, incorporated firms that need to draw on outside sources to finance their investments and operation, a sophisticated bookkeeping system is required to control cross-national costs and to manage inventories. This additional requirement is directly connected to the way in which production is organized. It means, among others, that the modern sector is an easy target for the tax collector, in contrast to the traditional sector where even primitive records are rarely kept. And for the same reason, minimum wage regulations are much better enforced in the modern sector than in the traditional sector. On the other hand, the modern sector has access to the formal credit market where it pays interest rates that are much lower than in the informal market. An illustration relating to a producer in the informal sector is presented in Box 5.1 in Subsection 5.2.2.

This multi-dimensional dichotomy between a modern and a traditional production sector is sometimes also referred to as the formal/informal dichotomy. It will be discussed in more detail in Chapter 5. But, it can be observed already here that the modern and traditional sectors are characterized by opposite scores of characteristics of exchange elements. As a consequence the respective actor groups operate in entirely different market and non-market exchange configurations.

The technological environment affects exchange configurations in various ways. For example, the technology employed leaves its imprint on the resulting product (the item exchanged). Many products – for example, footwear, bricks, furniture, kitchen utensils – can be produced in many ways employing different techniques, but with different results in terms of quality, appearance, homogeneity and so on. Further, as noted above, the employed production technology has a strong bearing on the form of organization of production and, thereby, on intra-firm transactions. Finally, the production technology applied is also a major determinant of the demand for specific labour skills, raw materials and semi-finished products. In all these cases the technological environment exerts its influence in indirect ways.

The magnitude of this indirect influence on exchange configurations becomes directly apparent following a technological change. When the change is marginal, the impact will likewise be limited. But technological development also proceeds by leaps and bounds and can then, as history illustrates, have spectacular consequences for exchange configurations.

### 4.4.3   The Socio-economic Environment

The dominating single aspect of the socio-economic environment in terms of impact on the formation of transactions is undoubtedly the stage of economic development. In a high-income environment massive income streams seek outlets. Such a situation has repercussions not only for the type of goods that is bought and sold, but also for the variety of goods that can be selected. Product differentiation catering to different preferences and needs is feasible only if demand is sufficiently large. This is particularly apparent in the financial sector in high-income countries where the accumulated wealth can be invested in a wide range of increasingly sophisticated (and risky) financial products. In low-income countries such diversity is less available; the needs and preferences exist but they do not generate a sufficiently large demand.

In low-income settings social security is typically provided within communities by the extended family, village or neighbourhood. This help to the more needy individuals is provided semi-voluntarily, in the sense that an unwillingness to provide it entails social costs. As income grows such private-support arrangement tends to be replaced by a system in which the state takes an ever larger role defining the criteria for entitlement and the size of the benefits, making payments and collecting the resources for its implementation. But the public sector can only play an active role in social-security programmes when its administrative capacity meets certain minimum requirements and the private sector's production capacity has become large enough to bear a heavier tax burden.

State intervention in social security has profound implications for transactions, in particular for transactions within the family (as intra-family support gradually loses a large part of its rationale) and on labour market transactions. As to the latter, especially state-provided unemployment benefits can have a strong impact, depending on the coverage of the scheme. Clearly the fact that these benefits render workers less dependent on their employers can influence worker mobility. Further, it may reduce the sense of urgency of finding new employment outlets among workers who have lost their job and it may raise the reservation wage, that is the wage that must be offered before new employment becomes sufficiently attractive.

Another characteristic of the socio-economic environment relates to the production structure, that is the sectoral composition and spatial dispersion of production activities. Its impact is most clearly felt in regions where only one production activity dominates. Especially labour-exchange configurations will be influenced by the geographical concentration of production, given the close connection that exists between production and labour. But other configurations may also be affected, for example, by strong seasonality in production or, in general, by the fortunes of a dominating economic sector. Such consideration applies with special force to developing countries with their characteristically narrow production structures.

In this connection the structure of industry also deserves mentioning as an important determinant of the form an exchange configuration will take. Some of the aspects distinguished in the vast literature on this subject – such as degree of competition, technology, protection and restriction to entry – have been mentioned under various headings above. Other important aspects are vertical integration and specialization, which tend to have entirely different consequences for exchange configurations. During a process of vertical integration the emphasis shifts from one governance structure to another as market transactions are replaced by intra-firm transactions. Specialization, to the extent that it results from a split-off from a previously integrated firm, has the opposite effect.

## 4.5 ACTORS

As a result of the wide variety of actor groups and of the functions they perform, the number of characteristics of actors which can influence the modalities of exchange processes is nearly endless. Below we consider only the main characteristics to illustrate how certain groups of characteristics of actors tend to impact on transactions. The role of actors as decision makers is taken up in Subsection 4.5.2.

### 4.5.1 Actors' Characteristics

The major characteristics or dimensions of actors which influence their (exchange) behaviour are: (1) the number and density of actors, the institutional and organizational forms assumed by the actors and their relative bargaining power; (2) actors' assets and liabilities, resource endowments (in terms of ownership of land, other physical and financial capital, and human capital), entitlements, and incomes; (3) objectives and preferences of actors, personal beliefs and attributes (such as age, gender, ability to learn, fitness) and class characteristics and constraints; (4) the relations which prevail among actors and the instruments at their disposal (which are, of course, related to their resource endowments and incomes); and (5) the level of information available to actors and their attitude towards risk and uncertainty. Each of these groups of dimensions of actors will be discussed below.

Actors engaging in transactions can consist of individuals, families and organizations[27] like firms, governments and other non-profit organizations. Thus, family farms, corporations, limited liability firms and cooperatives can operate at either end of exchange configurations. Also governments (local, provincial, national) can be major actors in a variety of settings, for example, as employers, borrowers, and purchasers of goods and services.

Another characteristic of actors belonging to the first group, and one discussed prominently in the field of industrial organization, is their number. It has implications for the degree of competition, from the case of large numbers of buyers and sellers leading to full competition, via ever smaller numbers of actors – giving rise to oligopoly and duopoly – to monopoly and monopsony. Each of these cases has implications for the price formation and the awareness of actors of possible reactions of competitors to own initiatives. Further, competitors may enter into coalitions and thereby affect the degree of competition, a subject analyzed in game theory. Still, the actual number of competitors may be less important than the potential number (a subject of study in the contestable-market theory). It may well be that the threat of new competitors, a threat that is especially potent in the absence of sunk costs, disciplines even a small number of actors in a specific market.

The second group of characteristics consisting of the resource endowment and entitlement of actors – as reflected by their possession of human capital, land and other capital assets – is an important factor in defining the profile of actor groups. It may seal off certain exchange configurations entirely for certain classes of actors based on their wealth or the lack of it. Thus, for instance, adequate material collateral may be a prerequisite for obtaining loans from the formal credit market; actors without such collateral are automatically excluded from consideration. Further, the size of the area of land a family owns determines on which side of the rental and labour markets its members operate, as landowners or tenants and as employers or workers. In the discussion of the wheat market in Pakistan (Subsection 2.3.2) the area of land owned also appeared to influence the revenue price of agricultural produce. Another, but closely related material asset, also of special relevance for individual actors and families, is the capital invested in an own business venture other than farms. The score on this characteristic differentiates between self-employed persons and other workers; it has immediate consequences for the responsibilities and the management of the activities of actors in these two groups.

Human capital is the accumulated knowledge and experience embedded in individual actors. As it is a personal attribute, it differs from the generally accessible knowledge presented in open publications that has a public-good character. It must be underlined that personal attributes can never be owned by firms and other organizations; they can become part of the profile of the latter actor groups only through labour-market transactions. This conclusion is of particular relevance for organizations operating in service sectors: their competence derives to a large extent from the personal characteristics of the persons they employ.

A strong factor determining the profile of firms in the non-service sectors resides in the kind of goods in which they invested. In these sectors of the economy, what count most are the machines, tools and equipment that firms employ and the goods they have in stock. The assets provide information about the nature and the quality of the commodities produced; they have important consequences for the market and intra-firm transactions that firms engage in. This conclusion implies that the assets must be described in some detail in order to make a meaningful contribution, indicating not only their general purpose, size, quantity and so on, but also their age, sophistication and state of maintenance. The scores make all the difference here. At the high end one finds the fully operational state-of-the-art factory and at the polar end the junkyard.

In the third group of characteristics figure actors' attitudes, partly shaped by many of the above resource endowments. They determine whether their behaviour is maximizing, satisficing or following a combination of the two, as under bounded rationality. When considering decision making by very poor persons, their limited capacity to absorb economic shocks needs to be taken into consideration. Thus, the behaviour of poor farm households is sometimes described as following a lexicographic preference function to protect them against a small probability of a catastrophic outcome. Similarly, the attitude of producers in developing countries is a key determinant of the choice of technology, resource allocation and planned output. Traditional small farm owners or petty producers in the informal sector may well select a technique which yields a lower expected outcome than an alternative, more modern technique, because the distribution of outcomes of the former displays less variance.

Another essential personal attribute of actors concerns their preferences. Preference patterns steer individual behaviour, but they are at least also influenced by the social norms and values which individuals internalize during their upbringing and life in a certain environment. Less well-known individual characteristics of a similar nature are work ethic, altruism and morality. Still other personal characteristics are genetically determined and possibly honed or blunted in later life, such as physical fitness, intellectual power, a talent for leadership and social skills. Evidently, the attributes described here have a particularly strong impact on the nature of transactions which are typically individual-related, such as labour-market and intra-firm and intra-family transactions. An attribute of a different nature, but also obtained at birth, is the membership of a group (family, clan or neighborhood) that brings with it a certain reputation as well as rights and obligations regarding protection and support. Membership in a lower caste may be an insurmountable barrier to entry into or exit from certain product or factor exchange configurations.

Fourthly, the nature of the relations that link and bind actors together similarly influences their behaviour and ultimately the nature and form of transactions. This issue is intrinsically connected with the underlying cultural environment. At one extreme, in a highly traditional setting, the exchange process is ritualized and follows informally prescribed channels. In such a setting, customs geared to the survival of the community predetermine exchange. At the other extreme, trade is at arm's length and based on legal arrangements. In many present-day market transactions, however, the relations between actors are positioned somewhere between these two extremes. In fact, a successful business performance partly depends on relations with other businesses and clients. Such relations are, therefore, often carefully constructed and nursed. As indicated in Box 4.5, Bourdieu (1986) reserves the term social capital for the potential resources stored in networks of relations, thereby giving the term a typically individualistic interpretation. Fafchamps and Minten use the term in a still narrower sense, namely as the network of business contacts that traders have. In an empirical analysis of three African countries they found that traders with more social capital, represented by the number of other traders known, obtain higher levels of value added (Fafchamps and Minten, 2001).

Finally, information is a crucial dimension influencing the behaviour of actors in exchange configurations. In the real world, in contrast with the neo-classical paradigm, actors have to operate with imperfect knowledge

---

# BOX 4.7    INTERLOCKING TRANSACTIONS

In sharecropping transactions two items (land use and labour) are exchanged simultaneously. In fact, these contracts often act as a screening device for the exchange of even a third item (namely credit) between the same participants. Landlords realize that sharecroppers will not go into hiding after having obtained a loan and that repayment of the loan can rather easily be enforced at harvest time. So sharecroppers are seen as relatively secure debtors. Thus, particularly in developing countries, the interlinkage of different factor-exchange configurations yields so-called interlocked transactions in reaction to the information problem faced by actors.

---

and information regarding the characteristics of other elements, such as the environment and attributes of other actors now and in the future. Thus, actors behave and make decisions under uncertainty and risks. It has been emphasized that the choice of an exchange system depends significantly on the cost of acquiring information about trading partners and the cost of enforcing contracts (Eggertson, 1991, p. 243). Several parallel exchange systems can be found within the same economy because individuals and exchanges are heterogeneous with respect to transaction costs.

Uncertainty can have a destructive effect on transactions. If buyers have less information than sellers as to the true quality of a product and must face the possibility of deceit by suppliers, it can be shown that the lower quality items tend to drive out the good ones. If buyers only know the average quality, the sellers of higher-quality items will be discriminated against compared to those offering lower-quality items. This will start a cumulative process of sellers of higher-than-average quality items removing themselves from the market until, at the limit, the market disappears altogether.[28] The destructive effect of asymmetric information can also be observed when, inversely, sellers are less well informed than buyers. This case occurs in some insurance markets and has become known as the adverse-selection problem (see Box 3.4).

When information is unevenly shared between buyers and sellers, there is an incentive to engage in activities which convey and yield information. Thus sellers of high-quality items will want to convey this information to potential buyers by way of 'signals'. An important signal in the labour market is education, which suggests productive potential, while product guarantees can tell something about quality in product markets. But also race or caste may be used by employers as an indicator of the perceived 'average quality' of a given group of workers.

Another example of how limited information affects exchange is obtained whenever prices are seen as carriers of information about quality. This case occurs when, for example, the willingness to accept a low wage is understood as an admission of a worker's low productivity, or the acceptance of a high rate of interest is considered as an expression of bad risk. In these instances, the market may no longer clear and unemployment and credit rationing result. As Shapiro and Stiglitz (1984) have shown, the market adjustment mechanism will then differ drastically from the neoclassical model, repealing the standard law of supply and demand.

Finally, regarding attitudes towards risk there is the need to recognize first of all the very considerable differences that can be observed among individual actors. The differences express themselves in diverse consumption, investment and other patterns of behaviour and in the measure of foresight actors show when taking (or avoiding) decisions affecting their future. But account should be taken also of general patterns in risk-related attitudes such as those Kahneman and Tversky identified in their classical 1979 article. In their study they found among several other things that actors react differently to possible gains and losses. Actors are systematically risk averse when the choice is between sure gains and expected gains whereas they are risk seeking in decisions between sure losses and expected losses. If they have a choice, people are clearly willing to pay a premium in order to avoid the regret brought about by unfortunate outcomes of earlier decisions.

### 4.5.2  Actors as Decision Makers

The special nature of actors in economic exchange has already been emphasized in Section 2.3. Actors take in information about the relevant exchange elements, process it and then, most important of all, take decisions and, thus, breathe life into transactions. Two types of decisions can be distinguished here. Firstly, actors must select the most appropriate exchange configuration for the transactions under consideration. Secondly, actors have to establish if they want to go ahead with a transaction, given its form and conditions. It is because of their unique decision-making powers that actors stand apart among the elements of exchange in exchange configurations. Brokers mediating between parties and lawyers specialized in drawing up contracts can also be involved with transactions, but if they do not take the pertinent decisions they are not considered as actors in that same sense.

By engaging in certain transactions actors can alter the characteristics of their own attributes. For example, a family can buy or sell agricultural land and by so doing bring about a radical change in the composition of its assets. Or an individual can enroll in a training course and improve his/her level of education. Or a firm can buy new machines, hire personnel with specific qualifications, or lease a patent and become an entirely different business unit. In fact, actors – and, among them, especially firms – have considerable room for recreating their profiles of assets and attributes.[29]

This observation leads to two very important conclusions. The first conclusion is that, while the principal relation in exchange configurations runs from elements of exchange to transactions, there can be another relation running in the opposite direction. Or, put differently, actors can use transactions to bring about change in an element of exchange. The second conclusion derives its importance from its immeasurable impact in the real world. For, in accordance with the main argument of the exchange-configuration approach, a change in an element of exchange has consequences for transactions. Therefore, by consciously changing an exchange element through transactions, actors can try to manipulate the preconditions for exchange and thus improve the outcomes of new transactions. With the latter conclusion we have identified one of the foremost dynamic forces to be discussed in detail in Chapter 7 which deals with the dynamics of exchange configurations.

# NOTES

1. Strictly speaking the factor of production to be discussed here is 'financial funds'. But financial funds are highly fungible, such that there are large numbers of financial instruments many of which are close substitutes. A discussion of these subgroups is far beyond the scope of this book. We limit ourselves to loan or credit transactions because they still are of overwhelming importance in developing countries.
2. Note that the risk involved in a lease transaction is considerably smaller: also in this type of transaction a certain item is transmitted for use by another party for an agreed period of time, but the item is not transformed.
3. Family members are excluded because loans among family members do not belong to the category of credit-market transactions. For a discussion of 'Friends and family' as an informal rural credit-exchange configuration see subsequent subsection.
4. This subsection is based on Thorbecke and Paternostro (1995) which discusses in detail the process of rural credit intermediation. For still another form of rural informal credit transactions, see Box 4.7 in Subsection 4.5.1.
5. For a more detailed treatment of these matters, see, for example, Agénor (1992).
6. Here we see another link with a characteristic of the exchange environment.
7. Structural imperfections in the rental markets of draft animals and agricultural machinery also contribute to the attractiveness of land-rental markets.
8. Marshall, Book 7, Ch. 11, 1890.
9. See Johnson, 1950 and Cheung, 1969.
10. Intra-family transactions are an exception to this rule: only the marriage decision (and assuming free choice therein) allows some room for selecting environmental components.

11. Note that the terms formal and informal have a different meaning in the context of the formal/informal sector dichotomy discussed in Subsection 4.4.2 and, in more detail, in Subsection 5.2.2.
12. For a discussion of this phenomenon, see Geertz, 1973, p. 255 ff.
13. See Beugelsdijk et al., 2002.
14. Reasons for the persisting, idealistic view of the state have been discussed in Schumpeter, 1950, 3rd edition, Chapter 21. See also Chapter 6.
15. In fairness to Tinbergen, his methodology allowed certain real life characteristics of the environment and actors to be incorporated as binding constraints in his system.
16. Actors, in turn, will often operate in such a way as to dampen and limit the effectiveness of these actual policy measures sometimes even through unofficial and illegal means. The 'rational expectations' approach emphasizes the countervailing reactions which actors adopt to undo the intended effects of policies (Lucas, 1976).
17. See Lindblom, 1977, p. 12 ff.
18. See, for instance, Brennan and Buchanan, 1985.
19. In Killick's words, the balancing acts which politicians must perform to maintain control are generally speaking more precarious in developing countries than elsewhere; Killick, 1976. See also Easterly, 2001, Chapter 13.
20. For example, it took 77 steps and approximately 13 years to acquire desert land for construction purposes and register property rights in Egypt and it took 168 steps and between 13 and 25 years to register informal property of residential structures in the Philippines.
21. See for an early contribution Skaperdas, 1992.
22. Kremer, 1993.
23. Diamond, 1998.
24. Veblen referred to this phenomenon as 'the instinct of workmanship'; Veblen, 1914.
25. Fogel, 1999.
26. Romer, 2006, Section 3.4 offers a more extensive analysis.
27. North defines organizations as 'groups of people bound together by some common purpose to achieve certain objectives'; North, 1994, p. 361. Also see Subsection 2.3.3.
28. See Akerlof's classical paper on 'lemons' in the used car market in the United States; Akerlof, 1970.
29. We came across this opportunity for strategic intervention in the discussion of organizational learning in Section 3.5.

# REFERENCES

Agénor, P.-R. (1992), 'Parallel currency markets in developing countries: theory, evidence and policy implications', *Princeton Studies in International Economics*, Princeton, NJ, USA: Princeton University.

Akerlof, G. (1970), 'The market for 'lemons': quality uncertainty and the market mechanism', *The Quarterly Journal of Economics*, **84** (3), 488–500.

Beugelsdijk, S., H. de Groot and A.B.T.M. van Schaik (2002), 'Trust and economic growth, a robustness analysis', *Tinbergen discussion paper 049/3*, Rotterdam, NL: Tinbergen Institute.

Bourdieu, P. (1986), 'The forms of capital', in J.G. Richardson (ed.), *Handbook of Theory and Research for the Sociology of Education*, New York: Greenwood Press.

Brennan, G. and J.M. Buchanan (1985), *The Reason of Rules*, Cambridge, MA: Cambridge University Press.

Cheung, S.N.S. (1969), *The Theory of Share Tenancy*, Chicago: The University of Chicago Press.

Christensen, G. (1993), 'The limits to informal financial intermediation', *World Development*, **21** (5), 721–731.

De Soto, H. (2000), *The Mystery of Capitalism: Why Capitalism Triumphs in the West and Fails Everywhere else*, New York: Basic Books.

Diamond, J. (1998), *Guns, Germs and Steel: A Short History of Everybody for the Last 13 000 Years*, London: Vintage.

DiMaggio, P. (1994), 'Culture and economy', Chapter 2 in N.J. Smelser and R. Swedberg (eds.), *The Handbook of Economic Sociology*, Princeton, NJ: Princeton University Press and New York: Russell Sage.

Djankov, S., R. La Porta, F. Lopez de Silanes and A. Shleifer (2002), 'The regulation of entry', *Quarterly Journal of Economics*, **117** (4), 1–37.

Easterly, W. (2001), *The Elusive Quest for Growth: Economists' Adventures and Misadventures in the Tropics*, Cambridge, MA: MIT Press.

Eggertson, T. (1991), *Economic Behavior and Institutions*, Cambridge, MA: Cambridge University Press.

Fafchamps, M. and B. Minten (2001), 'Social capital and agricultural trade', *American Journal of Agricultural Economics*, **83** (3), 680–685.

Fogel, R.W. (1999), 'Catching up with the economy', *American Economic Review*, Vol. **89**, No. 1, pp. 1–21.

Geertz, C. (1973), *The Interpretation of Culture*, New York: Basic Books.

Hall, R.E. and C.I. Jones (1999), 'Why do some countries produce so much more output than others?', *The Quarterly Journal of Economics*, **114** (1), 83–116.

Hofstede, G. (1980), *Culture's Consequences: International Differences in Work-related Values*, London: Russell Sage.

Johnson, J.G. (1950), 'Resource allocation under share contracts', *Journal of Political Economy*, **52** (2), 111–123.

Kahneman, D. and A. Tversky (1979), 'Prospect theory: an analysis of decisions under risk', *Econometrica*, **47** (2), 263–291.

Kanbur, R. (2003), 'On obnoxious markets', in S. Cullenberg and P. Pattanaik (eds.), *Globalisation, Culture and the Limits of Markets*, Oxford, UK: Oxford University Press.

Killick, T. (1976), 'The possibilities of development planning', *Oxford Economic Papers*, **28** (2), 161–184.

Knack, S. and P. Keefer (1997), 'Does social capital have an economic payoff? a cross-country investigation', *The Quarterly Journal of Economics*, **112** (4), 1251–1288.

Kremer, M. (1993), 'Population growth and technological change: one million BC to 1990', *The Quarterly Journal of Economics*, **108**, 681–716.

Lindblom, C.E. (1977), *Politics and Markets: The World's Political-economic System*, New York: Basic Books.

Lucas, R. (1976), 'Econometric policy evaluation: a critique', in K. Brunner and A. Melzer (eds.), *The Phillips Curve and Labor Markets*, Carnegie-Rochester Conference Series on Public Policy, Vol.1, pp. 19–46.

Marshall, A. (1890), *Principles of Economics*, London: Macmillan.

McClelland, D.C. (1961), *The Achieving Society* , Princeton, NJ: Van Norstrand.

Musgrave, R.A. and P.B. Musgrave (1973), *Public Finance in Theory and Practice*, New York: McGraw-Hill.

Nabli, M. and J.B. Nugent (1989), 'Collective action, institutions and development', in M. Nabli and J.B. Nugent (eds.), *The New Institutional Economics and Development: Theory and Applications to Tunisia*, Amsterdam: Elsevier.

North, D.C. (1990), *Institutions, Institutional Change and Economic Performance*, Cambridge, UK: Cambridge University Press.

North, D.C. (1994), 'Economic performance through time', *American Economic Review*, **84** (3), 359–368.

Putnam, R.D. (2000), *Bowling Alone*, New York: Simon and Schuster.

Putnam, R.D., R. Leonardi and R.Y. Nanetti (1993), *Making Democracy Work*, Princeton, NJ: Princeton University Press.

Romer, D. (2006), *Advanced Macroeconomics* (3rd edition), Boston: McGraw-Hill Irwin.

Schumpeter, J.A. (1950), *Capitalism, Socialism and Democracy* (3rd edition), London: George Allen & Unwin.

Shapiro, C. and J.E. Stiglitz (1984), 'Equilibrium unemployment as a worker discipline device', *American Economic Review*, **74** (3), 433–444.

Skaperdas, S. (1992), 'Cooperation, conflict, and power in the absence of property rights', *American Economic Review*, **82** (4), 720–739.

Speklé, R.F. (2001), *Beyond Generics: A Closer Look at Hybrid and Hierarchical Governance*, Rotterdam: ERIM.

Thorbecke, E. and S. Paternostro (1995), *Rural Informal Credit Configurations and Impact of Financial Liberalization*, paper prepared for the Institute for Policy Reform, Washington DC.

Tinbergen, J. (1956), *Economic Policy: Principles and Design*, Amsterdam: North-Holland.

Veblen, T. (1914), *The Instinct of Workmanship and the State of the Industrial Arts*, New York: Macmillan.

Zak, P.J. and S. Knack (2001), 'Trust and growth', *The Economic Journal*, **111** (470), 295–321.

# 5.  A typology of exchange configurations

## 5.1  OVERVIEW

A first and necessary step into understanding the process of exchange, undertaken in the preceding chapter, was to identify the most important specific characteristics of the exchange environment, the attributes of actors and the items traded. These characteristics, in different combinations, shape and capture distinct exchange configurations. In other words, each combination of environmental settings, nature of actor group and of the item they exchange results in relatively distinct configurations and homogenous transactions.

With a view to the very large number of widely varying characteristics of exchange elements discussed in Chapter 4 one may wonder if exchange configurations are a manageable concept. Each actor is unique, items are seldom identical, and the environment varies strongly over space, so, at the limit, it would be possible to define as many exchange configurations as there are individual transactions. Fortunately, however, this theoretical problem evaporates in practice. Section 5.2 addresses this matter systematically. The following arguments are discussed in some detail. First of all, many characteristics of exchange elements tend to have non-continuous and often bimodal distributions and tend to be highly interrelated. Furthermore, it appears that specific transactions derive from (small numbers of) specific characteristics of elements of exchange. These considerations appear to be robust and to apply generally. Thus, for any exchange configuration, the number of characteristics to be considered is modest and easily manageable. And, finally, the costs of developing new forms of transactions as well as the costs of operating in many different configurations tend to also restrict the number of transactional forms.

It also follows from the above arguments that operationally useful exchange configurations can be obtained even when painting with a relatively broad brush. By way of illustration we derive in Section 5.3 a set of prototypical product-exchange configurations from seven characteristics of exchange elements as they occur in many developing countries. The primary aim of this exercise is to illustrate the discriminative power of certain key characteristics such that the combination of only a limited number of them leads to recognizable categories of transactions. The discussion in that section also throws light on the question of whether another obstacle in the process of identifying exchange configurations can be overcome, namely that many dimensions of elements can only be measured in an imperfect way and often not quantitatively. We argue and illustrate with the help of detailed examples that qualitative or categorical estimates can be used without any serious loss of analytical rigor. The resulting aggregate product-exchange configurations appear to be recognizable and robust and yet to cover a wide spectrum. They are summarized in Table 5.2. Such aggregate configurations are worthy of consideration because of the understanding they provide per se and because they can help obtaining a grasp of more disaggregated variants.

## 5.2   ARE EXCHANGE CONFIGURATIONS MANAGEABLE?

As indicated in Subsection 2.2.2, an analysis of a specific exchange configuration entails a description of the specific combination of characteristics of the three elements of exchange, the process through which the corresponding transactions are formed and the characteristics of these transactions. Actors, when deciding on transactions, take the characteristics of exchange elements into consideration. But, as the previous chapter has amply demonstrated, the number of characteristics of elements conceivably relevant for the explanation of transactions is enormous. All these characteristics, each with its gamut of scores, can be combined in innumerable ways forming, in turn, myriads of distinct exchange configurations.

This consideration leads to the question: can exchange configurations be an operationally useful concept, if characteristics of elements and their scores – and, therefore, exchange configurations – exist in almost endless numbers? For a satisfactory response to these questions we have to move to a new layer of arguments. Below it will be shown in Subsections 5.2.1 and 5.2.2 that the number of scores of many characteristics of exchange elements is often small. Something similar applies to the number of characteristics that needs to be considered in analyses of exchange configurations. One reason for this derives from the strong interconnections prevailing among many characteristics such that one typical characteristic can represent a number of others (Subsection 5.2.3). Another reason derives from the practical observation that each specific set of exchange configurations is based on only a few relevant, discriminatory characteristics (Subsection 5.2.4). Finally, cost considerations limit the number of distinct forms of transactions observable in the real world (Subsection 5.2.5).

### 5.2.1 Non-continuous and Bimodal Distributions of Scores of Characteristics

It appears that a considerable number of characteristics of exchange elements have two (binary), or at most only a few states. This tendency for scores of characteristics of elements to be bimodally and/or non-continuously distributed can be observed especially in developing countries where many forms of dualism prevail. Moreover, when there are just two such states, they are each other's opposite. Obviously, this simplifies the distinction between exchange configurations and reduces the latter's number drastically. We present a few examples below of key characteristics of elements of exchange that tend to display the above features.

Thus, starting with *technology*, the choice of technique is not a continuous one. An entrepreneur or small farmer is generally faced with a few discrete alternative production techniques to choose from. The variables which together define a technology appear to fall in two sets along bimodal lines. These variables are, among others, the degree of factor intensity, that is labour and capital intensity (as measured by, say, the capital–labour ratio); the origin of the technology (imported vs. domestic); the vintage of the technology, that is modern (on the production possibility frontier) or traditional (within the frontier); and total factor productivity (the ratio of output to a measure of total inputs). Modern technology tends to be capital-intensive, imported and to display high factor productivity. In contrast, traditional technology tends to be labour-intensive, of domestic origin and to yield relatively lower total factor productivity. It is true that in some instances an intermediate technology exists, but in general, the distribution of alternative techniques – using the above indicators to define them – is approximately bimodal.[1]

The *form of organization* can range from a relatively self-sufficient and self-contained family firm or farm, oriented to the satisfaction of basic household needs, to a large corporation hiring factors internationally and producing for the world market. Even though there exists a whole spectrum in between those polar extremes, the alternative forms of organization tend to fall in two distinct groups, (1) family enterprises, which can be further subdivided into (a) household farms run under different tenancy types (i.e. owner-cultivator, fixed rent, or sharecropping tenancy); and

(b) informal enterprises in services and industry largely based on self-employment; and (2) unincorporated or incorporated enterprises.

The next element on our list is the *physical and locational environment.* Clearly, as the detailed discussion in Subsection 4.2.2 revealed, the most fundamental dimension of this composite element is the rural–urban dichotomy. As will be documented and argued subsequently, this is a crucial distinction in segmenting product, labour, credit and land markets. In fact, the classical example of a segmented labour market is the Harris-Todaro (1970) model, which, among others, provides an explanation of the determinants of the rural–urban migration.

Another crucial characteristic of the environment is the *political environment* as a whole, which can vary greatly from one setting to another. Economic policies are equally diverse affecting market and non-market exchanges. But there appears to be a predilection on the part of governments of developing countries to rely somewhat more on discretionary than on non-discretionary policy measures and to direct measures benefiting specific sectors, products and factors of production in efforts to protect the latter from foreign competition, to encourage industrialization or to provide cheap food to urban dwellers. Because of this, production sectors can often be grouped in accordance with the orientation of policy interventions. For example, a distinction can be made between sheltered and non-sheltered sectors. The latter category can be further subdivided into a sub-group, not subject to explicit government intervention, and another sub-group consisting of other sectors which are discriminated against. In developing countries the agricultural sector often belongs to the latter category when government intervention drives food prices significantly below world market prices.[2] Sheltered sectors, in contrast, may have access to cheap credit and/or foreign exchange and other privileges.

Many consumer goods tend to be sheltered to encourage import substitution and the industrialization process. In contrast, commodities competing in the world market would typically be non-sheltered, while such goods as food and transportation services might be subjected to negative sheltering taking the form, for example, of price controls of a discriminatory nature with the presumable intent to improve the welfare of the poorer classes. Likewise, the informal sector is often subjected to the same type of negative sheltering (see Section 5.2.2 for more detail). In summary, the extent of policy intervention tends to follow a binary scheme depending on whether products or industries are sheltered (inward oriented) or not sheltered (outward oriented). Government intervention, in turn, can be of a protective kind (shelter) or of a discriminatory type (negative shelter). The impact of policy intervention on factor markets is more complex. Firstly, to the extent that the demand for factors is derived from the demand for products, factors, used in sheltered industries, may indirectly benefit from that protection. Secondly, however, policymakers often intervene directly in factor markets through price and quantity controls, such as minimum wage legislation, subsidized credit, exchange control, and land use and zoning restrictions. Here again, the nature of intervention tends to divide actors in factor markets in two groups, those who benefit from the intervention and those who do not. Thus, for example many agricultural casual workers are either not covered by minimum wage legislation, or the legislation is not implemented or ineffective, in contrast with workers in the organized urban sector.

In connection with the *legal environment*, a distinction can obviously be made between the legal and the illegal state. The vital difference between this dichotomy and the formal/informal dichotomy should be emphasized as the next subsections make clear. When firms in the informal sector do not apply certain rules, this is not necessarily seen as an illegal act, because they may have been explicitly exempted or because their violation of the rules is condoned simply because an effective enforcement is impossible and/or counterproductive. Illegal or black economic activities, on the other hand, explicitly violate the rules and may at any time elicit a reaction by law enforcers.

The *socio-economic characteristics and attributes of actors* include their status in terms of income and resource endowment (physical, financial and human capital), their objectives as producers and as consumers, their tastes and preferences, their access to information and its distribution among them, their attitudes towards risk and uncertainty and the nature of relations among them. In developing countries, which typically have relatively skewed income distributions, these characteristics tend to be highly interrelated and constitute two distinct subsets of actors: (1) the poor, relatively uneducated and uninformed households, with little endowment (and practically no collateral), oriented in their production and consumption decisions towards the achievement of survival and subsistence; and (2) the educated rich (that is the non-poor) who are endowed with physical and/or human capital and receive relatively high income, have access to information, can afford to take risks and have 'conspicuous' tastes.

These two groups would also tend to differ significantly in their *cultural aspects*. The discussion of the impact of these aspects on exchange behaviour in Subsection 4.4.1 reveals that there exists a marked difference in the customs and personal value orientation of individuals operating in a traditional (typically agrarian) setting and the impersonal (arm's-length trading) attitudes displayed by individuals in a more modern setting. This dual breakdown among actors derives its analytical power from the fact that owners of assets have better access to formal credit markets, are in a better position to take risk and have greater political power. Of course, there will be many cases where a breakdown in only two groups is an excessive simplification such that a further division is required. Even then, the number of groups tends to remain limited.

### 5.2.2 Another Form of Bimodalism: the Formal–Informal Dichotomy

An important topic inherent in the development economics literature focuses on what has been somewhat loosely called the formal–informal dichotomy. In fact, three manifestations of this dichotomy can be distinguished, relating to the differences between (1) formal and informal sectors, (2) formal and informal forms of organization of production, and, (3) formal and informal transactions respectively. The discussion below describes the differences and connections between these three manifestations of the formal/informal dichotomy. It illustrates the pervasive and dominant nature of this bimodal distinction in shaping exchange configurations.

#### Formal and informal sectors

Two views on the informal sector can be distinguished in the literature. In the ILO World Employment Project publications, which helped to popularize the term, the informal sector is described strictly in the context of developing countries as a collection of informal production units providing income-earning opportunities to those unable to gain access to the formal/modern sector.[3] These publications emphasize the informal form of organization (see below) and the very meagre and irregular incomes that informal workers earn. In the subsequent literature, however, the informal sector has been characterized as the collection of economic activities avoiding official regulation that can occur in rich and poor countries alike.[4] This literature emphasizes, in contrast to the earlier approach, the dynamics of this sector and the opportunity it provides to earn incomes comparable to those in the formal sector. It also points out the connections that exist between the formal and informal sectors, for example, when workers cross over from jobs in one sector to the other or when they combine jobs in both sectors and when formal enterprises outsource activities to the informal sector.

Authorities in many developing countries have an ambivalent attitude towards the informal sector. They realize that it is indispensable as a source of income and as a supplier of goods and services for many families. But they feel frustrated by the fact that official rules are ignored and that informal stalls and workshops can be an eyesore. So, from time to time, authorities attempt to discipline the sector and physically remove the primitive stalls and shacks, even when such action unleashes strong reactions and tends to do more harm than good. The formal sector is often treated more favourably, notwithstanding its shallow roots in the local economy. It exemplifies modernity and brings in taxes and policy makers and bureaucrats can connect with it. In many countries this sector can be seen to profit from a wide variety of privileges.

### Formal and informal forms of organization

Strictly speaking, the formal and informal sectors are just sets of differently organized production units, or recognizably different actor groups engaging in exchange.[5] A formal form of organization applies to firms organized in accordance with a selected legal statute for enterprise. Firms adopting a certain formal form of organization are required to be registered and, thus, become taxable units. A system of accounting, even if unsophisticated, is mandated by the tax authorities, but is also a useful management tool allowing an advanced degree of division of labour within the firm. And, last but not least, adequate books open opportunities for obtaining external funds permitting a much larger scale of operation than would be feasible without them.

Informally organized units of production are not set up in accordance with a certain legal format. Also they are not registered and, as a consequence, they are largely immune to legislation pertaining to taxes, minimum wages, workers' safety and the protection of the environment. Informal production units are most common in economically underdeveloped regions where they are condoned because they provide a living for workers and entrepreneurs with limited capital and skills who cannot be absorbed by the formal sector at the going minimum wage and because they are in any case very hard for a bureaucracy to control. Accounting systems being too sophisticated an instrument, the great majority of informal firms has no access to formal credit markets and depends on its own capital for funding or on loans from family members and moneylenders. Because of their simple structure and limited access to external finance, production technology other than the unsophisticated, traditional kind is beyond the reach of informal production units. Thus, the range of their output is largely limited to such products and services as furniture, leather products, bricks, apparel, earthenware, construction work, car repair, short haul transportation and street selling. Box 5.1 provides an image of the operation of an informal shoemaker.

---

## BOX 5.1   THE INFORMAL SHOEMAKER

Our informal shoemaker has learnt his trade as an apprentice in his uncle's shop. When he started a business of his own, he obtained part of his tools and equipment from his uncle and purchased the rest from a colleague. The required funds were borrowed from a shoe trader/moneylender, but the shoemaker was fortunate that he could pay back the loan soon from credit on much softer terms provided by family members.

He runs his shop from a shed that he constructed with the aid of some relatives on a narrow stretch of unclaimed land along a railway track. So he pays no rent. He keeps no records. His eldest son and a nephew are his apprentices. They help him when there is more work than he can manage on his own, they run errands for him and guard the shop when he is away. He pays for their upkeep and sometimes, depending on the business, gives them some money for clothes or presents. They do not receive a regular wage.

His production capacity is very limited. He works in batches ordered by a shoe commission agent at irregular intervals. Competition for orders by commission agents is fierce. With the credit the agent provides him with each order he buys the materials he needs for the batch and works feverishly to deliver as early as possible and, thus, to minimize the interest costs which run at one per cent per day.

---

Formal units of production are much less constrained in terms of funding, technology, size and scope. In contrast to informal producers, they can operate on world markets and reap the full benefits of economies of scale that modern technologies provide. Many subsidiary companies established in developing countries to profit from the low local wages take this to an extreme when their entire production is exported in accordance with instructions from the parent company.[6] Their international orientation is often reflected in their imported technology and funds.

**Formal and informal transactions**
The above discussion has shown that formal and informal production units form two different actor groups operating in different legal and technological environments and producing different items. Hence, they tend to engage in distinct exchange configurations. Indeed we see that, when it

comes to the form of transactions, informal transactions dominate within the informal sector and formal transactions in the formal sector. But also the content of transactions differs between the two sectors.

Formal transactions are designed to be in accordance with contract law and other pertinent legislation and the terms are often fully specified in a written form. In this instance, the degree of formality or informality of transactions seems to relate only to the form. But the content of transactions also play an important role, for the drafting of formal contracts is costly and whether or not the costs are warranted depends on the content, that is, on the importance and complexity of the transaction. Value and time span often play a determining role here. The high costs of setting up a formal transaction are considered as an insurance premium willingly paid to establish one's position in case a conflict were to arise requiring legal recourse. Conversely, it would not make sense to draft a formal contract spelling out terms which are outside the law.

Informal transactions, in contrast with formal transactions, are drawn up in an informal way even though their content would often have warranted a formal approach. We observe this type of transaction between actors who lack the skills to draw up a formal contract, for example due to illiteracy. Informal credit transactions between moneylenders and their clients, where at best some notes on a scrap of paper serve as a reminder, are typical examples of such informal transactions as are transactions based on terms that cannot stand public scrutiny. Regardless of the cause for the informality of a transaction, the actors involved in these transactions do not have access to legal recourse. Not surprisingly, therefore, social control is strongly developed in the informal sector with severe social penalty for deceit.

### 5.2.3 Interrelations Among Characteristics of Elements

Many characteristics of exchange elements appear to be associated with specific characteristics of the same or other elements in the sense that low/high scores in one characteristic go hand in hand with low/high scores in one or more other characteristics. For all practical purposes these interrelations further restrict the number of exchange configurations. We identified such a string of interrelationships and correlating scores in the discussion of credit-market configurations in Subsection 4.3.2 and also in the preceding subsection on the formal/informal dichotomy, especially where the powerful interrelations between such different characteristics of exchange elements as production technology, form of organization, economic and social attributes of actors and cultural and legal aspects were highlighted. In fact, the interrelations between these characteristics and their bimodal nature lie at the heart of the formal/informal dichotomy; the latter would not exist without them.

By way of illustration two additional major nexus of interrelated characteristics of elements are discussed next. The first nexus consists of the interrelation among the item traded (product or factor), the physical environment (as captured by the rural–urban dichotomy) and the policy environment. The intercorrelation between product and location is obvious: agricultural products are, by definition, grown in rural areas and industrial production tends to be highly concentrated in urban areas, at least at the outset of the industrialization process. Further, the degree and form of government intervention is often associated with the characteristics of the item traded, such as type of use that is made of it, sectoral origin and tradability or non-tradability. The degree of competition appears to be sensitive to combinations of these interrelated characteristics.

In particular, policy measures can have a major impact on the degree of competition prevailing in different product exchange configurations. For example, tariffs and quantitative measures applied to imports to further the import-substitution process create a protected market in which competition is restricted. Alternatively, non-intervention in manufactured product markets ensures that these markets are linked to the highly competitive world markets. Furthermore, certain policy measures can elicit unofficial activities. Thus, the implementation of an artificially high exchange rate, rent control or minimum wage legislation, may induce unofficial – if not illegal – transactions culminating in a parallel market. Many policy actions, likewise, affect drastically the adjustment mechanism. More specifically, all attempts at controlling prices shift the burden of adjustment towards quantities.

The second nexus of elements which appear to be highly interrelated is that of technology and form of organization, economic and social attributes of actors, and cultural aspects. In this connection, based on the more detailed and specific discussion of elements in Chapter 4, the following observations can be made. Firstly, technology and form of organization are, in reality, two distinct elements which may be grouped together because they are, in fact, highly correlated as previously indicated. Secondly, the association of cultural characteristics and attributes of actors is obvious; cultural factors affect the preferences and attitudes of the actors and their status. Further, participants in a certain group, sharing the same culture, often also show remarkable similarity of resource endowments in terms of physical and human capital. Where actors are poor, uneducated, uninformed and trying to reap a subsistence income, the culture is oriented towards the community (or household). Alternatively, where actors are endowed with assets (including skills and education) and information, the culture is more impersonal and modern. Thirdly, the two polar types of cultural environments, just described, appear highly associated with a corresponding type of technology and form of organization. Specifically, traditional cultural characteristics are associated with traditional technology and a family type of enterprise, while modern culture is associated with modern technology and unincorporated or corporate firms.

To the extent that the four characteristics of elements, in this second nexus, are closely interrelated, any one of them could be selected as a proxy for the whole subset. In fact, technology and form of organization is a natural choice because the characteristics of this element are relatively easily measurable in quantitative terms (for example, various indicators can be used to identify technology), and qualitative terms (different legal status of the various forms of organization are readily observed).

### 5.2.4   The Selective Relevance of Characteristics

We know that the number of characteristics of elements of exchange that can in principle have an impact on the formation of transactions is extremely large. If each characteristic is thought to form an axis, one would obtain a space in a number of dimensions equal to this large number of characteristics.[7] According to the central argument of the exchange-configuration approach, groups of transactions differ in a systematic and consistent way with respect to the underlying characteristics of the exchange elements. As a result, one can imagine groups of transactions as being distinct swarms of points in this space. Expressed in terms of this spatial interpretation of the exchange-configuration approach, the impact of the considerations presented above will be clear: bimodality of scores of characteristics reduces the number of relevant swarms, and interrelations among characteristics allow the collapsing of the space into a smaller number of dimensions. By reducing drastically the numbers of (scores of) elemental characteristics that need to be considered in identifying distinct configurations this property contributes likewise to reducing the number of exchange configurations. We now come to an additional consideration that strongly reinforces the operational usefulness of the exchange-configuration concept.

Experience shows that the impact of the overwhelming majority of characteristics is very restricted. Specific characteristics of elements of exchange have an impact on specific configurations and little or no impact on others such that relatively small subsets of characteristics with genuine discriminatory power suffice in analyses of exchange. Two factors can explain this phenomenon. Firstly, most transactions are influenced only by the 'local' setting reflecting the prevailing local characteristics of elements which are only a fraction of the immeasurably large total number. Secondly, of the local characteristics only those are relevant that have a bearing on the subject of analysis which can relate to an item traded, a specific actor group or a component of the environment. So, returning to the spatial interpretation introduced above we can conclude that each swarm (and hence each type) of distinct transactions can be properly defined by only a relatively small and discriminating number of dimensions. Of course, in this era of globalization there are exchange configurations that operate world-wide, but even in such a global setting identifying the major discriminating characteristics is normally not an insurmountable obstacle.

The cases presented earlier can serve as an illustration of this last point. In the case of the primary wheat market in the Punjab of Pakistan (Subsection 2.3.2) we used ten dimensions. They were 'wheat' and 'batch size' for item traded; 'size of farm holding' and 'ownership of beasts of burden' (which we collapsed into one) for farmers' characteristics; 'state or private', 'morality', 'access to means of transportation', 'credit to farmers' and 'commercial capital' for buyers' characteristics; 'road connection from the village' and 'guaranteed wheat price in the secluded Pakistani market' for environmental dimensions. For the formal/informal credit markets (Subsection 4.3.2) nine dimensions appeared sufficient to capture distinct exchange configurations. But, as we have seen, such lenders' characteristics as 'mode of organization', 'scale of operation', 'intermediation' and 'quality of administration' are highly interrelated and may be represented by one proxy dimension, such that only six dimensions remain. For the land-rental markets (also Subsection 4.3.2) we distinguished seven dimensions. Of course, one may object that all these cases are of a stylized, illustrative nature which may not represent or reflect exchange configurations in the real world. However, it appears that empirically observed transactions display remarkable parsimony when it comes to the number of underlying elemental characteristics shaping them. Although a precise number is hard to give, it is safe to say that the analysis of any group of transactions will rarely require many more than a dozen characteristics of elements of exchange and often fewer to define an operationally useful typology.

### 5.2.5   A Limited Number of Transactional Forms

The argument presented under this heading refers to a pivotal issue in this book, namely the mapping from the characteristics of exchange elements to the form of transactions. Potential actors pondering the pros and cons of entering into a transaction play a decisive role in this process. They observe, consider and weigh the various relevant characteristics of exchange elements and decide on the form of transaction that presumably suits them best and minimizes their transaction costs.

In the preceding subsections it has been shown that the number of characteristics to be considered by actors in the decision process remains within reasonable limits. Even so, because all (potential) actors are unique and items are often not identical, there could be a tendency among actors to desire a relatively individualized format in each transaction they consider. Such tendency, if unmitigated, would result in a vastly larger number of transactional forms than we actually see in reality. The restraining factor in this regard resides in transaction-cost considerations acting as funneling devices that guide different combinations of characteristics of exchange elements towards a relatively small set of transactional forms.

There are, firstly, the costs involved in devising a separate transactional form for a new transaction. These are the costs related to the time and energy expended in preparing an unfamiliar transactional form and to the heightened uncertainty in executing the transaction. The estimated costs then have to be compared with an estimate of the benefit such newly designed transaction would bring. Not surprisingly, actors very often prefer the use of sufficiently suitable prevailing forms of transactions. In other words, transactions tend to be shaped in a limited number of moulds. Other cost considerations strengthen this conclusion. Actors incur costs also when preparing and engaging in entirely routine transactions. Thus, it pays to economize on the number of different transactions. This consideration explains, for example, the popularity of one-stop shopping when consumers purchase such different items as bread, vegetables, cough drops and detergents from the supermarket in a single, uniform and consolidated transaction.

The above conclusions have consequences for analyses of exchange and for the number of exchange configurations. Firstly, when transactional forms are robust, one can afford to paint the characteristics of exchange elements with a broad brush. Secondly, when the finer distinctions between characteristics of elements of exchange can be ignored, the overall number of configurations that need to be distinguished is clearly much reduced.

These are also the main reasons why typologies of exchange configurations make sense even though they cannot take account of all distinctions between exchange elements in minute detail. Such typologies are best derived separately for specific products (including services) and factors of production, as the item traded appears to be the predominant element determining the transactional form.

## 5.3   A TYPOLOGY OF PRODUCT-EXCHANGE CONFIGURATIONS: AN ILLUSTRATION

The conclusion that a meaningful analysis of transactions requires only a limited number of dimensions of elements of exchange holds generally. The level of aggregation of the analysis does not appear to make any difference; it only determines to what extent the dimensions of the elements of exchange are to be disaggregated. The exercise presented below, using a 'broad brush', shows how some general, but reasonably representative and distinct types of product-exchange configurations follow from only a small number of characteristics of exchange elements. In most practical (real-life) cases it will be necessary to 'unpack' and further disaggregate the dimensions that have been applied in the exercise which follows. There is obviously a trade-off between increasing the detail of the analysis which will yield more information for less diverse configurations each comprising fewer transactions, and increasing the level of aggregation of the analysis, which will yield less in-depth information but for a wider range of transactions. The former would be tantamount to reducing the size, density and internal diversity of the previous swarms while the latter would do the opposite. The degree of detail or aggregation necessary depends, of course, on the purpose of the analysis.

### 5.3.1   Selecting Discriminating Characteristics

The task at hand is one of systematic simplification by selecting the most essential elemental characteristics from a vast set, namely those characteristics which seem to have the greatest discriminatory power. The example which follows concentrates on identifying distinct prototypical product-exchange configurations within the setting prevailing in developing countries. It will be seen that certain characteristics of exchange elements suggest themselves as being more relevant than others. In other words, a hierarchy emerges in which characteristics of exchange elements have different ranks depending on the strength of their discriminative power. This hierarchy is not general and depends strongly on the starting points of the analysis. Thus, for example, if one analyzes exchange configurations relating to production factors instead of products, or if the environment relates to middle-income countries instead of poor countries, different characteristics of exchange elements will gain prominence and a different hierarchy obtains.

In order to illustrate the delineation of exchange configurations, an introductory, schematic approach will now be presented. The item traded provides a suitable starting point for such an exercise. For the present exercise we have selected as item traded the aggregate group of 'products, including services' (dimension #1). This is the first of seven dimensions to be distinguished here. Since all of them are of an aggregate nature, the resulting exchange configurations mirror this characteristic.

After the item traded, the next discriminating dimension (in this hierarchy) to be introduced refers to the exchange environment. This dimension can serve to express one aspect of the endemic nature of dualism in large parts of the developing world, as captured by the dichotomy between rural and urban areas (dimension #2). Another type of dualism derives from the technology (#3a) selected by actors as producers, where a distinction can usefully be made between modern and traditional technologies. Since technology, embedded in the machines and tools and labour skills employed, reflects a series of decisions by producers, it is considered here as an actor characteristic.[8] These two fundamental dimensions explicitly recognizing dualism, the first reflecting the gap between rural and urban areas and the second between traditional and modern technology, give rise to a dual–dual framework which provides the basis for the analytical scheme developed here.[9] With regard to the second dichotomy, it must further be recalled that technology is often strongly associated with the form of organization (#3b), another characteristic of actors as production units.

Figure 5.1 offers a graphical illustration of two of the propositions (relating to intercorrelation and bimodality) made in Section 5.1. The three axes in the figure represent the three dimensions of exchange elements introduced there: production technology (with scores ranging from very modern to very traditional), location (distinguishing rural from urban areas) and mode of organization (ranging from formal to informal). The scores of these three dimensions corresponding with individual market transactions in a prototype developing country can be plotted as swarms of dots in Figure 5.1. Because of the bimodal distribution of characteristics assumed in the dual–dual approach these dots will not be dispersed randomly within the space defined by the sides of the box, but will be concentrated in four corners. Further, the interrelations between modern technology and formal organization on the one hand and traditional technology and informal organization on the other results in empty areas in the lower right-side and upper left-side corners. It follows then that the three-dimensional scores of market transactions in developing countries will tend to form the four swarms appearing in Figure 5.1. Because of the strong correspondence between the dual scores of technology and mode of organization, the two dimensions can be collapsed into one (dimension

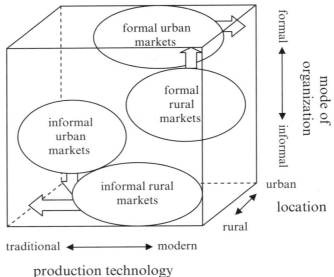

*Figure 5.1   Swarm formations of scores of selected characteristics*
*             of exchange elements for product-market transactions in*
*             developing countries*

#3) – say, technology – also representing the other. This is indeed how
'technology' is to be interpreted in the remaining part of this section.

The case represented in Figure 5.1, based on only three dimensions,
is, in general, too simplistic to yield an operationally useful taxonomy
of product configurations. Therefore we incorporate additional characteristics of elements to derive a more realistic taxonomy and typology
of product-exchange configurations. A natural next step is to divide the
aggregate item traded 'products, including services' (dimension #1) into
(a) agricultural products, further subdivided into staple food and other
agricultural commodities, (b) mining products, (c) processed goods, (d)
industrial products, and (e) services. These two-level subdivisions occupy
dimensions #4 and #5.

Another crucial step is to incorporate the impact of the policy environment (dimension #6). Typically, agricultural commodities in developing
countries tend to be discriminated against through a variety of policies.
Food prices are usually regulated by the government and maintained at a
level below the world (import) price. The reasons for such a policy include
the desire by the state to provide cheap food to urban workers, who are
a more effective pressure group than the rural poor, and to keep wages

low in order to promote industrial activity. In the case of export crops, state monopolies in the form of commodity boards that domestic producers have to sell to, though much less common nowadays than they were until the 1990s, still prevail in some countries. The 'stabilization prices' offered by these boards are normally below the world price and thus allow the state to squeeze out part of the agricultural surplus. This type of discrimination by the state (which could be called negative sheltering) invites corruption and illegal sales of export crops circumventing the commodity boards (not included below). Products relying on modern technologies (and forms of organization) outside agriculture may either be 'sheltered' or 'non-sheltered'.

A final distinction (dimension #7), applying to the traditional complex, relates to the nature of the relations among actors and, more specifically, whether the transactions are generated within a family or not. One rationale for this distinction is that it allows incorporation of the large proportion of food crops in developing countries that does not pass the farm gate and is consumed within the household that produced it. Another relates to the importance of familial forms of organization also in urban informal markets.

In the scheme the public or government sector has not been incorporated for two reasons. The first is that public goods – financed and provided, but not necessarily produced by the public sector – by their nature (being non-rival and non-excludable goods) cannot be provided through transactions. Therefore, these goods do not fit in a scheme on patterns of exchange. The other reason is that public sector enterprises, which do indeed produce transactable goods, are very diverse and cannot easily be incorporated in a general framework as the present one. However, it is certainly possible, and indeed useful, to incorporate public sector enterprises in a product-exchange configuration scheme for a specific country.[10]

### 5.3.2  Prototypical Product-exchange Configurations

The resulting analytical scheme applied to products is shown in Figure 5.2 where each cell represents a prototypical exchange configuration and where the dual–dual delineation (that is the contrast between the rural and urban areas and between traditional and modern technologies and forms of organization) is shown graphically by two sets of double lines. Clearly, the outcome of the exercise differs with the characteristics of exchange elements selected at the outset. Note, for example, that the hierarchical classification scheme embodied in Figure 5.2 defines different product-exchange configurations, mainly according to the characteristics of the

| | | | Technology | | | |
|---|---|---|---|---|---|---|
| | | | Traditional technology | | Modern technology | |
| | | | Negative shelter | | Non-sheltered | Sheltered |
| | | | Family | Other | | |
| Rural Areas | Agricultural products | Staple food | Family-farm system | Domestic and international staple food markets | | |
| | | Other | | Cash crops world markets | | |
| | Mining products | | | Regional/National | World markets | |
| | Processed goods | | | Local markets | Rural formal markets | |
| Urban Areas | Industrial products | | Urban informal markets | Domestic and world markets | Domestic and world markets | |
| | Services | | | Professional and financial services | Air-conditioned markets | |

*Figure 5.2    Some product-exchange configurations in the context of a developing economy*

producers or suppliers. In similar exercises relating to, for example, labour- or credit-exchange configurations, other characteristics of exchange elements suggest themselves. Also note that Figure 5.2 incorporates mostly market-exchange configurations. Intra-firm transactions are not included at all and intra-family transactions only so far as they relate to production activities. Again, other exercises emphasizing different combinations of characteristics at different levels of aggregation yield entirely different types of configurations.

Following these qualifying remarks, Figure 5.2 is described briefly to illustrate the taxonomic usefulness of the general framework. Starting with rural areas, the exchange configurations which have been identified are: (1) the family-farm system; (2) the domestic food markets which, on the supply side, are made up of two very different sources, that is the marketable surplus of the family farms and the commercial food production of (large) farmers in those countries, where a bimodal food production structure prevails; (3) the markets for cash and exports crops; (4) the rural traditional markets; and (5) the rural formal markets (which could, depending on the specific conditions, be differentiated further according to the prevailing policy regimes). The intra-family farm system, in its purest form, would not be considered a market since the transactions are typically open-ended. However, in reality, it is almost impossible to find a case of pure subsistence farming. Even very small farms sell a part of their output, so that within the family-farm system, decisions have to be made by household members regarding the distribution of output between self-consumption and marketed surplus.[11] The farm-household exchange configuration is thus closely connected with another configuration, that is the commercial food market in which the marketable surplus is sold, even though this market might be dominated by larger farmers using modern techniques. In fact, in some countries traditional farmers produce cash crops (for example, tea and coffee) and, hence, connect with cash crop markets. These connections are shown in Figure 5.2 by way of broken lines.

In the urban areas the major configurations which appear are (1) the urban informal sector; and (2) a number of configurations characterized by producers relying on modern technology and form of organization, but subject to different types of government intervention. Also here a further distinction could be introduced in accordance with the prevailing government policies differentiating, for example, between regulated and protected commodity markets (which are, in turn, likely to give rise to official and parallel markets). Next, these configurations are very briefly discussed.

Notice, first, that all these configurations operate as markets, with the exception of the family farm within which a number of transactions occur among family members that take the form of implicit barter transactions. The farm household must reach decisions regarding (1) what and how much to produce for home consumption and for the market; (2) what and how much to consume; and (3) how family time should be allocated to different activities such as on- and off-farm employment and leisure. Many of the resulting transactions are virtual, implicit exchanges among the same actors on both the demand and supply sides. A complicating factor in analyzing behaviour within the household farm is that transactions in product- and factor- (particularly labour) exchange configurations are jointly and interdependently determined. For example, there is an implicit exchange of labour by household members working on-farm for present and future food consumption. Since the objective is to economize on transaction costs, the family structure must have a lower level of these costs than markets, in order for the given set of exchanges to occur within the family, rather than in the distinct market configurations associated with products and factors.

The family-farm configuration is unusual, if not unique, in that it deals in many different items, such as food and labour (on-farm), and at least two types of insurance. Firstly, old-age insurance is provided to older members receiving support from their children in exchange for care received in their youth. Secondly, by tying together the production and consumption of essential foodstuffs, the family is able to provide some insurance against state-contingent uncertainty. The marketable surplus that the family-farm supplies to the staple-food configuration constitutes only a small part of all transactions occurring within that configuration. For a further discussion of the family farm, see Subsection 6.3.2.

Staple food products, as is typical of agricultural goods, face a relatively price inelastic demand. The same applies, at least in the short run, to supply which also depends on unpredictable weather conditions. These two factors result in volatile price movements. Supply adjustment takes at least one growth season and often longer and can result in cobweb cycles of over- and undersupply. Staple food products are mostly destined for domestic consumption; only a small percentage reaches the world market which thereby tends to become still more volatile. Governments in developing countries often make efforts to dampen price movements in the domestic staple food markets by establishing guaranteed maximum prices which remain in most cases significantly below the long term world market prices. In isolated communities where only a few people possess the necessary means of transportation monopsonistic situations can easily arise. In other cases however, the exploitation of farmers by professional merchants in staple food markets seems to be a much less serious problem than the literature and political rhetoric often suggest. As a rule, merchants purchasing staple food make the most of their scarce funds by maximizing turnover. Access to this market is easy, so competition among traders tends to be fierce and trade margins low.

The major share of cash crops is meant for export which has consequences for the corresponding exchange configuration. The crops must meet specific quality standards regarding appearance, maturity, hygiene and disease and pest control and must be available in large quantities in a timely fashion for packaging and transportation. This obviously requires close coordination between grower/supplier and exporter expressing itself in long-term, detailed contracts which sometimes develop into full-scale mergers. Prices are typically quoted in international currency.

Processed goods might have undergone such simple operations as tanning, milling, threshing, drying and fermentation, but even then the technology applied – and, thus, the resulting products – can differ drastically. For example, the wheat that families retain for own consumption is milled in very small batches in local mills applying a traditional technology. This flour is not the same as the flour produced by large-scale modern mills and neither are the transactions. The transaction between the farmer and the traditional miller is a casual affair and the fee is typically a certain, customary portion of the milled wheat. Modern mills use regular contracts with negotiated fees and expect payment into their bank accounts. On occasion they buy and process wheat and sell the flour when the prices are right or when the mill is short on commissions. These mills may also accept their fees in kind. Modern mills may have to seek regular (that is, privileged) provision of electricity for their survival.

Mining products, being raw materials, are characterized by a low price elasticity of demand and a high sensitivity to (world) economic cycles. Most of these products are exported and traded in large quantities in world markets at prices denominated in international currency. Hedging contracts are often used to insure against currency risk and price volatility. Transportation of these bulk products in the producing countries requires a well-developed system of roads, railways and port facilities. Certain other mining products, such as lignite and clay, are primarily for domestic use. Such products are traded in entirely different exchange configurations. This goes to show that finer distinctions in this as well as in other product categories uncover the variety of relevant configurations to be distinguished at lower levels of aggregation.

Moving from essentially rural-based product configurations to essentially urban-based product configurations, the urban informal sector comprising such diverse items as simple consumer goods, furniture, and a variety of services ranging from security guards to parking lot attendants has been described in great detail in an earlier subsection (5.2.2) to which the reader is referred. As entry into this market is easy, competition among suppliers in markets of products manufactured by the informal sector is intense. Due to scarcity of funds and the technology they employ, informal producers can supply only small batches, often commissioned by middlemen on partial prepayment.

The industrial products' formal exchange configurations are concentrated in urban areas. Formal sector products are supplied in large quantities directly to world markets or for subsequent sale by parent companies. In the latter case transactions are basically arranged internally as between departments of the same corporation. Major parts of formal sector production often profit from state aid in the form of access to under-priced foreign exchange, a regular electricity supply and other privileges such as tax deferrals. When sold on domestic markets formal sector products are often protected from international competition by a variety of measures. Even if these measures were meant to provide strictly temporary support to infant industries, they often appear to be hard to eliminate.

Services cannot be stored, must directly be used and, thus, are offered mostly in urban areas where economic activity is geographically concentrated, although, with the advent of new communication technologies, the geographical distance between providers and users is now hardly a matter of concern for some particular services. Entry into markets for professional services (provided by, for example, doctors and lawyers) is restricted as professional qualifications and licenses are often required before a practice can be opened.

## NOTES

1. The Green Revolution technology in wheat and rice production relying on high yielding varieties (HYV), irrigated land and intermediate inputs (mainly fertilizer) is sometimes considered an intermediate technology between the traditional labour-intensive and mechanized alternatives. In fact, this biological-oriented technology may be quite capital-intensive when all the irrigation infrastructure and intermediate capital input costs are properly accounted for. Furthermore, for land scarce countries, the viable alternative technologies are the modern biological HYV technique and the traditional local one. The mechanized technology is not an appropriate alternative in a land-scarce, labour-surplus setting, in contrast with a land-rich, labour-scarce setting.
2. This treatment is in stark contrast to that extended to the agricultural sector in developed countries which profits from strong government support.
3. The ILO Kenya report (International Labour Office, 1972, p. 6) describes the informal sector as 'a way of doing things': to start a business in this sector very little capital and no diplomas or licenses are required, the technology used is traditional and labour intensive and the workers are often members of the same family.
4. See, for example, Portes, 1994.
5. They also form recognizably different environments for intra-firm transactions.
6. Such networks are very important phenomena in international trade. See, for example, Rauch, 2001.
7. By analogy with discriminant analysis, one can consider the elements to be discriminating variables. For a good description of a spatial interpretation of discriminant analysis, see Klecka, 1980, p. 16.
8. Note that, in a different context, 'technology' can be seen as a dimension of the exchange environment. A discussion of this matter is presented in Subsection 4.4.2.
9. For a discussion of this framework, see Pyatt and Thorbecke, 1976, pp. 74–84 and Santiago and Thorbecke, 1988.
10. This observation holds with special force for analyses of the financial sector in developing countries where many banks and insurance companies are still state-owned. Financial institutions of the latter type differ from private institutions because they are often used as instruments of government policies while being insulated from disciplining market forces.

11.  By analogy, an intra-family labour exchange configuration can be visualized as one within which decisions are reached regarding the family labour time allocation to production on the farm and off the farm, to household activities and leisure.

# REFERENCES

Harris, J.R. and M.P. Todaro (1970), 'Migration, unemployment and development: a two-sector analysis', *The American Economic Review*, **60** (1), 126–142.

International Labour Office (1972), *Employment, Incomes and Equality in Kenya*, Geneva: International Labour Office.

Klecka, W.R. (1980), *Discriminant Analysis*, Series Quantitative Applications in the Social Sciences, London: Sage Publications.

Portes, A. (1994), 'The Informal Economy and Its Paradoxes', in N. Smelser and R. Swedberg, (eds.), *The Handbook of Economic Sociology*, Princeton, NJ: Princeton University Press and New York: Russel Sage Foundation.

Pyatt, G. and E. Thorbecke (1976), *Planning Techniques for a Better Future*, Geneva: International Labour Office.

Rauch, J.E. (2001), 'Business and social networks in international trade', *Journal of Economic Literature*, **39** (4), 1177–1203.

Santiago, C.E. and E. Thorbecke (1988), 'A multisectoral framework for the analysis of labor mobility and development in LDCs: an application to postwar Puerto Rico', *Economic Development and Cultural Change*, **37** (1), 127–148.

# 6. Systems of exchange in different phases of development

## 6.1 OVERVIEW

This chapter is concerned with exchange configurations in different phases of development. Even though the time dimension is prominent throughout the chapter, the approach adopted has mostly a comparative static nature. A truly dynamic approach is reserved for the next chapter, where a systematic description is presented of the various ways in which configurations evolve and of the forces that cause the change. The present chapter sets the stage for the dynamic approach of exchange configurations.

A very broad distinction between different forms of exchange is the one between exchange in subsistence and in market economies. For most of history, since man left the hunting and gathering stage behind and settled down to concentrate on agriculture, subsistence-oriented exchange relations dominated. Section 6.2 presents the types of exchange relations prevailing in subsistence communities, while Section 6.3 discusses the emergence of markets and the spreading of market participation. The first part reviews some broad theories speculating on the conditions under which markets come into existence as a new phenomenon and on the ways in which whole communities move from community-based to market systems. The second part concentrates on the decisions for or against market participation among individual present-day rural households in developing countries. Finally, Section 6.4 presents and discusses the exchange configurations corresponding with three broad phases of development while paying special attention to the differences between the exchange elements in these phases and to the nature and focus of the apparent changes in them.

## 6.2 FORMS OF EXCHANGE IN SUBSISTENCE ECONOMIES

Markets became a common institution only relatively recently. Intra-community (including intra-family) transactions were the rule during most of history, as a number of rather stringent conditions had to be satisfied before market exchange could emerge. First of all, there had to be a certain excess production such that goods were available for trading, and a certain form of order for a minimum degree of safety for the actors and their wares. Under these conditions a barter exchange could develop. Further, only after this exchange had intensified and information about the terms became available to other actors, such that a genuine price formation occurred, did barter transactions turn into market transactions.

At the early stages of development, people have few means to control their natural environment for productive purposes. Under these conditions a community-based organization of economic life offers better chances of survival, so sharing of production and assets is a custom that can often be observed in combination with other customs that test or express members' loyalty to the group. Interpersonal relations are of overwhelming importance in such communities, and their codes and institutions regulate activities connected with production, distribution, consumption, exchange and transfer. For example, in the widely practised custom of gift-giving, the subjects (persons involved in the exchange) are more important than the objects (presents exchanged). However, as economic development proceeds and surpluses are produced over and above subsistence needs, inter-household and intra-community relations evolve and lead to a different exchange process. Whereas mutuality and sharing were essential traits for survival in a subsistence setting and may continue to exist in some form or other, they cease to be the dominant principles of economic activity in a setting in which surplus is generated.

Clearly, in self-sustaining, subsistence communities decisions on production and distribution for consumption are complicated processes and need to be guided by rules and traditions for a regular and predictable pattern of participants' behaviour to result. Polanyi[1] distinguishes between three 'forms of integration' that provide unity and stability to community-based economies: reciprocity, redistribution and exchange. These forms of integration do not represent stages of development and may occur side by side.

Reciprocity relations entail symmetrical arrangements among groups that recognize each other as such. In the classical example of the Tobriand Islands studied by Malinowski (1921) inland communities are paired with coastal villages in a pattern of barter exchange of inland breadfruit for fish. In many cases such transactions are disguised as reciprocal exchanges of gifts. Symmetrical arrangements in the form of an exchange of gifts may also develop within groups (families, clans, neighbourhoods) in efforts to establish and maintain goodwill between group members.

Redistribution, on the other hand, hinges on the existence of a strong central authority, for example, a head man, a priest or a group of elders. The output is channelled from the periphery to the centre from which it is then distributed to group members often according to well-defined rules. Different forms of redistribution arrangements can be found in primitive hunting tribes, but also in ancient Egypt and Babylonia, in the ancient Greek estate and the Roman familia, in the medieval manor as well as in many present-day subsistence farm households.

The use of the term 'exchange' by Polanyi to contrast with the other forms of integration is somewhat misleading in the sense that all three forms involve exchange transactions of some sort or other. Polanyi seems to only consider true exchange to take place within markets. In our framework all three alternatives are exchange configurations, with the first two being of the non-market type.

Finally, it is worthwhile noting that the inter-personal relations in community-based economies and the (mostly informal) institutions that sustain these relations can easily be threatened by market exchanges. Negotiations between parties on opposite sides of a market exchange process introduce an element of antagonism that cannot be permitted in communities where solidarity is to be maintained for protection and survival. This is why in some such communities, gainful transactions involving food items were banned (Polanyi et al., 1937, p. 255).

## 6.3  TRANSITIONS TOWARDS MARKET EXCHANGE

Markets have often been regarded with suspicion and the overall evolution from the early community-based economies to the present-day market economies has by no means been a linear one. Some regions that were at the forefront of transactional innovation in a given period experienced stagnation and regress in other periods. Communist countries even abolished the market system as a whole. And it is only five or six centuries ago that the volume and value of market transactions could begin to sustain the development towards the myriads of refined transactional forms that we see today.

In a discussion of the transition towards market exchange a distinction must be made between situations where market exchange evolved from barter exchange as a new phenomenon and situations where certain individual actors gradually make the transition from an autarchic way of living towards participation in existing markets. In the first case a new and previously unknown type of exchange is coming into existence–testily one would presume – and where, over time, market transactions are made more frequently as they turn out to be profitable. Initial experience with such transactions among actors did not exist and the latter can learn about transactions only through active participation. In the second case, however, a newcomer to market exchange finds that the forms of transactions have already been mostly established. Also he/she can learn about market exchange beforehand from observation and hearsay. Both cases will be discussed below.

### 6.3.1　Origin and Spread of Markets

At first sight it may seem strange that rather little is known about the origins of such a vastly important phenomenon as market exchange. Of course, market exchanges must have occurred already before physical market structures – such as the agora of ancient Greece or, even earlier, the permanent retail shops in Lydia – were built. So the latest date for the emergence of markets would be around 500 BC. For the previous period records are rarer, but the transition towards market transactions is likely to have been so gradual that people present were not even aware of being witness to an historical development. Barter trade between individuals as well as groups, sometimes across considerable distances, occurred since the earliest civilizations long before 500 BC. Therefore, the mere fact that somewhere at one point in time barter of certain goods had become sufficiently frequent and information about the terms sufficiently diffused that price formation, as we now call it, started to take place and the thin line towards market exchange was being crossed, most probably remained unnoticed by participants and observers. The latter were unprepared for the rather abstract meaning that present-day economists attach to the term market exchange.

In this connection, it can be added that, in the seventh century BC, the Lydians had invented money coins as a standard means of payment. Although there is no supporting evidence, it is most tempting to assume in accordance with the exchange-configuration arguments that such an important change in the transactional environment as the introduction of money did promote the spread of market exchange. Conversely, while economic agents seem to have been slow in adopting money as a useful device in economic exchange, it seems likely that the spread of market transactions contributed to the use of money.

Two main theories of the origins of markets and fairs and of the transformation from subsistence forms of organizations to market exchange have been proposed.[2] The first, dating back to Adam Smith's *Wealth of Nations*, starts with an agrarian society in which surpluses develop, permitting a basic form of division of labour to emerge from the propensity of individuals to barter the surpluses. This leads to the establishment of a specialist group of artificers (smiths, carpenters, wheelwrights) located in a village central to the farmers they serve and with whom they exchange. With further specialization and larger surpluses inter-regional trade follows intra-village exchange. The transformation is caused by a sequence of internally triggered changes along evolutionary lines.

The alternative approach, which is espoused by Polanyi (1957) and Pirenne (1936), reverses the sequence, claiming that trade and markets can never arise within communities, for trade is external, involving different communities. Berry (1967, p. 109) sums up the essence of this last approach:

> Markets do not develop out of the demands of purely local or individual commerce, but are primarily induced by external exchanges of complementary products with an alien population, and are thus the result rather than the starting point of long distance trading. The sequence is seen as one of trade routes, fairs established on these routes, and local (periodic) markets developing around the original parent market as a network of tracks or roads spreads.

From an analytical point of view the two approaches are not mutually exclusive. Indeed, not only may both be correct, there may well be still additional explanations. Market exchange seems to have come up independently in different ways and in different places when barter exchange intensified and the terms of the exchange became known to other actors who used the information as input for new transactions. In early India and Greece, for example, periodic national assemblies and religious gatherings, during which hostilities were suspended, offered opportunities for participants to trade goods on a more or less regular basis. In a different setting, fishermen and cattle herders (occupational travellers well-equipped to connect different settlements) seem to have been initiators of a regular exchange, as well as pirates and brigands in need of an opportunity to trade their booty for provisions. Alternatively, market exchange can have originated from the elaborate bartering ceremonies in which bands of people engaged in early civilizations, or from the formalized, bureaucratically implemented exchanges of goods between the courts of rulers in ancient Mesopotamia and Egypt,[3] or from the kind of exchanges referred to in the Code of Hammurabi.[4]

In all these instances, the transaction costs were extremely high. This was partly caused by an often hostile exchange environment characterized by the near absence of roads, primitive means of transportation and the lack of safety for travellers. In addition, the difficulty of communicating with other actors whose language, customs and reliability were mostly unknown must have raised transaction costs considerably. This immediately explains why the items exchanged were limited to commodities of high value and low weight and to actors best equipped to protect themselves and their possessions.

Another question is how incidental market exchange widened to become a market system. An attempt at explaining the transition from one system of social and economic relations to another has been made by Ishikawa.[5] He makes a distinction between community- (and family-) type activities and market-type activities which corresponds to a large extent with Polanyi's differentiation between reliance on the reciprocity and/or redistribution principles and reliance on the market principle. He further distinguishes between families whose permanent income barely assures a minimum subsistence level of living and families that are better off and that are assumed to represent the landlord class. Under primitive conditions, subsistence families will prefer the organization of production and distribution to be in accordance with community relations and not with market relations which will yield to them a lower income as long as marginal labor productivity falls short of subsistence income. Land-owning families, however, will have a preference for a market type of organization.

But this will change drastically if, after introduction of improved technologies, marginal labour productivity rises above the subsistence income. Of course, the new technology will not be adopted simultaneously by all subsistence families in a given community, so there may be a conflict between the early and the late adopters regarding the desirable distribution mechanism. Furthermore, the early adopters, whose marginal productivity is now higher than the institutional (average product) income, will favour a move towards an exchange system entailing accordingly higher remunerations. Ishikawa underlines that this general description has in reality many variants in terms of speed of adaptation, emerging class structure, distribution of benefits and so on, and suggests that the original social organization (for example, hierarchical, caste or communal) is a particularly powerful factor in influencing the move to a market system.

Rather than seeing the community and the market as rival institutions, a growing group of authors maintains that community norms can further trade relations and facilitate the initial development of markets.[6] Further, Hayami[7] argues that markets and communities are largely complementary in those cases where community transactions and relations are entered into to correct and remedy pervasive failures in the markets for land, credit, insurance, labour and products. This issue is elaborated below, where we examine a formal model of rural households switching between intra-family and market transactions in reaction to market failures. Note that in this case, and in contrast to situations of newly developing forms of market exchange described above, markets are already present and that households can opt for market or non-market exchange, or both.

### 6.3.2    Modelling Rural Households in Developing Countries

Above we examined the attitude towards market participation of whole communities. In the present subsection we adopt a micro approach and discuss the impact of different settings on the behaviour of agricultural households vis-à-vis market exchange. It serves three purposes. First of all, as is fitting in a section on transition towards market exchange, the discussion is meant to throw light on the reasons why rural households in developing countries decide for or against participating in market transactions and why different households come to different conclusions in this respect. Secondly, an analysis of the transition process towards market participation helps to illustrate how complex the relations between exchange configurations can sometimes be. More specifically, it will appear that the operation and performance of one market configuration can have a strong impact on the operation and performance of other configurations. A market failure has repercussions elsewhere. Even the non-existence of certain markets can have a strong effect. Thirdly, the discussion illustrates how the theory one selects to describe and explain the operation of a configuration influences the interpretation of its behaviour and performance. This is of particular importance when evaluating the likely impact of government policies or exogenous shocks on the performance of the exchange configuration under scrutiny. Whereas our approach provides a taxonomy and conceptual framework for the analysis of different exchange settings, it has to rely on existing theories to explain the actual operation of configurations. In the next chapter we shall return to this issue.

There is a vast body of literature analyzing the effects of constraints on the decision-making process of rural households in developing countries. There are good reasons why this actor group has attracted so much attention: in many developing countries members of rural households still form the majority of the population and they often belong to the poorest sections. But it is only relatively recently that the predicaments of this population group arising from market failures have become better understood.

The family farm combines a whole set of market transactions with virtual, implicit and internal (non-market) transactions occurring among members. It is the hybrid nature of the family farm which makes it such a fascinating organization to study. Family farms and their members are closely connected, through their marketed surplus, with the domestic food market and, to a lesser extent, with the cash crops market (for example, smallholders producing tea or coffee). On the labour side they are also linked to the rural labour market. In short, family farms are key actors in a number of market configurations, while they act as governance structures for internal transactions among family members.

The major constraints faced by rural households relate to their access to land, credit, agricultural inputs, schooling and information about prices. These constraints often apply in combination, and affect farm households in varying degrees of severity. As expected, the limitations on the availability of such vital inputs and types of information have strong, negative repercussions on various aspects of agricultural life, such as on poverty, factor productivity, investments, product mix, migration and market participation.

De Janvry and Sadoulet (2006) summarize the results of a wave of studies – many of them inspired by Singh et al. (1986) – investigating the impact that market failures due to transaction costs have on rural households in developing countries. They distinguish three broad types of transaction costs, that is, direct transaction expenditures (consisting of trade and transport margins and search costs), costs due to uncertainty and risk and collateral-related costs.

**Direct transaction expenditures**
The most familiar market failures are those caused by direct transaction expenditure. A key question relates to the behaviour of peasant households in terms of their reliance on internal (non-market) transactions vs. market transactions.[8] In other words, how do farm households decide on the extent to which they engage in intra-farm household transactions such as production for own consumption, and family-farm labour applied to own farm production, as opposed to participating in transactions in existing market configurations for the same items? De Janvry et al. (1991) have provided a formal framework within which this question can be addressed. They start by offering an interpretation of market failure for labour and food that is specific to the household and not to the commodity. They proceed to derive within an integrated farm-household model (acting as a producing and a consuming unit) the household response to changes in the price and productivity of cash crops, changes in the price of manufactured and consumption goods, the levying of a monetary tax, and availability of new technological opportunities in the production of food. Translating their model into the framework developed in this study, it could be said that they formalized the behaviour of the farm-household configuration.

According to de Janvry et al. (ibid., p. 1401),

> [a market fails] when the cost of the transaction through market exchange creates disutility greater than the utility gain that it produces, with the result that the market is not used for the transaction. Either surrogate institutions will emerge to allow the transaction to take place or the transaction simply does not occur. Non-existence of the market is thus the extreme case of market failure. In a more general sense, the market exists, but the gains for a particular household may be below or above costs, with the result that some households will use the market while others will not.

They postulate that for commodities such as labour and food that can be sold and bought by peasant households, their sales price is a fraction of the purchase price. The width of this band depends on a whole set of transactions costs. 'The poorer the infrastructure, the less competitive the marketing systems, the less information is available, and the more risky the transactions, the greater the size of this band' (ibid., p. 1402). Thus we see that the width of the price band (which is directly affected and constrained by the characteristics of the elements constituting the configuration) is a crucial determinant of the household behaviour. The novelty of this approach is that the model yields shadow prices for intra-household transactions as well as for market transactions. When the shadow price of a product or of labour produced and used by a farm household falls within the price band, no trade takes place; the household reverts to self-sufficiency (subsistence) and relies on internal transactions.

The main conclusion is that the chronic inelasticity of supply response, particularly within the context of sub-Saharan Africa, may be explained 'as a structural feature associated with missing markets and not as an inherent behavioral trait of peasants' (p. 1410). Again, within the more comprehensive analytical framework used in the present study, this implies that a number of specific characteristics of elements operates as binding constraints on the behaviour of actors within the farm-household configuration. In turn, the more inelastic supply response in the African context, relative to say Southeast Asia, can be attributed to the fact that most, if not all, elements are less structurally rigid in the latter case illustrating once more the importance of context specificity in evaluating behaviour.

The policy implication flowing from the above analysis is that it pays to relax the structural constraints (that is, yielding an upward shift and narrowing of the price band) so as to elicit greater market responsiveness on the part of peasant actors. This effect can be achieved by infrastructure investments, increased competitiveness among local merchants, better access for peasants to credit markets, technology transfer and a more elastic and low-price supply of manufactured consumption goods such as textiles, footwear, processed foods and some inputs.

### Risk and uncertainty

A second category of market failures has to do with the fact that agricultural households in developing countries are prone to severe risks and uncertainties, most of which are directly related to the nature of their production activities. For example, production in agriculture depends strongly on the occurrence of diseases and pests and on the vagaries of the weather. Now it is true that these are usually risks, that is the probability density of the outcomes can be calculated approximately. But the problem here is that losses due to these risks occur mostly simultaneously in large regions, which renders them uninsurable. The use of pesticides and insecticides can reduce risk, but only for those relatively well-to-do households that have the means to buy such inputs. In order to cope with these risks, rural households resort to self-help insurance arrangements to the detriment of production efficiency.

Rural households also have to cope with specific types of uncertainty. One cause of uncertainty is moral hazard which affects, for example, the lease market of draft animals. Knowing that the health and performance of their animals depends on how well they are looked after, owners will be reluctant to rent them out even if they cannot fully employ them on their own land. Moral hazard is of course of great importance also in the market of labour services where the performance of hired labour is uncertain and supervision costly. Other problems affecting the agricultural labour market derive from the concentration of demand in the peak seasons of sowing and harvesting and from the considerable travelling costs in rural areas. When such imperfections in the labour market apply, production and consumption decisions reached within the family farm are non-separable.

### Rural credit and collateral-related costs

Finally, consider the effects of imperfect rural credit markets on rural households' decisions. One of the complications relates, again, to the simultaneity of agricultural activities which causes demand for credit to be concentrated in certain periods while there are other periods when financial funds remain idle. This periodicity of demand would be far less pronounced if credit markets were better integrated, such that funds could move between urban and rural areas but the lack of experience with other actor groups and with a different environment creates a persistent barrier. Another serious constraint has to do with the availability of collateral. As indicated on earlier occasions, households without material collateral,

## BOX 6.1   AN ALTERNATIVE APPROACH

The Locay-model applies a neo-classical approach to explain the transition process from families to firms as production units (Locay, 1990). When comparing this approach with that presented by de Janvry et al. (1991), it appears that entirely different stylized facts are emphasized. In the Locay model, the production functions of families and firms are both characterized by economies of scale. Families have lower monitoring costs which gives them an advantage over firms. However, although market imperfections are practically ignored, only firms can hire labour and capital and purchase intermediate goods. So firms can reach much higher production levels and reap more economies of scale, if markets are large enough. As markets tend to grow with economic development, firms will gain in competitive advantage and gradually replace family production. This goes to show how different theories emphasize different characteristics of exchange elements and, thus, describe different exchange configurations and generate different conclusions.

which are typically poor households, have, at best, access to informal credit lines, some of which are known for their uncommonly harsh terms. A result of all this is that those households that are sealed off from credit and without means of their own are unable to purchase the inputs needed for application of more efficient agricultural technologies.

Clearly, rural households in developing countries are a very diverse actor group as a result of variation in attributes like size, age and gender distribution, access to land (size and quality, owned or rented) and equipment and distance to product markets. Not surprisingly, these attributes determine through their impact on transaction costs the extent to which and the conditions under which households participate in market activities. Certain households are likely to be locked in suboptimal technology resulting in a small potential marketed surplus. Further, where households cannot separate production and consumption decisions, their surpluses and deficits must be absorbed internally which also results in efficiency losses. Finally, because poorly endowed rural households are less active in market transactions, public policy measures can hardly reach them. It is for these reasons that de Janvry et al. (1991) argue that market failures in agriculture tend to be household-specific rather than commodity-specific.

## 6.4    EXCHANGE ELEMENTS IN DIFFERENT PHASES OF DEVELOPMENT

In this section we examine exchange configurations corresponding with prototypical present-day economies in different phases of development, paying special attention to the elements of exchange and the types of transaction characteristic within each phase. Because these are prototypical economies that do not directly correspond with actually existing countries, we abstract from such more or less stochastic changes in exchange elements as wars, diseases, discoveries of mineral deposits and so forth. that often contribute to the uniqueness of the development of individual countries. The main purpose of this exercise is to compare present-day exchange configurations in different phases of development and, thus, to obtain a first impression of the nature and the centres of gravity of the forces that change and propel configurations.[9] For this purpose we consider only three types of economies, namely an early, middle and a late development phase. In this section we limit ourselves to a description of each of these phases, leaving the discussion of the dynamics of the evolution process from one stage to another to Chapter 7.

The dual–dual framework[10] is the analytical tool used here for identifying the phases and their corresponding key configurations. As indicated in Section 5.3, the two most important manifestations of dualism in large parts of the developing world appear to be related, first, to the physical and locational environment and, second, to the technology and forms of organization adopted. The first manifestation captures the dichotomy between rural and urban areas and the second between traditional technologies and family farms or enterprises, on the one hand, and modern technologies adopted in more complex forms of organization, on the other. This yields a four-way classification that identifies and delineates four broad sectors, that is, (1) subsistence (small scale) agriculture applying traditional labour-intensive technologies on family farms and producing mainly domestic food crops; (2) commercial, large scale (for example, plantation-type) agriculture using more capital-intensive technology and being oriented more toward export crops; (3) the informal urban sector; and (4) urban modern industry and services. This gives rise to what Thorbecke (1997) terms the dual–dual economy.

Kuznets (1966) describes the period since the industrial revolution of the mid-eighteenth century as the epoch of 'modern economic growth' which is characterized by the extended application of science to problems of economic production. Accordingly, the modern sector in the dual–dual framework comprises those production activities that use current scientific knowledge and participate in genuine innovation. From this it follows that the modern sector is an evolving phenomenon. In comparison, the pre-modern, or traditional sector is essentially static. Of course, changes occur also in the traditional sector: people move from one production activity to another, or move from the countryside to the city, workers and production units step over to the modern sector, and so on. But the dominant properties of this sector in terms of the elements of exchange (see Figure 6.2 and the left-hand side of Figure 6.3) remain unchanged.

### 6.4.1   The Early Development Phase

In countries that are still in an early phase of development, traditional agriculture predominates and production and transactions are generally concentrated in the northwest quadrant of the dual–dual framework as shown in Figure 6.1.[11] The discussion below therefore concentrates on the transactions connected with this configuration. Food production constitutes the bulk of total output. During this phase household and cottage enterprises appear in the form of various crop processing units, carpentry, masonry, handicrafts and so on. The technology used is very traditional and the form of organization is informal. Urban activities are limited and relate to various artisan crafts, trade and services, public administration, military and education.

Traditional agriculture in this phase is characterized by certain distinct features that largely determine the kind of transactions likely to emerge.

| Geographical Location and Nature of Product | | | **Technology and Form of Organization** | |
|---|---|---|---|---|
| | | | Traditional technology and family or self-employed enterprises | Modern technology and large enterprises |
| | rural | agricultural | Family farm configuration (for details refer to Figure 6.2) | Undeveloped |
| | | non-agricultural | Beginnings of cottage enterprises | |
| | urban | | Handicrafts, textiles, masonry, services | Relatively undeveloped |

*Figure 6.1   Exchange configurations in the early development phase*

Firstly, traditional agricultural is subject to much risk. Vagaries of the weather, pests and diseases cannot be controlled and cause substantial variations in food production of each household. The available technology does not allow storage of output for more than one production period. The nuclear household is too small to spread the risk of harvest failure or animal disease, so the larger kinship unit or horizontally and/or vertically integrated families become the insurance collectivity in many such cases.

Secondly, the produce of traditional agriculture varies not only in quantity, but also in quality. A standard quality cannot be guaranteed and modern marketing techniques like grading and the use of brand names are ruled out such that export markets are largely beyond the reach of this configuration. Further, as discussed in Subsection 6.3.2, the high transaction costs that are common in the early development phase often preclude participation in the domestic market. These are additional reasons why traditional agriculture tends to be inward-looking.

Thirdly, the biological processes inherent in agricultural production are highly sensitive to the care devoted before, during and after the growth cycle. Thus it matters a great deal whether a labourer performs his work with careful attention and adjustments in response to variations in ecological conditions. Such work quality is very difficult to monitor as agricultural operations are generally spread over a wide space. This leads to serious principal-agent problems for owner/tenant-operators (who therefore often use family labour, thus further strengthening the family as the production unit in traditional agriculture) as well as for owner-landlords.

Because of the characteristics associated with traditional agriculture – production and quality uncertainty, limited participation in markets, asymmetric information and incentive problems – transactions with other actors than members of the family tend to be interlinked. A prominent example of interlinked transactions, widely studied since the 1980s, is sharecropping tenancy,[12] in which the tenant agrees to pay a certain proportion of the total produce as rent. This arrangement, although in existence for many centuries, is demonstrably inefficient under neoclassical assumptions. The paradox can be explained, however, because sharecropping has two important advantages. Sharecropping, as opposed to pure wage contracts, helps to overcome the problem of incentives and monitoring (the tenant shares in the fruits of his labour) and, in contrast with pure rental contracts, helps to overcome the problem of missing insurance markets (as the rent varies with the size of the harvest). Usually, the landlord also advances credit for production and consumption purposes. In this case the landlord–tenant relation acts as a collateral for the loan. Braverman and Stiglitz (1982) have pointed out that the landlord,

| Actors | Items | Environment |
|---|---|---|
| • Typical actors:<br>- members of family farms.<br>• Other actors:<br>- landlords, middlemen, lenders (often in combination).<br>• Form of employment:<br>- largely self-employed.<br>• Behavioural characteristics:<br>- risk averse;<br>- custom bound values.<br>• Education:<br>- trained in traditional skills, formal education rare.<br>• Assets:<br>- largely in the form of land, cattle, tools, precious metals.<br>• Productivity/Income:<br>- low. | • Products:<br>- narrow range of products;<br>- food products dominate.<br><br>• Credit:<br>- collateral options limited due to:<br>(1) land lacks sales value (see under Environment);<br>(2) no major investment in machinery.<br>- material collateral mostly precious metal; personal reputation otherwise.<br>- loans tend to be small, short-term and for consumption.<br><br>• Labour:<br>- largely trained in traditional skills, formal education rare<br><br>• Land:<br>- partly communal;<br>- rights to privately owned land often unclear; plots often unconnected. | • Infrastructure:<br>- rudimentary transport and communication systems.<br>• Level of urbanization:<br>- low.<br>• Value system:<br>- strong community feelings;<br>- kinship ties very strong.<br>• Technology:<br>- traditional;<br>- limited division of labour;<br>- very labour intensive;<br>- scale economies unimportant;<br>- physical capital restricted to hand tools and cattle.<br>• Organization of production:<br>- mostly self-employment;<br>- family farms.<br>• Legal:<br>- property rights not developed;<br>- customary law prevails.<br>• Government:<br>- limited reach of measures;<br>- very limited revenue and expenditure. |
| **Transaction type** | • Personalized, non-monetary, implicit and interlinked.<br>• Terms of contract governed by custom.<br>• Governing principle behind exchange is that of reciprocity or redistribution rather than economic gain. | |

*Figure 6.2    The family-farm configuration in the early development phase: characteristics of actors, items, environment and transactions*

by adjusting the terms and the amount of the loan that he makes available to the tenant, can induce him to increase his work efforts or to undertake projects more to the liking of the landlord.

Due to the multi-stranded nature of exchange relationships in traditional agriculture, it does not make much sense to analyze land, labour, credit and product exchange configurations separately. Most intra-family transactions are virtual and implicit and in sharecropping the exchange of land, labour, produce and credit all hang together.

Figure 6.2 lists in detail the main characteristics of the exchange elements and of transactions in the family-farm configuration. The characteristics mentioned there are only selectively discussed in the text. It is important to note that many countries that by now have reached a higher level of development have in the more or less distant past also gone through this phase. And, although times were different then, the characteristics of the exchange elements were to a very large extent similar to those described in Figure 6.2. This implies that, even though this section presents a cross-section of today's prototype economies in different phases of development, we can compare exchange elements in the early phase with those especially in the middle phase and identify the shifts and changes the latter have undergone over time. In other words, the importance of the early development phase for the present discussion also derives from the fact that this phase can serve as a point of initial reference.

### 6.4.2   The Middle Development Phase

Only a handful of present-day developing countries are still in the early development phase; the great majority has reached the middle phase. In the latter group of countries, the family-farm exchange configuration still plays an important role, but modern production units are contributing significantly to total production and urban centres have come up. Precisely this situation is captured by the dual–dual framework. Comparing Figure 6.3 with Figure 6.1, we see how the northwest configuration is being encroached on from the east (through the use and application of modern technology and form of organization and their related characteristics of elements) and from the south (through the increasing importance of urban production and associated characteristics).

One comment regarding Figure 6.3 is in order before we examine the differences between the two sets of exchange elements. The dual–dual framework also brings out the tensions that many present-day developing countries experience. For the differences between rural traditional agriculture, on the one hand, and modern agriculture and the modern urban sector, on the other, go beyond the outward appearances of the applied technology and form of organization. An examination of characteristics of exchange elements in the various configurations presented in Figure 6.3 reveals clearly that the dichotomy between traditional and modern configurations is also one of inward as opposed to outward orientation, of personal versus impersonal relations and of domestic versus foreign influences. In other words, there are strong cultural and social and, thus, also political overtones in the distinctions between especially the configurations on the left- and on the right-hand side of Figure 6.3. These tensions may have a dynamics of their own. Resistance against what are considered as alien elements may flare up and slow down, limit or rule out further

| | | **Technology and Form of Organization** | |
|---|---|---|---|
| | | Traditional technology and family or self-employed enterprises | Modern technology and incorporated or unincorporated enterprises |
| | Rural; Agricultural | Family Farm Configuration<br>• Actors:<br>- (members of) family farms;<br>- subsistence oriented; risk averse;<br>- personal and custom bound value orientation.<br>• Item:<br>- generally food crops, beginnings of cash crops.<br>• Environment:<br>- traditional technology;<br>- poor infrastructure;<br>- land rights begin to emerge. | Large Scale Farms/Plantations<br>• Actors:<br>- large scale farms/plantations;<br>- foreign dominated/domestic;<br>- hired labour;<br>- profit oriented.<br>• Item:<br>- cash crops/plantation products.<br>• Environment:<br>- modern technology applied;<br>- capital intensive technology<br>- often sheltered by the government. |
| Geographical Location and Nature of Product | | • Transaction type:<br>- personalized, interlinked;<br>- some monetization appears.<br>• Market structure:<br>- fragmented markets. | • Transaction type:<br>- impersonal, monetized.<br>• Market structure:<br>- linked with foreign product markets;<br>- emerging domestic markets. |
| | Rural and urban; Non-agricultural | Non-Agricultural, Informal<br>• Actors:<br>- family and cottage enterprises;<br>- traditional orientation;<br>- risk averse.<br>• Item:<br>- food processing, textiles, furniture, artisinal products, construction, services, transport and trade.<br>• Environment:<br>- simple, traditional technology;<br>- limited effective regulation;<br>- tax laws scarcely apply;<br>- hostile government. | Modern, Mostly Industrial Sector<br>• Actors:<br>- emerging large factories;<br>- advanced management techniques;<br>- profit oriented.<br>• Item:<br>- consumer goods for domestic use;<br>- assembled products for re-export;<br>- emerging professional services.<br>• Environment:<br>- modern, relatively large scale, capital intensive technology;<br>- formal legislation applies;<br>- protective government. |
| | | • Transaction type:<br>- generally monetized, often personal.<br>• Market structure:<br>- regional markets;<br>- some links with formal sector;<br>- strong competition. | • Transaction type:<br>- formal, impersonal, monetized.<br>• Market structure:<br>- domestic markets linked;<br>- limited competition domestically;<br>- where applicable: strong competition on international markets. |

*Figure 6.3    The middle development phase: emergence of four major product-exchange configurations*

change away from traditional settings. The movement out of traditional toward modern configurations is by no means a steady and linear one.

We now come to a discussion of differences between the characteristics of elements of exchange in the early and the middle development phase.

As indicated before, these phases represent present-day prototypical economies in different stages of development. But if it is correct to argue that present-day, more-developed countries all had their starting point in an essentially similar early phase the differences can be interpreted as the outcome of changes over time. In this sense, the present discussion prepares the ground for a detailed analysis of the dynamics of exchange configurations in the next chapter.

From the point of view of the exchange-configuration approach it is important to distinguish between changes emanating from configurations themselves – or, more precisely, from decisions of actors participating in transactions within current configurations under review – and changes that come from outside. The former will be called endogenous, the latter exogenous changes.[13] We start with the exogenous changes.

Recalling the inward-looking attitude of actors in the family-farm configuration as discussed in the foregoing subsection, it would seem likely that, at least in the first instance, the transition from the early to the middle phase is mostly exogenously driven. This is indeed what often happened in many countries through the influx of foreign enterprises,[14] introducing modern technology and related management techniques combined with government initiatives that are meant to reduce transaction costs and raise economic efficiency. The changes that foreign enterprises bring may well relate to all three exchange elements: new types of actors, new products and new technology. Government initiatives affect primarily the exchange environment through pertinent regulation and the financing of infrastructure projects.

Endogenous changes, taken individually, are in the majority of cases much less spectacular than exogenous changes. It is only due to sheer numbers that their impact can be at least as important. This is not to say that all endogenous changes necessarily have a modest effect; there are many examples of major enterprises born of an initiative of one person. But the typical endogenous change affects at most the initiating individual actor and those in his immediate surrounding. An example is the member of a rural family who decides to try his luck in the city. On a macro-scale this decision by itself is only of minute importance, but the contrary applies to the waves of urbanization that many developing countries witnessed when millions of others decided similarly. Another example connects with the discussion in Subsection 6.3.2 about consequences of high transaction costs for participation of certain groups of farm households in product markets. As transaction costs drop, one household after another will decide to offer an increasing part of its production on the market. In the course of time this may lead to specialization, investments and eventually a cross-over to modern methods of agricultural production. While each of these decisions is hardly noticed, accumulated they have sweeping consequences for the agricultural sector and beyond. Many more of such examples of various types of endogenous changes can be given. Chapter 7 presents a systematic treatment.

### 6.4.3 The Mature Development Phase

The dual–dual set-up, while particularly useful in the middle development phase, is less suitable for analysis of countries in the mature phase. The main reason for this is that in many present-day developed countries the concept of a traditional sector, as distinct from a modern sector, no longer applies, or may never have applied. In order to clarify, it is useful to distinguish between early and late starters.[15] Here we define 'early starters' as countries which, by the end of the nineteenth century, had secured individual property rights, national markets for a wide range of commodities, diverse specialized financial institutions and widespread commercialization of land and labour. Amongst the early starters are most of the West European countries and the United States and Canada. Those are also the countries that have joined in the industrial revolution from an early date on and, as a result, gradually absorbed technological and managerial developments as they were introduced. And even though some industrial sectors were not as quick as others on the uptake, the difference was never so prominent as to merit a distinction between modern and traditional configurations.

This is not true for the late starters. But some of them, such as Taiwan, South Korea and Japan, followed consciously a unimodal strategy of agricultural development and, as a consequence, avoided the marked dualism in agriculture between a modern and a traditional subsector. And in other countries in this group the traditional sector has meanwhile vanished. Only in a few remaining countries is it still a real but dwindling phenomenon.

As the traditional sector is non-existent or disappearing in the mature phase, its transformation cannot be a source of development. But other opportunities remain, such as raising efficiency through continued specialization and investing in commodity and process innovation. In addition there are opportunities to profit from the international division of labour through trade with and direct investment in countries in other phases of development. Note that all such initiatives have an endogenous nature as they stem from decisions by actors venturing on a new course. They give rise to the continuous introduction of new items of exchange, types of agents and aspects of the environment, very often replacing existing exchange elements.

While governments of countries in the mature phase of development

| | | | Technology and Form of Organization | |
|---|---|---|---|---|
| | | | Traditional | Modern (also see the main text for a description of some important characteristics of exchange elements) |
| Geographical Location and Nature of Product | Rural | Agriculture | Disappearing (if applicable) | 'Industrial' methods of production. Strong government intervention: environmental regulation combined with extensive protection in land-scarce countries. |
| | | Non-Agriculture | | Geographical decentralization of production activities blurs the distinction between rural and urban non-agriculture. |
| | Urban | Industry — Tradable | Disappearing (if applicable) | Highly specialized production units connected with other such units in global networks. Importance of bulk and mass products rapidly diminishing. Agents invest continuously in product and process innovation, adaptation, imitation. |
| | | Industry — Non-tradable | | In the era of globalization the magnitude of non-tradables is dwindling in the mature phase. |
| | | Services — Salaried | | Services become the largest sector as the complex operations and transactions that are characteristic of this phase require professional financial, logistic, fiscal, technical, legal, accounting, computational and other support. Various levels of government are major actors in labor, land and capital markets. |
| | | Services — Self-Employed | | Increasingly, self-employed professionals are becoming incorporated. |

*Figure 6.4   The mature development phase: myriads of specialized exchange configurations*

have much in common with those in countries in other phases of development, there are also some major differences. For example, the former often possess more and more detailed information about economic agents and have a stronger administrative capacity allowing them to target taxes with greater precision and collect more tax revenue. Thus, they can also exert greater and more discriminative influence on economic activities. Such (exogenous) actions create an entirely different exchange environment as compared with countries in the early or middle phase. Furthermore, government outlays on social protection in mature economies are relatively much higher than in other countries thereby strongly reducing the need for traditional networks for mutual assistance and eventually eroding the informal rights and obligations among (extended) family members, neighbours, and members of the community. Thus social and cultural aspects of the environment are affected with consequences for the form and content of transactions.

The forces of globalization and the increasing integration of the world economy have led to a significant reduction in the powers of national and sub-national governments to intervene in and influence and regulate their domestic economies. Many goods and factors have become global in scale. But even more remarkable has been the enormous growth of new exchange configurations focused on global multinational and transnational corporations.

## NOTES

1. Polanyi, Chapter 13 in Polanyi et al., 1957.
2. The present brief description of these two theories relies heavily on Berry's synthesis. See Berry, 1967, p. 108.
3. Polanyi, Chapter 2 and Revere, Chapter 4 in Polanyi et al. (eds.), 1957.
4. Hammurabi's Code, drawn up around 1780 BC, regulates among many other things a variety of transactions, such as selling cattle and slaves, taking loans, renting out or selling land with or without maintaining usufruct and hiring animals and boats. So, already at this early date individual actors of a certain status were regularly involved in exchanges of very different items.
5. See Ishikawa, in Reynolds (ed.), 1975.
6. See Aoki and Hayami (eds.), 2001.
7. Hayami, 1989, p. 4.
8. The following discussion of the conditions under which a family farm decides to produce for the market, or alternatively opts for subsistence draws extensively on Thorbecke, 1993.
9. The present exercise is complemented by another one, presented in Chapter 7, examining historical cases of exchange configurations in widely differing periods of time.
10. See Thorbecke, 1997.
11. The discussion that follows draws on an earlier paper by Thorbecke and Mehra, 1994, which describes the evolution of the pattern of exchange from an early development stage to a mature one with an application to Sub-Saharan Africa.
12. See for example, Bardhan, 1980 and 1989 and Basu, 1983.
13. More will be said about this distinction in Chapter 7.
14. This is one reason why land-locked countries without mineral deposits, unattractive to foreign investors and traders, have great difficulty in moving away from phase 1.
15. There are several ways in which the early starters can be separated from the late starters and the composition of the groups differs somewhat with the criterion applied.

## REFERENCES

Aoki, M. and Y. Hayami (eds.) (2001), *Communities and Markets in Economic Development*, Oxford, UK: Oxford University Press.

Bardhan, P.K. (1980), 'Interlocking factor markets and agrarian development: a review of issues', *Oxford Economic Papers*, **32** (1), 82–98.

Bardhan, P.K. (ed.) (1989), *The Economic Theory of Agrarian Institutions*, Oxford, UK: Clarendon Press.

Basu, K. (1983), 'The emergence of isolation and interlinkage in rural markets', *Oxford Economic Papers*, **35** (2), 262–280.

Berry, B.J.L. (1967), *Geography of Market Centers and Retail Distribution*, Englewood Cliffs, USA: Prentice-Hall.

Braverman, A. and J.E. Stiglitz (1982), 'Sharecropping and the interlinking of agrarian markets', *American Economic Review*, **72** (4), 695–715.

Hayami, Y. (1989), 'Community, market and state', in A. Maunder and A. Valdez (eds.), *Agriculture and Government in an Interdependent World*, Proceedings of the 20th International Conference of Agricultural Economists (Buenos Aires), Sudbury, MA, USA: Dartmouth and Brookfield, VT, USA: Gower Press.

Ishikawa, S. (1975), 'Peasant families and the agrarian community in the process of development', in L.G. Reynolds (ed.), *Agriculture in Development Theory*, New Haven, CT: Yale University Press.

de Janvry, A., M. Fafchamps and E. Sadoulet (1991), 'Peasant household behaviour with missing markets: some paradoxes explained', *The Economic Journal*, **101** (409), 1400–1417.

de Janvry, A. and E. Sadoulet (2006), 'Configurations and transactions: frontiers in the modeling of rural households' behavior', in A. de Janvry and R. Kanbur (eds.), *Poverty, Inequality and Development; Essays in Honor of Erik Thorbecke*, Heidelberg: Springer.

Kuznets, S. (1966), *Modern Economic Growth: Rate, Structure and Spread*, New Haven and London: Yale University Press.

Locay, L. (1990), 'Economic development and the division of production between households and markets', *The Journal of Political Economy*, **98** (5), 965–982.

Malinowski, B. (1921), 'The primitive economy of the Tobriand Islanders', *The Economic Journal*, **31** (1), 1–16.

Pirenne, H. (1936), *Economic and Social History of Medieval Europe*, New York: Harcourt.

Polanyi, K., C.M. Arensberg and H.W. Pearson (eds.) (1957), *Trade and Market in the Early Empires*, Glencoe, IL: The Free Press and The Falcon's Wing Press.

Singh, I., L. Squire and J. Strauss (eds.) (1986), *Agricultural Household Models*, Baltimore: The Johns Hopkins University Press.

Thorbecke, E. (1993), 'Impact of state and civil institutions on the operations of rural market and nonmarket configurations', *World Development*, **24** (4), 591–605.

Thorbecke, E. (1997), A *Dual–Dual Framework to Analyze the Process of Development*, Conference in Memory of John C.H. Fei, Taipei.

Thorbecke, E. and R. Mehra (1994), *The Evolution of the Pattern of Exchange in Developing Countries*, Washington DC: Institute of Policy Reform.

# 7. The dynamic forces in exchange configurations

## 7.1 OVERVIEW

This chapter is concerned with the dynamics of exchange configurations. So the main task here is to explain how one state of exchange configurations springs from the foregoing. In the following pages it will be argued that a multitude of forces can be distinguished that move configurations from one state to another. As will be seen, these forces differ from each other in their origins and in the ways they make their impact felt.

In the following, we sometimes use the term 'evolution' as an alternative for the dynamics of exchange configurations. Social scientists attach different and sometimes unclear meanings to the term.[1] Hence, in order to avoid confusion, it must be added that we use 'evolution' in a non-Darwinian sense. As will be seen below, the dynamics of exchange configurations are driven to a large degree by considered, even if sometimes ill-fated, decisions taken by actors/decision makers and public policy makers. Clearly, such a view conflicts with a strictly Darwinian concept of evolution.

The number of dynamic forces that modify exchange configurations is fairly large. As they also vary strongly in nature, it is necessary to group them in order to bring structure into the discussion. Therefore, Section 7.2 starts by distinguishing four main groups of forces of change applying two criteria, 'endogeneity' and intention. The intentional dynamic forces in exchange configurations are nearly always triggered by an evaluation of the outcomes of existing transactions. This is why Section 7.3 is devoted to a brief discussion of evaluation processes and the different criteria that appear to be relevant for the dynamics of exchange configurations. Thereafter, the various forces in each of the main groups are discussed in Sections 7.4 to 7.6. Section 7.7 presents a graphical summary.

The impact of forces of change can be formidable. Many of these forces that occurred in the past made it to the history books. Section 7.8 presents six historical cases referring to different, but sometimes overlapping periods. They describe the evolution of exchange configurations as a result of the various dynamic forces identified in earlier sections. Each case represents a move away from earlier patterns of exchange. The cases demonstrate firstly the impact of exchange elements and their changes on patterns of exchange. Thus, they underline the historical applicability of the exchange-configuration approach as presented in the foregoing chapters. Secondly, they show that exogenous changes in exchange elements are not the only driving force in the dynamics of exchange configurations. Actors not only adapt to the new conditions resulting from exogenous changes in elements, but also shape and reshape exchange elements and thereby create new configurations endogenously. Thirdly, the cases discussed illustrate the dynamic role that transactions themselves can play when transactions and exchange elements transform one another in dynamic loops.

## 7.2   FOUR MAIN GROUPS OF FORCES OF CHANGE

The nature of forces of change that drive the evolution of exchange configurations varies widely. Thus in this section we set out to form a few main categories of forces in order to prepare for the discussion of individual forces of change in subsequent sections. For this purpose we shall distinguish between endogenous and exogenous and between intended (or premeditated, or planned) and unintended forces to obtain four main categories.

We define endogenous forces of change as the changes emanating from decisions by actors in the exchange configuration(s) under consideration. The definition reflects the central role played by actors as decision makers in the formation of transactions. Inversely, exogenous forces do not originate from actors' acts and decisions in the exchange configuration(s) being considered. Further, intended dynamic forces comprise decisions and acts which are meant to affect transactions or, at least, which are the result of conscious deliberation taking account of the effects on transactions. Unintended forces do not satisfy the latter criteria.

Figure 7.1 shows the four-way distinction that obtains from an application of the above-mentioned criteria. Each quadrant contains a particular group of dynamic forces with entirely different origins and impact. The nature of the forces in each group is indicated in the quadrants. Subgroups and individual forces in each of these main groups will be discussed under these headings later on in this chapter. The four main groups are described briefly in the following paragraphs by way of introduction.

Firstly, consider the actor-triggered dynamic forces deriving from the tactics and strategies actors apply in exchange (in the top-left corner of

|              | endogenous                              | exogenous          |
| ------------ | --------------------------------------- | ------------------ |
| **Intended**   | Actors' tactics and strategies          | Public policies    |
| **Unintended** | Loops or feedbacks in systems of exchange | Shocks           |

*Figure 7.1    Four main groups of forces of change*

Figure 7.1). These forces represent a major extension of the role given to actors in the preceding chapters. By tactics we mean short-run responses to the current state such as, for example, the kind of responses to which actors were limited in earlier chapters when we discussed their reactions to exogenous changes in elements of exchange establishing a new state. Strategies, however, encompass decisions and devices meant to change the state variables. In other words, the strategies in this group consist of those actions by actors in exchange configurations that lead to changes in the elements. The fount of initiatives opened up by widening our perspective of actors in this way reveals a dynamic force that is easily the most important one in the exchange-configuration approach.

The public policies in Figure 7.1 include in any case the interventions by different levels of government that are meant to influence transactions directly or indirectly. They can be of a relatively simple, low-cost nature, such as a change in the level of an import duty. But they can also be highly complex, such as a tax reform and entering into an international trade agreement, or very costly, such as most infrastructure projects. Public policies also include budget policy. The latter is often meant to impact on the aggregate level of transaction activity in the context of macroeconomic stabilization policy. But even if budget policy is not applied as a stabilizing instrument, policy makers consider its effect on transactions.

Many decisions and acts by actors resulting in transactions have very significant effects on specific aspects of elements of exchange even though they are unintended. These effects create loops and feedbacks in systems of exchange (in the bottom-left quadrant). The loops capture and transmit the indirect effects and externalities of these decisions. Examples of these effects are pollution and congestion which change the exchange environment. The accumulated effects of transactions on the income and wealth position of actors and the information which transactions provide to outsiders are other examples.

Shocks form the fourth main group of dynamic forces. They have an accidental nature. Examples of shocks are natural disasters, epidemics and religious struggles. A birth or death in a family, a fire and a burglary are shocks on a micro-scale.

The categories of dynamic forces outlined above appear to be robust and useful in the organization of the subsequent discussion of more specific individual forces. Still, it must be added in fairness that a certain measure of ambiguity cannot always be avoided. For example, we have chosen to include wars under 'Shocks'. But one only has to think of von Clausewitz's famous dictum about wars being the continuation of politics with different means to see that wars could also be made part of public policies. Indeed, many armed struggles had their origin at least partly in trade conflicts.

A second example of ambiguity concerns new technologies and innovations: are they an exogenous or an endogenous force of change? On one hand, one can only agree with Solow (1994, p. 51) when he argues: 'There is probably an irreducibly exogenous element in the research and development process, at least exogenous to the economy.' On the other hand, innovations have always also had an endogenous character. In the past they were introduced by artisanal inventors to improve the results of their transactions. Also nowadays firms consider the efforts they direct towards innovation as an instrument to gain an advantage over their competitors. Similarly, universities promote and encourage the production and publication of innovating concepts in order to maintain or improve their reputation in the configuration called academia. For these reasons we treat innovations below as an endogenous, intentional force of change to be included among 'Actors' strategies and tactics'. It is true that the great majority of successful innovations are acquired and used by actors who had no part whatsoever in their development. From the viewpoint of these actors such innovations drop from thin air. But such asymmetry – one actor in a configuration taking all other actors by surprise – is characteristic of many strategic moves (also see Subsection 7.4.1).

In an analysis of exchange the intentional dynamic forces are more interesting than the unintentional forces. This is not to say that the latter are unimportant. In fact, the forces we include under 'Loops' in exchange systems and under 'Shocks' often are the source of major changes in exchange configurations. Still, they just happen. Intentional forces of change, however, (grouped under 'Actors' tactics and strategies' and 'Public policies') are the outcomes of learning and decision-making processes. They are more complex and analytically more challenging. This is also why they are examined in more detail below. The next section prepares the ground by discussing processes of evaluating transactions which are often the starting point of efforts by actors and governments to improve outcomes.

## 7.3    EVALUATING OUTCOMES OF EXCHANGE CONFIGURATIONS

The appraisal of outcomes is a crucial part of economic exchange. In transactions one thing is traded for something else, so it is only natural that the result of this give-and-take is assessed at some point of time. Of course, not all transactions are evaluated with the same frequency and intensity, business transactions scoring higher in this regard than intra-family transactions. But, in general, evaluations are practically inevitable. For the present discussion, evaluations derive their importance from the fact that they generate forces of change, as actors or governments (representing the general interest) or both may attempt to improve the outcomes.

As a preliminary to Sections 7.4 and 7.5, this section presents a discussion of evaluation processes within the framework of exchange configurations. The literature in the tradition of the structure–conduct–performance (SCP) approach (discussed in Section 3.4) provides a useful starting point. But it must be kept in mind that the exchange-configuration approach covers a much wider range of transactions. As a result, the reviewers to be considered here (for example, various types of individual actors, firms, family members, government institutions, and so on) and the criteria applied (economic, social, political, legal, ethical, emotional criteria at different levels of aggregation) show much greater diversity. The following general observations regarding evaluations of market and non-market transactions can serve as an illustration.

Evaluations of market transactions by individual actors are relatively simple. A comparison of utility derived from the terms of the transaction with transaction costs often suffices. Stronger still, many day-to-day transactions rarely generate much thought. But there can be complications, such as when the transactions involve durable consumer goods where only time can tell if actual utility lived up to expected utility. Further, utility often has many dimensions requiring some form of weighting in order to allow a conclusion.

In the business sector market transactions are mainly evaluated as aggregates. Generally speaking, attention focuses on the overall results of buying and selling operations as expressed in terms of a whole range of accounting ratios. As each ratio, or criterion, indicates only one aspect of the total performance of business units, a weighting system must be applied in order to arrive at an overall judgment. The weights as well as the criteria often appear to change over time (Meyer, 1994, p. 556).

The public sector is not concerned with individual market transactions. As the guardian of the common good, it derives the criteria for judging market transactions from market failures in a general sense. Familiar criteria for assessing market failure are (1) market efficiency (threatened by external effects, market domination and asymmetric information), (2) equity, and (3) economy-wide stability and the rates of employment and growth. But before implementing any measure to correct for market failure, governments should also test for government failure which occurs when public intervention fails to improve on the existing situation.

Among the non-market transactions those concluded within organizations, and especially those involving labour relations, have attracted most attention in the economic literature. The labour-management literature and the principal-agent theory provide ample illustration of the difficulties in assessing the performance of intra-firm transactions due to monitoring problems. The considerable costs organizations are willing to spend on staff and systems monitoring and motivating employees provide further evidence of the complexity of the problem. The criteria applied in these assessments are partly of an economic nature. But we should be aware also of the importance of criteria of a social nature in evaluations of the performance of intra-firm transactions by the individual participants. The performance of internal transactions in organizations other than firms – such as government organizations, hospitals and schools – is particularly difficult to measure given their objectives and the nature of their 'products'. The inadequacy of the available criteria often results in excessive attention to forms and procedures (Meyer, 1994).

The argument presented above, stressing the importance of non-economic considerations in intra-firm labour relations, holds a fortiori in intra-family transactions. Individual assessments of intra-family transactions tend to depend strongly on the feelings members harbour towards each other, and on members' personalities, tasks, capabilities, position and interpretations of the norms that hold in the family and on the emotions that close contacts can produce.

Governments are also concerned with non-market transactions, especially with the safety and health aspects of intra-firm transactions and with the observance of rights and duties among spouses and rights of children in intra-family transactions.

|              | positive                        | normative                                          |
|--------------|---------------------------------|----------------------------------------------------|
| analytical   | Why are the results as they are? | Why do the results deviate from the norms/objectives? |
| hypothetical | What happens if ...?            | What must be done to achieve the norms/objectives? |

*Figure 7.2    Four second-round questions in evaluations of performance*

We now come to a discussion of evaluation processes. Evaluations are not made for their own sake; they must lead to a conclusion. Often the final conclusion in evaluations of the outcomes of exchange configurations is reached in a number of rounds. The first round often consists of such activities as collecting the necessary information, selecting criteria and deciding whether the outcomes are satisfactory or not. In the first case the evaluation may end there. But, especially if the stakes are large, the reviewer may wish to understand what causes the outcomes to be satisfactory and/or which events could threaten the outcomes. The latter (positive) questions, requiring a second round of search, appear in the left-hand-side column of Figure 7.2. In the second case, where the results were found to be unsatisfactory, obvious questions for a second round concern the causes and/or the possible actions that may be undertaken to improve results. These are the kind of normative questions that appear in the right-hand-side column.

Note that the questions in the second round can be addressed only with the help of appropriate theories that help to provide explanations of the phenomena under review. It is not always directly apparent which theory is the appropriate one for a particular question. Take the category of 'What if . . .?' questions indicated in the bottom-left corner of Figure 7.2. Examples of such hypothetical questions are: 'What happens if my boss retires . . .? A competitor enters into the market . . .? The opposition wins the next election. . .? The housing market collapses?' Clearly, the appropriate theory is to be selected from a wide array covering simple and complex, economic and non-economic issues at different levels of aggregation. The exchange-configuration approach can be helpful in this regard. After all, the central thesis of this approach is that transactions derive their form and content from the characteristics of the underlying exchange elements. Thus, for an understanding of how transactions have come about, it pays to examine carefully the relevant elements of exchange and then to select the theory that incorporates the characteristics of these elements best.

Armed with an appropriate theory, the positive-analytical, second round questions on the left-hand side of Figure 7.2 can be tackled. The evaluation may well end there. Clearly, however, the conclusions drawn from the exercise can give rise to new questions, especially so if an improved understanding shows that the outcomes depend, for example, on chance occurrence. In other words, conclusions from a positive analysis of outcomes can lead to a reformulation of criteria and to asking normative questions like those on the right-hand side of Figure 7.2.

The latter are also the questions evaluators ask right away when the outcomes are found to be unsatisfactory. Note that compared with positive-analytical questions, the train of the argument when examining normative-analytical questions is reversed: from outcomes to causes. Where, in terms of the exchange-configuration approach, positive analysis is meant to explain how (given) characteristics of aspects of exchange elements explain the form and content of transactions, normative analysis aims at finding out how (given) outcomes can be traced back to the exchange elements. Finally, when addressing policy questions like those in the bottom-left corner of Figure 7.2, another round of analysis is needed in order to establish which instruments – that is variables that (1) affect the outcomes, and (2) can be manipulated – are available and which set of instruments is likely to be most effective.[2] More will be said about policy instruments in the sections below.

Before concluding this discussion of evaluation processes, attention must be drawn to the crucial role learning – or, more precisely the cognitive variant of learning[3] – plays in each stage. In fact, without learning evaluation becomes meaningless. Below it will be shown how evaluations of outcomes of transactions by actors and public policy-makers drive some of the most prominent dynamic forces. In other words, the importance of the underlying learning processes for the evolution of exchange configurations is not easily overestimated.

## 7.4 ACTORS' TACTICS AND STRATEGIES

The central role of actors as decision makers in exchange configurations has been emphasized on various occasions in this book. Still, the range of decisions by actors discussed so far has been strictly limited for reasons of presentation. In this section, however, we relinquish this limited view. We now explicitly recognize the role of actors/decision makers in effectuating the full range of forces of change distinguished in the top-left corner of Figure 7.1. Subsection 7.4.1 discusses this more extended role of actors as agents of change. Thereafter, in Subsection 7.4.2, attention will be given to the instruments that various categories of actors in different exchange configurations have at their disposal.

The changes discussed in this section are those brought about by actors/ decision makers with the intent to improve the outcomes of existing transactions. Clearly, the result of their actions may differ from the intended outcomes. There are all sorts of reasons for this: actors err in their analysis of unsatisfactory results; their efforts may be thwarted by other actors with different preferences; and chance events may alter the exchange environment. But such deviations from intended outcomes do not concern us here. It is the intention that counts, not its success.

As the title of this section suggests, we distinguish below between tactical and strategic decisions by actors. There are many different meanings attached to these terms. But for our purposes a definition introduced in a discussion of industrial organization and game theory is particularly useful (Shapiro, 1989, pp. 125–137). According to this definition strategic moves are devices to manipulate the rules of the game by changing the state variables. Strategic decisions involve a long-lasting commitment, that is they cannot be easily (costlessly) reversed. Tactical moves, on the other hand, are short-run responses to the current state. They are played out in a setting defined by the state variables. In other words, tactical moves have an adaptive character, whereas strategic moves are typically innovative.[4] Translating the above into the terminology of the exchange-configuration approach, strategic decisions are meant to alter aspects of exchange elements, whereas tactical decisions take the prevailing exchange elements as given.

The effect of a single actor's tactical or strategic decision is generally less dramatic than the effect of a single external event. Still, by sheer numbers, decisions by actors prove to be a formidable force in socio-economic development. In fact, it can be argued that the changes deriving from decisions by actors in an exchange configuration give, more than anything else, a true indication of the dynamic character of that configuration.

### 7.4.1   Actors/Decision Makers as Agents of Change

In the foregoing chapters actors/decision makers operated in a mostly static setting. Confronted with certain combinations of properties of exchange elements, decision procedures and properties of transactions, it was their role to decide whether to enter into a certain exchange or not. Only when an exogenous change in one or more exchange elements occurred, the multidimensional world of transactional opportunities would be altered. In that case the outcomes of unchanged transactions might prove to be unsatisfactory, so actors could have reason to adjust procedures and/or the form and content of transactions, depending on the costs of adaptation.

Here we identify these reactions of actors to changes in exchange elements as a separate force of change. Clearly, the changes in elements themselves are dynamic forces in their own right. They will be discussed in the following pages. But it is important to realize that there is not a direct and inevitable relation between changes in elements, on the one hand, and the repercussions they may or may not have for the form and content of transactions, on the other. It is true that configurations change when exchange elements change. But transactions may remain unaffected. Whether or not transactions change depends on how actors react after having considered the new conditions. In other words, decisions by actors form a separate force of change determining if and how changes in elements are translated into new transactions. These reactions, to the extent they occur, take the new state of exchange elements as given. So they are to be counted among the actors' tactical moves.

In addition to responses to changes in exchange elements, actors make many other tactical moves. The latter, a second category of tactical decisions, are taken together here to form an additional force of change. They include, in principle, all other changes actors introduce within a given set of exchange elements, such as reactions to other tactical moves and own experiments. Examples of such tactical decisions in the context of market configurations regard adaptations in prices, payment and delivery conditions and modifications in logo and packaging. In intra-firm transactions this type of tactical change occurs, for example, when tasks are redistributed among employees while hierarchy, functions and salaries remain the same. Among this category of tactical decisions some minor changes in elements may be included. Exactly what can be considered to be 'a minor change' depends entirely on the context. When a small private firm hires an additional employee, that firm's attributes change. This change is likely to be of no significance in the market in which the firm operates, so it may be ignored for all practical purposes. However, even such a small shift may very well be of major importance for the firm's internal transactions.

Having identified two types of tactical moves by actors/decision makers, we now turn to the category of strategic decisions which generate forces of change of an entirely different nature. Strategic moves involve conscious and autonomous manipulations of aspects of exchange elements. So, by intervening in the state variables, they change the game. On the whole, therefore, strategic moves by actors in exchange configurations express more ambition and daring than tactical moves. They are also much more complex, so it stands to reason that they are preceded by a more careful, farther-reaching evaluation process. The importance of strategic decisions by firms can hardly be overestimated. According to Schumpeter they are the 'fundamental impulse that sets and keeps the capitalist engine in motion' by creating new consumer goods, new methods of production or transportation, new markets and new forms of industrial organization. They incessantly revolutionize 'the economic structure from within, incessantly destroying the old one, incessantly creating a new one' (Schumpeter, 1950, p. 83).

We note, first of all, that actor-generated (endogenous) changes in elements occur next to the exogenous changes that were presented in the foregoing chapters as the prime movers of actors' adaptive decision processes. Clearly, endogenous changes in elements (that is actors' strategic moves) can have the same effect. So actors embarking on such moves are well-advised to take account of the possible reactions by other actors. Secondly, and partly in reaction to the previous consideration, strategic moves are often prepared in secret so as to optimize their impact or minimize costs. This consideration applies to market configurations (when firms launch new products, announce a merger), in intra-organizational configurations (when employees accept a job elsewhere) as well as in intra-family configurations (when partners separate). Thirdly, manipulation of exchange elements requires a certain measure of power in one or another form. Such power is distributed unevenly among actors such that those actors who are better equipped than others have more room for manoeuvre. Finally, of all actor groups, firms have by nature more strategic instruments at their disposal than others, as will be illustrated in the next subsection. It is symptomatic in this regard that the economic literature on strategic decisions – such as the literature on industrial organization and game theory – refers mostly to the business sector.

Innovations – that is the development and introduction of new products, services, production technologies, management techniques and so on – stand out among the strategic moves because of the radical changes they often bring. Individual innovations are, of course, primarily meant to improve the outcomes of transactions in which the activating actors are engaged.[5] But, taken together, all these individual innovations are of overwhelming importance in the dynamics of economic systems. Even adherents of such antipodal schools of thought as neoclassical growth theory and evolutionary economics look upon innovations as the most powerful engine in economic development.

When considering actors' tactical and strategic moves, one cannot avoid recognizing the immense importance of learning processes.[6] Especially when these moves are preceded by evaluation procedures as described in

Section 7.2 information must be collected, selected, processed, interpreted and analyzed. This type of learning processes, called cognitive learning (see Section 3.5), consists of conscious, goal-oriented efforts. But behavioural learning, which is mechanistic and merely results from performance feedback, is also very relevant in this context as is the passive absorption of observations and experiences that participants in social activities accumulate.[7]

The significance of learning helps to explain why some actors are better equipped than others to deal with new transactional conditions. It is also a reminder of the learning costs – in terms of money, time and effort – of considering transactional change. Further, if it is true that making sense of new information depends on existing knowledge and understanding, large jumps in insight are rare. This consideration is compounded by the risks and uncertainties that change brings. Especially doing new things (to be distinguished from doing existing things better) entails Knightian uncertainty[8] which can stifle an urge for change. The result of these counter-forces can be that exchange configurations go through periods of stagnation, not necessarily caused by conservatism. On the other hand, of course, the fact that all sorts of decision makers continuously apply a gamut of instruments with hopes of improving the net benefits derived from transactions testifies to their readiness to face the challenges that a dynamic world offers.

### 7.4.2 Instruments of Actors/Decision Makers

The arsenal of instruments that actors/decision makers can apply ranges widely. First of all, actors can, by their nature, directly change the form and content of transactions. Secondly, they can manipulate an array of characteristics of items and actors, but not so much of the exchange environment. It is worthwhile noting here the remarkable contrast between exchange actors' instruments and the set of instruments governments can apply. As will be shown in Section 7.5, governments can rarely influence the form and content of transactions directly. Further, though they can have a formidable impact on aspects of the exchange environment, aspects of the other exchange elements (items and actors) are mostly beyond their reach. These differences between the sets of instruments of actors/decision makers and governments reflect of course the complementary character of governmental tasks in market economies.

Obviously, in order to be able to apply any instrument an actor/decision maker must have some power: the power to manipulate and also the power of understanding how transactions come about (see the foregoing subsection). Decision makers scoring low on either point may just

accept the outcomes of transactions as they are. The choice they then have
is between opting in or out of transactions. But they may also try to create
an instrument such that their options are widened, for example by learning
a new skill, accumulating savings, expanding their social network. Still,
as actors often operate in large numbers of different configurations, it is
rare that they are powerless in all of them. And indeed it can often be seen
that an event in one configuration – say, a rise in sales taxes causing price
increases in markets of consumer goods – triggers a reaction in another
configuration where affected actors can exert their influence – say, a labour
market where workers press for a wage rise so as to compensate for the
drop in the real wage rate.

The list of instruments potentially available to individual actors/decision
makers taken together is nearly endless. As a result the discussion below
cannot be complete. Its main purpose is to illustrate the very considerable
differences between the instruments that different actor groups have at
their disposal in different types of transactions.

Figure 7.3 presents a variety of instruments available to actors/decision
makers through which they can aim to alter exchange configurations.
It distinguishes three dimensions: types of transactions (market, intra-
organizational and intra-family transactions), types of actors (firms and
individual actors in market transactions, employees in intra-organizational
transactions and family members in intra-family transactions) and types
of instruments (terms and form of transactions, decision procedures and,
especially, elements of exchange). Regarding the instruments, it is necessary to keep in mind the hierarchical relation that exists between the three
types distinguished here. As long as the prevailing elements of exchange
remain in place, the room for autonomous change in decision procedures
and form and content of transactions is limited. So it is precisely through
changes in elements of exchange – the strategic moves – that decision
makers obtain and widen opportunities for applying the other two types
of instruments. Or, put differently, decision makers doing little to alter
exchange elements cannot expect to come to a position where they can significantly modify decision procedures or transactions to their advantage.

Even though the list of instruments in Figure 7.3 is neither detailed nor
exhaustive, it illustrates the great variety of exchange elements that are
used as handles on transactions. It also shows the differences between the
instruments available to different groups of decision makers. For individual decision makers in market transactions, the most easily accessible
instruments have to do with their own attributes as actors; they can decide
to acquire information, save, invest, take a loan, improve their skills, and

| Types of actors | Categories of instruments | | |
|---|---|---|---|
| | Form and content of transactions | Decision Procedure | Elements of exchange |

### *Market transactions*

| | | | |
|---|---|---|---|
| Individual actors | Adapt, where possible and desired. | Collect info; search for options; consult mediators. | Migrate; participate in collective action; seek rent. Change size/composition of assets/liabilities; change/improve skills. |
| Firms | Adapt, where possible and desired (mostly as a follow-up of changes in exchange elements). | Collect info about competitors, potential partners, related transactions. Inform/ misinform others. Advertise reliability, commitment, credible threats. | *Item related*: Add/drop products/services; advertise; establish product standard; change product design; create/improve products. *Environment related*: Move/expand elsewhere; participate in pressure groups. *Actors' attributes related*: Start a firm; change legal status; form alliance; collude; merge; acquire other firm; alter reputation; file for bankruptcy; seek rent. Change size/composition of assets, funds, liabilities; invest/divest; apply improved production technology; invest in R&D. Acquire info/knowledge/experience; hire/fire. |

### *Intra-organizational transactions*

| | | | |
|---|---|---|---|
| Workers in firms | *All*: Excel; adapt, where possible and desired. | *Managers*: Optimize procedures/ incentives. *All*: Collect info; participate in relevant decisions | *Managers*: Change mode of organization (degree of formality, hierarchy, control), chart of organization, internal culture (loyalty, manners, result orientation, attitude to change and creativity); apply outsourcing, HRM (career management, promotion of learning). *All*: Change/improve skills; invest in network; impress; participate in collective action. |

### *Intra-family transactions*

| | | | |
|---|---|---|---|
| Family members | Adapt, where possible and desired | Collect info; participate in relevant decisions | Establish authority (change/improve skills, improve income, invest in relations); adapt intra-family values; marry/divorce; have children; arrange insurances; move elsewhere. |

*Figure 7.3    A selective list of instruments by types of transactions and actors*

so on. And since these are mostly individual decisions and actions, they are relatively easy to implement. They have, in principle, a few other categories of instruments at their disposal, but the effects of these are more difficult to control. A similar argument applies to individual decision makers in other types of transactions, as Figure 7.3 shows.

Compared with the other groups of decision makers, firms can choose from a particularly wide array of exchange elements they may attempt to change in order to improve the outcomes of their market transactions. It is not coincidental that entrepreneurs are considered to be the prime agents of change in various economic theories. Still, the actual room for manoeuvre of individual firms is often a function of their size. Small firms tend to have only a fraction of the opportunities that large firms have to change exchange elements to their advantage. And this holds a fortiori for the production organizations in the informal sector which we also include in this group.

The instruments available to firms are presented and discussed in great detail in a vast literature in which the industrial organization literature (see Section 3.4) figures prominently. With a view to the present topic, the distinction that is made in the structure–conduct–performance literature between the structuralist and the behaviouralist approach is particularly relevant. According to the structuralists, the market structure dominates any possible action by individual firms. Behaviouralists, on the other hand, maintain that market structure is not completely exogenous and stable, but at least partly subject to firm action.[9] This distinction, when translated into the terms used in the exchange-configuration approach, corresponds with the question of whether or not individual firms are capable of manipulation of exchange elements. In the first case the behaviouralist approach applies, in the second case the structuralist approach.

Of course, for persons engaged in intra-organizational transactions the opportunity to adapt exchange elements depends strongly on their position in the hierarchy. Those in a position of authority, indicated crudely as managers in Figure 7.3, have many more instruments at their disposal than the others. Managers may wish to change internal transactions on the basis of new insights they developed autonomously or which they derived from the management literature. But one can observe a certain correspondence between the aspects of exchange elements determining a firm's position in market transactions and the organizational mode it has adopted. Firm size is a powerful determinant in this respect and so are the products/services it produces and the nature of its production technology. Therefore, strategic moves with respect to market transactions are often followed by corresponding changes in the organizational mode. But the influence may also run in the opposite direction: there is evidence that the mode of organization influences the tendency to test and adopt innovations in production technology.

The dominating performance criteria applied by firms have to do with profitability and survival. These criteria are relatively clear-cut and imperative; managers can refer to them and introduce drastic changes in intra-firm transactions. Other types of organizations, like non-profits (for example, hospitals and schools) and governments, are in a different position. Their internal transactions are governed more by procedures aiming at expected outcomes. Employees often have a say in these matters and can, thereby, influence internal transactions.

Intra-family transactions are characterized by close and durable personal relations and the lack of an easy exit opportunity. So the quality of these relations strongly determines the performance of the transactions. Even minor frictions – of no import, or easily avoidable in market transactions – can develop into serious problems. But a family member who finds the outcomes unsatisfactory will note that instruments to alter the status quo are relatively few and costly. Especially in cultures where the position of individual members depends on age and gender, the opportunities for independent action are very limited.

## 7.5   GOVERNMENT INTERVENTIONS

Government interventions or policies have been classified in Figure 7.1 as exogenous and intended forces of change. Hence, they typically have a deus ex machina character. Although governments also operate in markets as regular actors (employers, borrowers, and so on), they typically introduce the overwhelming majority of their interventions in their role of outsiders endowed with special powers to improve the outcome of transactions. Being outsiders, their actions are exogenous, that is they are not explained by the exchange-configuration approach.

Interventions are meant to prevent or modify events. So, in the context of the exchange-configuration approach, government interventions are considered as conscious manipulations with the intent to prevent or modify the outcome of certain market or non-market transactions. These interventions differ in a number of ways from non-governmental interventions. Governments – whether operating at the national, state/provincial or local level – are subject to public law from which they derive very special and sometimes far-reaching power for their exclusive use. Also the criteria they apply when evaluating transactions have a special nature.

Before they can act as agents of change, governments must learn just like actors/decision makers must learn (see Subsection 7.4.1). But, compared with actors, the task for governments is often more complex if only because the objects of policy (for example, a failing market, a social-welfare system, a lagging region) tend to be more aggregate and abstract and riddled with conflicting interests. Another problem derives from the fact that compared with the private sector, policy failure in the public sector is less easy to detect and less speedily punished. Thus, learning from feedback is less compelling.

Many government interventions are aimed at the form and/or content of (aggregates of) market and non-market transactions. Given this aim, it is important to realize that governments themselves do not decide on form and content. Rather, the points of application of government policies are the various aspects of the elements of exchange. From this it follows that there is a gap between the point of impact of most public policy measures, on the one hand, and the objectives, on the other. This gap is bridged, of course, by the reactions of actors, as argued in the exchange-configuration approach. But governments are outsiders to the processes underlying such reactions; they cannot be sure that the results conform to their expectations. Even pertinent prescriptions may be ignored. Decisions about the actual form and content of transactions remain the prerogative of the actors.[10]

Still, this handicap is counteracted by the formidable, exclusive and wide-ranging powers that governments possess to steer present and future transactions. Governments can make laws and other rules specifying the limits of permissible behaviour and they can enforce their observance. They can raise taxes and issue subsidies, prohibit and prescribe the use of certain items and they can fix their price. With these and other measures governments directly impact on the legal environment of transactions. Further, they can use tax revenues for the provision of physical infrastructures and thereby shape the physical environment. The transfers made within the framework of social-security systems must also be mentioned. They directly influence an important attribute of recipients by raising the latter's purchasing power. Another crucial policy instrument affecting actors' attributes consists of the funds spent on education and health that contribute to the stock of human capital.

All the above-mentioned instruments of government intervention impact on aspects of an element of exchange, so they have a strategic nature. Also note that the instruments are concentrated on aspects of only one element, namely the exchange environment. There is one exception. Governments sometimes also pursue their objectives by operating as actors in certain markets, for example in order to stabilize prices. Such action is, at least in the first instance, also a strategic move. In this case the entry of government agencies – with considerable financial means and with objectives that deviate from those of private actors – has a strong impact on the composition of the group of actors. Nevertheless it can safely be stated that the great majority of instruments of public policy apply to aspects of the exchange environment. This observation, together with the fact that public policies can influence the form and content of transactions only indirectly, highlights the limitations of what governments can do despite their exceptionally powerful instruments.

Regarding market transactions, governments owe their remarkable power to the prevalence of major market failures in the form of inefficiency, inequity and instability of market outcomes. The causes, consequences and possible remedies of these failures are the object of study of the public finance literature. Here we confine ourselves to some selected comments.

Among the goods which markets fail to provide efficiently are public goods like national defence systems and street lamps. Such goods are characterized by a rare combination of properties: the provider cannot practically exclude users from using them (and, therefore cannot charge a price) and users do not inhibit the use by others (marginal costs of use are zero). Lacking an adequate supply by the private sector, the public sector provides these goods from tax revenues. Other markets, like those for disablement and unemployment insurance, fail because of the adverse-selection problem as a result of asymmetric information. Governments can make these insurances compulsory such that the insured include not only the 'bad', but also the 'good' risks. Note that in both cases the goods in question are uniform for all. Neither quantity nor quality can be adjusted to individual preferences, unlike goods provided by the private sector. Note further that public goods and social-insurance services are provided to users without individual consent and payment. Therefore, these provisions do not involve transactions.

Another type of failure giving rise to government intervention may be called consumer failure. It derives from a paternalistic value judgement by lawmakers observing that many individual consumers do not compose their consumption baskets in accordance with their best interests. In other words, consumers, if left free, tend to use too little (too much) of so-called merit goods (demerit goods). A whole range of instruments is applied to push consumption in the right direction: prescriptions (safety belts, crash helmets), subsidies (theatres, museums), excise taxes (tobacco, alcohol) and prohibitions (soft and hard drugs).

Markets can also fail collectively resulting in over- or underemployed economies. Governments may attempt to restore equilibrium through countercyclical budgetary and/or monetary policy. In practice, attempts at macroeconomic stabilization have had mixed results; in fact, governments have often been the source of instability. A market failure of an entirely different nature has to do with the fact that there is little reason to expect that an uninhibited operation of markets will generate equitable, just or morally acceptable outcomes. Clearly the motivation for government intervention here has a non-economic character. Social-security schemes – absorbing about 20 per cent of GDP in some developed nations – are the most conspicuous reactions to this failure. The transfers made in the context of these schemes have a direct bearing on the attributes of the recipients and thereby on transactions, but, being one-sided, they are not themselves transactions. For an illustration of a different type of morally unacceptable outcomes of market and non-market transactions, see Box 4.2.

Government intervention in non-market transactions is mostly inspired by non-economic considerations relating to human rights. For example, intra-firm transactions are often explicitly constrained by regulation promoting health and safety at work and protecting against harassment and discrimination. Some countries also provide workers a say in certain management decisions. Similarly, concerning intra-family transactions, family law specifies the rights and duties between husband and wife and between parents and children. In other words, the policy instruments that governments apply to non-market transactions concentrate on formal rules specifying desirable behaviour in lasting interpersonal relations. Several of these formal rules echo the informal rules embodied in conventions and standards of behaviour. Their purpose then is to strengthen informal codes of conduct through the threat of sanctions. But in many cases their purpose is to improve rights and treatment of groups of people suffering from negative discrimination under existing informal institutions.

It lies in the nature of government policies that their efficiency and effectiveness are constantly challenged. First, government provisions simply cannot take account of individual preferences. They typically consist of goods and services to be used by all members of society, and of regulations that apply uniformly. A country has, for example, one national defence system that serves all citizens simultaneously, including the pacifists among them. The magnitude and quality of such provisions are at best a reasonable compromise of the different opinions that voters express during elections. Further, market failures are real and manifest to those affected by them. But the real costs and effects of corrective policy instruments remain largely uncertain until implementation. The disparity of the arguments – one relating to real failure, and the other to expected cure – tends to distort the decision-making process in favour of intervention. The problem is compounded by the fact that politicians cannot always ignore pressure groups demanding action even if it conflicts with the common interest.

## 7.6    UNINTENDED FORCES OF CHANGE

We now turn to the unintended dynamic forces in exchange configurations. The 'Loops in Exchange Systems', which will be discussed first, are endogenous forces. Although they derive from (conscious) decisions by actors in transactions, they are the unintended side effects of these decisions. Shocks are straightforward; they have their origin outside exchange configurations.

### 7.6.1    Loops and Feedbacks in Exchange Systems

The various types of unintended forces of change resulting from especially market transactions show remarkable variety. The first type consists of external effects. In the literature external effects are connected only with market transactions. Positive external effects raise the utility level of parties other than those involved in the market transactions that create the effect. Negative external effects reduce utility to other parties. Examples of the latter are pollution and traffic congestion. In the terminology of the exchange-configuration approach they change aspects of the exchange environment.

Another type of loop covers the continuing streams of information that markets provide to a wide variety of actual and potential actor groups. If markets have virtues, this is one of them. Markets inform about changes in prices, volumes, products, queuing periods, decision processes, and so on, giving rise to reactions by actors in the same and other markets. The fact that the information becomes available in a spontaneous, casual, self-evident way does not diminish its immense value to market configurations. New information changes the perception of individual actors and thereby creates a second type of loop.

The third type derives from the connections among markets mostly as a result of the above-mentioned flows of information. Thus, events that disturb anticipated market patterns in one section of an economic system reverberate elsewhere, affecting not only the volumes of supply and demand but also the general mood (expectations) among actors. When these effects hold and spread and become self-reinforcing the business cycle takes a new turn. Although the actions and reactions of actors are uncoordinated, they have a common direction and thereby create a formidable force of change affecting the economic environment.

Fourthly, markets are instrumental also in furthering structural economic development. They help to improve the allocation of scarce resources, allow a continuously refining division of labour, create opportunities for reaping economies of scale and diffuse the commodities embedding technological innovation. These developments do not come about by themselves. Where they occur, they are the result of a series of successful decisions and actions by individual actors in various exchange configurations intended to improve on the outcomes of existing transactions. But, taken together, they change the economic environment through an economy-wide structural rise in purchasing power. An historical case in which the above-mentioned growth promoting factors combined to form a virtuous spiral of economic growth is described in Section 7.8 on 'The commercial revolution (after AD 1200)'.

The last type of loop we mention here has to do with the fact that the novelties introduced especially by market transactions are not always welcomed. First of all, the process of creative destruction obviously inflicts damage to specific actor groups. Further, the market economy, in general, and international trade and foreign direct investments, in particular, intensify contacts with attitudes, societies and cultures that may be considered alien by sections of the population who feel that existing values and traditions are threatened. The general attitude towards market transactions may take an unfavourable turn and, thereby, change the exchange environment. This effect is strengthened when the aversion of the afflicted groups is translated into effective collective action and governments find it opportune to intervene. For reasons explained in Subsection 6.4.2 such developments tend to be more likely in countries in the middle development phase.

### 7.6.2 Shocks

Shocks include the forces of change that are both exogenous and unintentional. They come in very different forms and have different impacts. Some of them make themselves felt worldwide, while others affect the fortunes of regional and local communities, or of individual families, firms or persons only. They can also differ in speed, arising suddenly like an earthquake, or slowly and gradually like the silting up of a river.

Armed struggles, like wars and invasions, can have profound and lasting consequences as history books amply demonstrate. The inherently destructive nature of armed struggles will dominate at least in the first instance and may, also in the long run, never be compensated. But in other cases armed conflicts also have positive effects, such as when they help to establish a benign rule of law and order, or open up trade opportunities. History abounds with examples of large-scale armed confrontations that can be argued to belong to one or the other group.

Terrorist acts are meant to create fear. They may or may not be committed in the context of a war. In the first case their aim is often to smother resistance. In the second case they are designed to influence the political and social agenda through violent means targeted at particular individuals, population groups, commodities or infrastructural projects. All these targets are dimensions of elements of exchange, so terrorism is likely to also affect exchange configurations. Even just a terrorist threat can have strong consequences for transaction costs.

Religious, social and cultural revolutions can coincide with armed struggles. But here we refer to those revolutions that lead to power shifts between population groups and to cultural change. They give rise to an overhaul of the body of law and governmental priorities, and to changes in people's attitudes and preferences. Revolutions alter the formal and informal institutions.

Massive demographic developments form a different type of shock. The impact that population explosions and migration flows have on transactions has been, and still is, amply demonstrated in different parts of the world. Epidemics have made havoc of cultures and populations and, thus, have changed conditions of exchange in wide areas especially in the past. The diseases that the Europeans brought to the indigenous peoples of the American continent are one illustration. The plague in Medieval Europe is another example. In the latter case, the need to repopulate devastated regions induced feudal rulers to grant rights to groups of people who used to live in a state of practical serfdom. The present-day HIV/AIDS epidemic belongs to this type of catastrophe.

The shocks described above typically have large-scale, wide-reaching effects on exchange configurations. Other types of shocks have a more limited range of effects. Such shocks as death or illness in a family affect existing relations and transactions among family members and give rise to new ones. The higher the rank of the deceased in the family hierarchy, the more profound the changes tend to be. Other shocks, like a birth and a coming of age, change intra-family relations in an entirely different way. Actor-related shocks as death, illness, retirement and injury on the work floor make their impact felt also inside organizations. Shocks of a different nature are fires and burglaries. They affect the asset position of families and organizations concerned (even if insurance policies cover all damages) and change internal behaviour patterns.

## 7.7   A GRAPHICAL REPRESENTATION

In the foregoing sections we have introduced and discussed seven main types of forces of change in exchange configurations. They are summarized graphically in Figure 7.4, which is an adapted, dynamic version of Figures 2.1 and 2.2. Block arrows indicate the basic train of argument of the exchange-configuration approach and single arrows represent the seven types of dynamic forces discussed above. Arrows and text boxes relating to exogenous forces of change are printed in bold type.

In earlier chapters it has been emphasized that exchange configurations change with the exchange elements. However it should be noted that, for simplicity of presentation, all shifts in exchange elements in Figure 7.4 connect with one, seemingly unmoving configuration. Another major simplification derives from the fact that only the main types of dynamic forces have been pictured. In reality the multitude of individual dynamic forces form a much more complex system. Further, many individual forces of change evoke a reaction, and so on, such that various interrelated loops may be active at any point of time even in narrowly defined configurations. Still, by bringing together the various categories of interacting, often unpredictable forces, Figure 7.4 helps to see why decision makers in a dynamic world collect information selectively, analyze imperfectly and decide by rules of thumb. The next section presents six historical cases of profoundly changing configurations. The cases illustrate empirically the diversity of individual dynamic forces within the seven main types distinguished in this chapter.

'Exchange configuration A' in Figure 7.4 represents the configuration that is being analyzed. Other configurations affecting configuration A, individually or as a group, are also included. Their role here is to illustrate the dynamics of interaction among exchange configurations. The impact of configuration A on the other configurations has not been indicated in order to keep the figure as simple as possible. Note that the figure applies to market as well as non-market transactions. Note further that actors, who are included among the exchange elements at the lower end of the figure, also appear in a separate box in their role of decision makers. In fact, as we have seen, the special position that actors assume among the exchange elements appears to be particularly prominent in the context of endogenous dynamics of exchange configurations. The forces of change in Figure 7.4 are numbered in the same order as they have been introduced in this chapter.

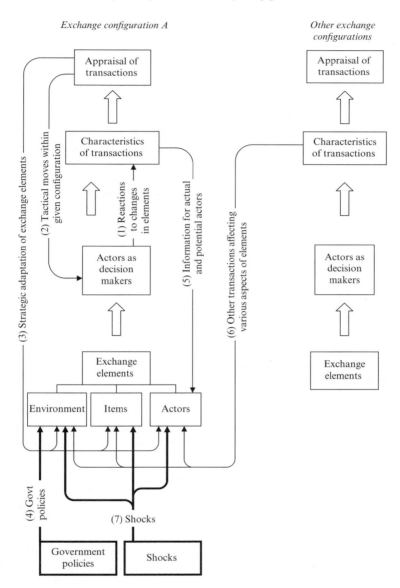

*Figure 7.4   Dynamic forces in exchange configurations*

We start with the forces of change discussed in Section 7.4. The first subgroup to be mentioned consists of the reactions by actors/decision makers to changes in exchange elements; it is part of the central argument of the exchange-configuration approach. These reactions are indicated by (1) in Figure 7.4. In earlier discussions, where endogenous change had not yet been introduced, they were considered as responses to exogenous changes in elements only. Note, however, that endogenous as well as exogenous forces altering exchange elements can trigger these reactions. Arrow (1) directly connects actors with characteristics of transactions. Obviously, reactions of type (1) are often based on evaluations of the outcomes of transactions after the change in elements took place. But this part of the process is ignored in the figure in the interest of simplicity.

The second type of dynamic force, also of a tactical nature, consists of a variety of moves. Prominent among them are experiments by actors adapting the form and/or content of transactions even though the exchange elements remained unchanged. Another large group consists of reactions to these experiments and of reactions to changes of type (1). This type of dynamic force is represented by arrow (2). The arrow's starting point indicates that these moves are based on at least some form of appraisal. The arrow connects with the box representing actors/decision makers who take the actual decisions affecting the characteristics of the transactions (not indicated).

Like the two dynamic forces mentioned above, the third type of force of change is both endogenous and intentional. But it differs fundamentally from the other two: as it modifies aspects of elements of exchange it has a strategic nature. Also, this force of change requires a lasting commitment by the decision makers activating it, so in most cases its effects are much more profound. The three-pronged arrow (3) illustrates the versatility of this force which can affect aspects of all three elements of exchange. In Section 7.4, we mentioned that this force can be seen as the true indicator of a configuration's internal dynamics. It follows that the totality of these forces, at work in the configurations that together form an economic system, are the true movers of that system.

Government interventions, discussed in Section 7.5, are an intentional force of change. They are expressly undertaken by governments after an evaluation of the outcomes of exchange configurations with the intent to influence these outcomes. The difference lies in the fact that the interventions are typically exogenous to the extent that governments, when implementing the interventions, are not at the same time actors/decision makers. So arrow (4) and the text box representing 'Government policies' are printed in bold type. Note that the arrow connects only with aspects of the exchange environment. Governments can influence the form and content of transactions in this way only indirectly. Even then public intervention is of the utmost importance where it can redress structural failures in the operation of exchange configurations. Governments can also choose to implement policy by participating in a configuration, for example by buying, storing and selling products in order to stabilize prices. When they do so they first cause an exogenous change in the composition of the actor group in that configuration as government institutions have different objectives and financial resources. This type of strategic move has not been indicated in Figure 7.4. As actors government institutions can activate also endogenous forces of change.

The remaining subgroups of dynamic forces are all unintentional, at least from the viewpoint of the actors in the exchange configuration(s) considered. First we mention the endogenous forces, that is the forces emanating from decisions by actors in exchange configurations as discussed in Subsection 7.6.1. The flow of information about transactions to actual and potential actors in the same configuration (arrow (5)) is particularly important in market configurations. When the data change, the flow will alert actors and may cause them to act. For example, when it becomes known that a firm needs additional personnel, workers from elsewhere may decide to apply. Or the volume of transactions may reach the critical mass that warrants specialization.

The subgroup indicated by arrow (6) that emanates from characteristics of transactions in other configurations consists of a great variety of forces of change impacting on various aspects of elements of exchange. Among those connecting with 'Actors' are the information flows between exchange configurations as well as the incomes and assets gained and lost in transactions that change the attributes of individual actors. Then there are the new products and services developed in other configurations that change the nature of the 'Items' traded elsewhere. Finally, there are the various forces in this subgroup that change the overall 'Environment'. Many of these are of a macroeconomic nature, such as the movements of business cycles and the socio-economic development which whole systems of exchange configurations bring about. Other examples are pollution and congestion.

The last type of change listed here (indicated by (7) in Figure 7.4) consists of external changes in elements of exchange, other than through government interventions. For brevity's sake we referred to them as 'Shocks' (see Subsection 7.6.2). Some have a limited impact (like illness or death may affect only one intra-family exchange configuration), while others (like wars) have a massive impact on the 'Environment' of a great number of exchange configurations. Such shocks disrupt without purpose. They are interesting from an analytical point of view only because of their impact.

## 7.8   SIX HISTORICAL CASES ILLUSTRATING THE DYNAMICS OF EXCHANGE

This section introduces six historical cases of dynamic exchange conditions referring to different, sometimes overlapping periods. Because descriptions of broad historical developments rarely allow unshakeable delineation, the periods have been indicated only approximately. Each case represents a move away from earlier patterns of exchange. Together they illustrate the conditions and processes by which exchange configurations emerge, change and expire.

The cases to be discussed demonstrate, first of all, the impact of exchange elements and exogenous changes therein on patterns of exchange, the connection to which we limited ourselves in earlier chapters. But they are especially meant to provide empirical support for the full-scale dynamic arguments put forward in this chapter. They illustrate the great variety of strategic moves that actors have used to create fundamentally different exchange configurations over time. The cases also show how transactions and exchange elements can be connected to each other in dynamic loops: changes in transactions resulting from changes in certain aspects of exchange elements can in their turn alter other aspects of exchange elements, and so on. Finally, the discussion serves as a reminder of the fact that, whatever the nature of an initial change in exchange elements, the effect on exchange configurations depends on the reaction of the pertinent actor groups. Thus, the course exchange configurations take is driven to a large extent by the attitude of actors, their capabilities and other attributes and, we should add, by their good or bad luck.

The cases are presented in two stages. In the first stage we briefly describe in general terms the characteristics of the case considered. Thereafter, we indicate in more detail what triggered the change, which exchange elements were affected mostly, and how exchange configurations were affected. The types of dynamic forces (indicated as 'df' below) at work in each case are indicated by the numbers given to them in Section 7.7.

### 7.8.1   Early Market Places (From Around 500 BC)

In the early Greek societies, during the classical period, individual property rights were strictly limited. The right to dispose of items like land, cattle and slaves was restricted to citizens with the appropriate status. Work in the service of others – on the farms, in the mines and workshops, or as domestic servants and scribes – was mostly left to slaves and serfs. But where they applied, property rights were protected. The resulting decline in transaction costs contributed to the rise of markets. On the whole, however, self-sufficient landholdings producing a variety of goods for own consumption formed the foundation of the economy.

In the towns – centres of public administration, worship and industrial activities – land-owning families would be supported by the produce of their land. Further, those who were considered as proper citizens could call on some support at public expense. Other town dwellers, however, profiting from the urban concentration of purchasing power and making a living by selling the products of their labour, depended on a regular marketed supply of surplus agricultural production. In fact, towns could not exist without it. At the same time, their geographically concentrated demand turned the chain of market transactions that sustained the inflow of goods into a profitable business. Market places emerged in Phoenician and Greek towns for trade in products for daily use. Such trade was considered natural and therefore socially accepted, unlike for-profit trade in other products. While this development allowed towns to rise, communities were still overwhelmingly self-sufficient due to the very modest yield-to-seed ratios that were obtainable under the prevailing agricultural technologies.

One of the initial forces of change in this case derives from the growing numbers of individuals possessing no land while individually responsible for their own survival (a demographic shock, df 7). These actors had to make a living by selling whatever they produced in exchange for basic goods. An urban environment offered the best opportunities for the sale of their products and services (df 3). Simultaneously, their demand for foodstuffs and other basic items created a profitable trading opportunity for individual suppliers. Information about transactions was readily available, so the latter could truly be called market transactions (df 1). These developments were supported by the establishment of property rights and citizenship (df 4) and by the earlier invention of money coins, a major change in the exchange environment (another type of shock, df 7).

Markets not only thrive on specialization, they also promote it. So, with the emergence of markets new actor groups, engaged in trading and manufacturing activities, entered the stage (df 3) and their additional economic activity altered the environment. This development shows how new forms of transactions, resulting from changes in exchange elements, can be the source of further changes in elements.

### 7.8.2   Manors (After AD 500)

After the fall of Rome, as the road system fell into disrepair and cities lost much of their vitality, economic activity in Europe during the Merovingian/Carolingian period reverted to redistributive agricultural communities (manors) where peasants worked the fields, mostly bound to the land as serfs. Manors were relatively small-scale organizations that combined economic, administrative and military functions and provided some protection against invaders and marauding bands. They were part of a hierarchical tenure system in which the central ruler granted a privileged elite rights to land areas in return for payment mostly in commodities and military services. Over time these rights would obtain a hereditary character.

At the manor, the peasants spent part of their working time on the local landlord's fields and the rest on the land conceded to them. They were not free to leave the land or even to marry without the landlord's consent. Hence, the notion of free employment did not apply. Transactions were cleared nearly exclusively in kind.

Here we see the effects of a regress in the exchange environment (df 1 as a result of df 7). With the disappearance of a strong central government the quality of the physical infrastructure and the security of traders and their wares dropped dramatically. Transaction costs became prohibitive, so towns lost their economic foundations. People moved to the countryside and the money economy evaporated.

The new organization of society (df 4) was characterized by a rigid system of rights and duties between strictly separated social classes. In this environment most transactions, involving rights granted for payments in kind, were an inseparable part of the system. They expressed the far-reaching power relations between the actors and covered nearly all aspects of life, especially the specific use of land and labour. As a result they tended to have an obligatory, non-negotiable character which distinguished them from market transactions (df 1). Commercial exchange outside this system was relatively rare, if only because of the scarcity of tradable manufactured goods. Even towards AD 1000 a linen shirt could be traded for a slave and a coat of mail (armor made of rings for flexibility) would cost the equivalent of the harvest from five acres of land.

### 7.8.3   The Commercial Revolution (After AD 1200)

In thirteenth century Europe the rapidly rising importance of courts, profane and religious, created geographically concentrated areas of very strong demand for services and luxury goods. Courts acted like magnets attracting large numbers of people with widely different backgrounds and skills hoping to profit from the new opportunities as craftsmen producing for the courts.[11] Further, the changing techniques of warfare and the growth of the money economy eroded the function of knights and castles in favour of standing armies answering to a central ruler. Nation states in need of large amounts of fiscal revenues began to arise.[12]

Only part of the commodity demand exerted by the expanding towns could be met from local and regional supply. Other goods had to be imported from far away. High-quality cloth, for example, was produced only in the two industrial centres of the time: the Southern Netherlands and Tuscany. Other luxury commodities like spices were imported from Asia and the Levant and re-exported from Northern Italy. But the towns also needed large quantities of foodstuffs – such as grain, salt, wine and beer – in addition to what was supplied from surrounding regions. And, finally, increasing amounts of raw materials like wool, iron ore, timber and olive oil had to be brought in to satisfy the requirements of the manufacturing activities. Thus, the importance of long-distance trade increased enormously. It reached the critical mass allowing specialization in trade, finance and transportation activities and supporting improvements in infrastructure. It also invited introduction of new technologies facilitating the management of the unprecedented money and commodity flows. Many of these new technologies were first adopted in Northern Italy[13] from where they spread to other parts of Europe following the trade routes.[14]

The commercial revolution of the thirteenth century hinged on a succession of radical changes in exchange elements, causing changes in transactions that caused further changes in elements, and so on. The developments were triggered by a period of rapid population growth (df 7). The resulting population pressure allowed landlords to demand rent payment in money and no longer in goods and services, a clear example of how a change in an exchange element can affect the content of transactions (df 1). Rulers now had an opportunity to settle down and establish a court. This set in motion the train of reactions that led to the urban concentrations of purchasing power as indicated above, an example of how transactions can profoundly affect the environment (dfs 5 and 6).

The increased long-distance flows of luxury goods, foodstuffs and raw materials achieved a degree of regularity that had consequences also for the organization of trade. Where each long-distance commercial trip had been arranged as a separate venture in earlier days, trading families in Italy now set up business units with continuity under one name in which financiers could participate with transferable shares (dfs 3 and 5). Further specialization involved transportation, storage and money exchange (dfs 3 and 5). Italian trading firms introduced agents as their representatives in other commercial centres (df 3). Thus, new actor groups, new services and therefore also new types of transactions came into existence (df 1). The increased complexity of commercial enterprises necessitated the introduction of sophisticated accounting techniques.

The interdependent combination of increased trade, growing specialization and international division of labour and improving technologies and infrastructures generated a remarkable rise in value added. For the first time in history traders and bankers surpassed landowners in income and wealth (df 6). Clearly, this upward leap in the level of economic activity required an equally large increase in money supply. Indeed, mining areas produced more silver. But the rising supply of bullion alone could not have sustained the economic expansion. The introduction of bills of exchange created an essential addition to the money supply (df 3). Note that the use of bills of exchange, by changing the way payment is arranged, alters the content of transactions (df 1). Note further that this change became possible only after the development of actors as business units with continuity, frequently engaging in market transactions and thus establishing a reputation of creditworthiness.

### 7.8.4   Town Guilds (From AD 1300)

Guilds would cover services as well as artisanal activities. In the latter case, guild regulations prescribed the ingredients to be used in production,[15] working methods, the just product price, labour relations and the maximum number of workers per shop, among other things. Vocational training was provided exclusively by the guilds through apprenticeships and only those who had obtained such training could become a member of a guild. Thus, the content of commodity transactions under this regime was strongly affected by the guild regulations. Opportunities for competition were severely reduced – directly because prices, production methods and ingredients were regulated, and indirectly because the system controlled the number of new entrants. Also labour-market transactions had to do with guild instructions.

With so many actors being restricted by guild regulations, shirking and cheating were a constant threat. So sanctions – that could derive from church law, urban common law and merchant law – were introduced to enforce cooperation and compliance. Expulsion not only meant loss of income, position and privileges, but also loss of church and priest and support at times of illness and death.[16] Eventually, merchants in Western

Europe engaging in international trade would set up separate production units for large-scale industrial production outside towns and thus began to erode the power of the guilds.

All aspects of life in the Middle Ages were imbued with religion. Under the influence of the prevailing religious philosophy of Scholasticism, nature, man and morals were all considered to be part of a harmonious and static world plan (df 7). In the new, crowded, walled-in towns that arose at cross-ings of main roads,[17] social conflicts, health hazards and fires were major issues. In agreement with Scholastic thought, local administrators address-ing these issues introduced guilds that were meant to strike a balance between the interests of producers, consumers and workers (df 4).

This case illustrates the profound effect that exogenous environmental change can exert. The guild system not only dictated directly major parts of the content of commodity and labour transactions (df 1). Guild regula-tions also bore on actors (for example, their training and freedom to act) and the nature of products (their ingredients and the way they were pro-duced) and thereby even intensified their impact on transactions (df 1). Clearly, the system also stifled internal competition and initiatives.

### 7.8.5   Commercial Capitalism (After AD 1500)

For post-Copernican Europe – confronted with the fall of Constantinople, the discovery of the Americas and the sea-route to Asia – the pattern of long-distance trade routes underwent revolutionary change. New European nation states that had emerged from protracted armed struggles and religious revolts realized that trade followed the flag and exported their confrontations to other continents and the open seas. Further, depending on the outcome of internal power struggles, European states developed different incentive systems, more by accident than by design.[18] In countries like France and Spain where rulers held absolute power, fiscal revenue could be conveniently collected from established monopolies, the sale of privileges and confiscation of private property. In other countries, like the Dutch Republic and England, where fiscal power was more decen-tralized, tariff concessions were exchanged for rules establishing individual property rights, thus creating structural incentives for economic growth.[19]

The new, truly worldwide international trade that arose carried in its wake a few more important changes. The practice of concluding contracts on inspection of samples sprang out of necessity, batches began to be traded before delivery and a genuine trade in futures developed with con-comitant heavy speculation. The functions of financier and entrepreneur were gradually assumed by different persons. Next to traditional family firms and maritime firms (with one travelling and one sedentary partner) other, more refined organizations emerged such as joint-stock companies and the monopoly-based merchant companies which offered their share-holders a liquidity as well as a risk premium. From the professional money trade emerged a well-functioning short-term credit market and even a long-term capital market. More than before, time obtained an economic value and credit operations expanded despite continual disapproval and censure.[20]

Unprecedented opportunities for worldwide trade arose in the sixteenth century from some remarkable changes in the exchange environment (df 7). But in order to make the most of the opportunities still other aspects of exchange elements had to be adapted.

The requirements derived directly from the characteristics of the long-distance trade expeditions, such as the many dangers that had to be coped with and the massive long-term investments that were required. For example, merchants needed strongholds in the lands of destination and on the coasts en route. Bullion brought in to pay for purchases made, and storage rooms for goods to be shipped and for materials, equipment and provisions needed military protection. Also, on the high seas, mer-chant vessels could not do without such protection most of the time. Thus, the active involvement of some form of public authority was necessary to help protect the common interest by force (df 4). But still other factors – such as storms, diseases and navigation errors – seriously endangered mer-chant vessels on their trips. Expeditions were very risky enterprises. They also demanded huge investments in ships, provisions and bullion, for long periods of time. No individual financier could be expected to invest these large sums at the real risk of losing everything. So new types of actors were created by refining existing forms of enterprise (df 3). Multiple expeditions organized by these enterprises evened out the risk for investors.

Where these conditions were met, the new configurations of exchange elements brought about new types of transactions (df 1). Salable shares gave rise to the first stock exchanges and enhanced the attractiveness of participation in the enterprises concerned. Bourses were established, extended and refined to reduce transaction costs.

### 7.8.6    The Rise of Industrial Capitalism (After AD 1750)

The cost advantages that the industrial revolution offered could only be fully reaped if complementary developments occurred, such as the build-ing of an infrastructure facilitating the movement of raw materials and finished goods and reducing their transportation costs; introducing or strengthening patent law, contract law and bankruptcy law; introducing standardized units of measurement; and so on. Many of these novelties had a public-good character and required government action.

Specialization and the increased scale of production resulted in interconnecting commodity, labour and credit and capital markets. The industrial production system gave rise to a targeted search for technological innovations on the basis of scientific knowledge, thus breaking away from the artisanal approach to technological improvement that had dominated until then. While the specific outcomes of the drive for innovation remained mostly unpredictable, as a stream they allowed production to outpace population growth. The Malthusian trap could be dismantled. Still, the large-scale introduction of machines directly threatened existing employment opportunities and labour income of many workers in traditional occupations. The clash of interests of owners and workers, the inhumane labour conditions in factories and mines and the ensuing social struggles together with new ideas about human rights eventually had political consequences on local, national and world scales.

The gigantic upward leap of the efficient scale of production caused by the introduction of mechanization reduced the number of production units proportionately (dfs 3 and 7). Consequently market structures and transactions also changed (df 1). Exchange relations between actors could take a monopolistic or monopsonistic turn. The much increased batch sizes gave rise to more formal transactional forms and to the addition of layers of intermediate traders, up- or downscaling batch sizes within production columns (df 5). Further, industrial production techniques produced standardized commodities of fairly constant quality. This would lead to new phenomena like the creation of brand names and advertisement campaigns (df 3).

Also the intra-firm labour relations underwent drastic change and, with them, labour transactions (df 1). From here on people lived by the clock. In the mechanized production units anonymous workers produced impersonal goods in which the hand of the maker could not be discerned. Workers were seen as instruments and treated as such. In reaction to a multitude of abuses governments gradually introduced corrective regulations. But governments also adopted a pro-active stance where they participated in the build-up of infrastructure and in the drafting of legislation that facilitated transactions and reduced transaction costs (df 4).

In this period we see the beginnings of the complex, intricately interwoven economies of today in which practically all aspects of exchange elements are in a state of flux.

## NOTES

1. For example, Jones, 2000, p xxxiv, writes: 'Evolution is to the social sciences as statues are to birds: a convenient platform upon which to deposit badly digested ideas.'
2. For the first systematic descriptions of the relation between positive and policy analysis in (macro-)economics, see Tinbergen, 1952, Chapter 4 and Tinbergen, 1956, Chapter 1.
3. See Section 3.5.
4. Fusari, 2005, presents an exercise merging adaptive and innovative activities.
5. Innovations presented in scientific publications have a different nature. They are typically public goods, so the new insights they propound contain freely accessible, 'disembedded' knowledge. These innovations do not generate private returns. As a result also their motivation and funding differ from the innovations referred to above. See Romer, 2006, Section 3.4, for a more detailed discussion.
6. North, 1994, p. 362, labels these processes 'the most fundamental long-run source of change'.
7. The relatively new field of social economics emphasizes the link between individual behaviour and group outcomes through the direct influence that other people's choices have on individuals' decisions. See, for example, Schelling, 1978.
8. Nooteboom, 2003.
9. See Den Hartigh, 2005, p. 52 ff. for an overview.
10. This is in essence also what the Lucas critique is about: actors take into account the changed conditions created by new government interventions, adapt their decisions and so undo the intended effects; Lucas, 1976.
11. For a detailed treatment of the events described here, see Spufford, 2002.
12. See, for example, Chapter 6 in North and Thomas, 1973.
13. Several originated in Islamic countries.
14. For example, Pacioli's description in 1494 of the existing Venetian practice of double-entry bookkeeping was soon translated and adopted in commercial centres outside Italy.
15. Even today many modern German brewers voluntarily adhere to the old Purity Law (the *Reinheitsgebot* of 1516) prescribing the three exclusive ingredients for beer: barley, hops and water. History matters!
16. See Richardson, 2005.
17. Despite the rising flow of trade, rural and even urban communities still had a strong inward orientation. Prices of bread could differ considerably between one town and the next.
18. North even argues that rulers typically produce inefficient property rights, North, 1981.
19. For illustrations, see Chapters 10, 11 and 12 in North and Thomas, 1973.
20. A succession of popes reaffirmed restrictions on lending at interest up until the eighteenth century.

## REFERENCES

Den Hartigh, E. (2005), *Increasing Returns and Firm Performance: An Empirical Study*, Rotterdam: ERIM.

Fusari, A. (2005), 'A model of innovation-adaptation mechanism driving economic dynamics: a micro representation', *Journal of Evolutionary Economics*, **15** (3), 297–333.

Jones, S. (2000), *Almost Like a Whale: The Origin of Species Updated*, London: Transworld Publishers.

Lucas, R. (1976), 'Econometric Policy Evaluation: A Critique', in K. Brunner and A. Meltzer (eds.), *The Phillips Curve and Labor Markets*, Amsterdam: North-Holland and New York: American Elsevier, pp. 19–46.

Meyer, M.W. (1994), 'Measuring performance in economic organizations', Chapter 22 in N.J. Smelser and R. Swedberg (eds.), *The Handbook of Economic Sociology*, Princeton, NJ: Princeton University Press and New York: Russell Sage Foundation.

Nooteboom, B. (2003), 'Managing exploitation and exploration', Chapter 9, in S. Rizzello (ed.), *Cognitive Developments in Economics*, London: Routledge, pp. 218–242.

North, D.C. (1981), *Structure and Change in Economic History*, New York: W.W. Norton.

North, D.C. (1994), 'Economic performance through time', *The American Economic Review*, **84** (3), 359–368.

North, D.C. and R.P. Thomas, (1973), *The Rise of the Western World: A New Economic History*, London: Cambridge University Press.

Richardson, G. (2005), 'Crafts, guilds and Christianity in Late-Medieval England: a rational choice analysis', *Rationality and Society*, **17** (2), 139–189.

Romer, D. (2006), *Advanced Macroeconomics* (3rd edition), Boston: McGraw-Hill Irwin.

Schelling, T.C. (1978), *Micromotives and Macrobehavior*, New York: W.W. Norton.

Schumpeter, J.A. (1950), *Capitalism, Socialism and Democracy* (3rd edition), London: George Allen & Unwin.

Shapiro, C. (1989), 'The theory of business strategy', *The Rand Journal of Economics*, **20** (1), 125–137.

Solow, R. (1994), 'Perspectives on growth theory', *Journal of Economic Perspectives*, **8** (Winter), 45–54.

Spufford, P. (2002), *Power and Profit. The Merchant in Medieval Europe*, New York: Thames and Hudson.

Tinbergen, J. (1952), *On the Theory of Economic Policy*, Amsterdam: North-Holland.

Tinbergen, J. (1956), *Economic Policy: principles and design*, Amsterdam: North-Holland.

# 8.    Some concluding messages

## 8.1    OVERVIEW

A summary of the content of this volume has already been presented in Chapter 1, to which the reader is referred. Instead, the present chapter contains a series of selective 'messages' (that is lessons derived in the previous chapters) to illustrate and highlight the relevance of the exchange-configuration approach to the investigation of a number of issues related to the interdependence between exchange and development. The messages are discussed in the context of the following six issues: (1) The interrelationship between the process of exchange and economic development; (2) Why is the exchange process so different in poor countries to that in rich countries? Some characteristics of the exchange process in countries at an early stage of development; (3) Development and the roles of actors and governments; (4) The vital role of learning in the dynamics of exchange; (5) The contemporary global financial crisis explored within the exchange-configuration approach; and (6) How does the exchange-configuration approach differ from and contribute to the neo-classical framework?

## 8.2    A SELECTION OF MESSAGES

### 8.2.1    Interrelationship Between the Process of Exchange and Economic Development

In present-day economies at an early stage of development, characterized by an essentially agrarian economy dominated by subsistence farmers, many transactions occur within the family, community or village. As was described in some detail in Chapter 6 these transactions tend to be implicit within the farm household with different members contributing to producing a meagre food output. The exchange process among family members tends to be virtual, largely based on local customs and norms. Most household members exchange their labour for a share of the food produced on the farm and access to other basic needs such as shelter. Transactions among households (farm and off-farm) are often barter arrangements. A farmer will trade some food with the village artisans for cloth or simple tools. The use of money in the exchange process is limited as is the size of the market.

The organization of production on small farms, largely for own consumption, is influenced by missing or failed rental and credit markets. The transaction costs in the few exchange configurations prevailing in this early development setting are very high and result, consequently, in exchange configurations characterized by relatively few and, on average, small transactions. Given those initial conditions both market and non-market configurations are 'thin' and the process of socio-economic development remains stagnant. There is practically no scope for scale economies in either production or exchange.

At some point, some exogenous forces (such as new trading routes, an improved farm technology or physical infrastructure investment in, for example, village roads) will reduce transaction costs and facilitate a move from an early- to a middle-development stage. Small farmers facing lower transaction costs and a more productive technology will be able to produce more than they consume and enjoy a marketable surplus. Consequently they will be able to spend more on consumer goods – benefiting thereby the local village traders – and invest in land improvement raising land and labour productivity and starting a cumulative growth process. The various exchange configurations will expand, contributing to economies of scale, and the relative importance of market configurations will increase. Gradually, a dual–dual structure of production tends to evolve, characterized by four main sectors: small-scale subsistence agriculture producing domestic food crops; commercial agriculture producing cash and export crops; a formal industrial and service sector; and an informal sector.

As agricultural productivity and output grow, workers can start migrating to more urban areas with only a few fortunate enough to find employment in formal activities and the bulk of the migrants ending up in the informal sector. Here again, improvements in the exchange environment – a key concept underlying our exchange-configuration approach – such as an improved road network and improved human capital formation benefiting the rural actors facilitates the migratory flow and raises the likelihood of migrants landing formal employment slots. Successful migrants will be in the position of remitting some of their earnings back to their rural families raising further rural incomes. Under the impetus of economic development, markets and later, intra-firm configurations grow almost exponentially and spread inter-regionally and internationally. As this development process continues, an economy reaches the stage of maturity as discussed in Chapter 6, characterized by a preponderance of market and intra-firm exchange configurations and the gradual decline, if not disappearance, of intra-family transactions.

The interrelationship between the evolution of the exchange process and that of socio-economic development is striking. In the pre-take-off stage, stagnation reigns and whatever exchange takes place is based largely on traditional, normative and often ritualized transactions. There are no endogenous forces within that setting to start the cumulative growth path. Once the impetus for change is triggered through some of the mechanisms mentioned earlier, the cumulative development process can start. As incomes slowly rise, the division of labour and more specialization are encouraged. Existing exchange configurations expand in size and adapt to the new circumstances. The increasing scale (mass) of potential exchange leads to new configurations as well as changes in existing configurations. Actors see new opportunities and apply or help devise new trading instruments such as limited liability, share-cropping and interlocking factor transactions (for example, the linking of wage and credit contracts between landlords and wage labourers). Denser, more efficient and new configurations facilitate trade and economic growth by acting as its life-blood and the resulting growth further improves the operation of configurations. The bi-directional link between exchange and development is mutually reinforcing.

Of course, the mutual progression is not always positive. History is replete with examples of exchange configurations that failed and slowed down the pace of development. The failure of the global financial configuration for credit default swaps discussed in this chapter is a case in point. The good news is that the net effect of the positive reinforcement between exchange and development throughout history has much more than compensated for the negative episodes that have sometime led to temporary recessions and even depressions. Chapter 7, painting with a broad brush over an extended historical period, reveals clearly how the interdependence between these two forces was crucial in the undergirding economic growth.

### 8.2.2   Why is the Exchange Process so Different in Poor Countries to That in Rich Countries?

There are fundamental differences in the exchange process in poor developing countries compared to rich developed countries. At the most general level this can be explained by the differences in the characteristics of the exchange elements which are the pillars of our framework: (1) the item exchanged; (2) the actors involved; and (3) the environment in its multiple dimensions. At an early stage of development average income is low, there is a high incidence of poverty, the physical infrastructure and, in particular, the road network is rudimentary. The structure of production in those countries is typically characterized by two types of dualism (regional: urban/rural; and technological: modern/traditional). Transportation and other transaction costs are very high and the obstacles to trade are much greater than in the industrialized world.

The economies of poor countries are hardly diversified. Only a few *items*, such as staple food, some agricultural export crops, some mining products, simple consumer goods and largely informal services dominate the economic landscape. Limited diversity in production and consumption, relatively few high value-added commodities, low average and unequally distributed incomes, dualism, and major impediments to trade translate into conditions of inadequate 'marketing mass' and overall purchasing power. The consequence is great fragmentation in terms of the items traded (essentially similar items are exchanged in different configurations) and regional coverage, with large numbers of distinct exchange configurations operating side by side. In contrast with more industrialized societies, markets are only imperfectly integrated and many markets, as those for credit and insurance, are missing for the poor households. Alternative, non-market exchange configurations have sprung up to substitute for the missing markets.

Also *actors* possess different sets of attributes. The set of attributes (in terms of income, education, health, assets and access to social security) of representative actors in poor countries contrasts significantly with that of rich countries. In the cities of developing countries actors with low incomes, little education and few assets are essentially sealed off from employment in the formal sector. Many of those unable to find employment in the formal sector must turn to the informal sector. The production units in this sector form a very special actor group – often centered around the family – engaging in transactions that deviate from those of their better educated and more skilled counterparts in the formal sector. Also the intra-organizational transactions in both groups differ sharply. In agricultural areas low-income and asset-poor actors lack access to formal credit. In addition, they have to cope with failures in rental markets and with high transaction costs in labour and agricultural-product markets. In reaction to these problems they often organize their economic activities within families largely producing for own consumption. Such families form another actor group with characteristic intra-family transactions. These diverse actor groups, common in developing countries, give rise to a differentiation between types of transactions that hardly applies in developed countries. The prevalence of a series of regional exchange configurations contributes to the fragmentation of transactions in developing countries causing pronounced differences in prices for the same product in different regions. In contrast in mature economies, national – if not global – markets dominate the scene and lead to a process of integration around standard and brand name items with relatively low price spreads.

In addition to the major differences in actors' attributes and the physical *environment*, another key distinction between the developing and the developed world relates to the role of the public sector. In many dimensions, the public sector in developing countries tends to display some characteristic properties that contrast greatly with how it functions in more developed societies. Here we limit ourselves to mention only two such properties. Firstly, the administration and protection of property rights often leaves much to be desired to the detriment of trust and the rule of law, which are the lubricants of exchange activity and the generation of income. Secondly, public sectors in developing countries rarely possess the tax and administrative capacity needed to implement a social-security system. So actors engage in self-help schemes providing support to needy members within social groups as families and neighbours based on a mix of voluntary and compulsory participation. Such schemes reinforce the significance of cultural considerations as important determinants of the form of exchange in developing countries.

### 8.2.3   Development and the Roles of Actors and Governments

Economic development is a highly multi-dimensional concept. It occurs when the welfare of a society improves. The set of relevant attributes in the welfare function yielding the state of development includes income, level of education, state of health, access to information, security, and even such intangibles as justice and freedom of thought enjoyed by all members. A key issue relates to the relative importance of efficiency versus equality. Would the majority of the population prefer a slightly lower average per capita GDP combined with a relatively more equal income distribution (and similarly for the other attributes) in case a trade-off actually exists between those two objectives? Whereas the neoclassical theory argued that an uneven income distribution was a pre-condition to growth, because the rich save a higher proportion of their incomes than the poor and a larger flow of savings-cum-investment translates into a higher GDP growth rate, the new political economy of development maintains that greater inequality can be an obstacle to future growth for a number of reasons and, particularly, because of the political and social instability that it may engender.

If this new doctrine is correct a relatively more equal income distribution over some range (say a fall in the Gini coefficient from 0.4 to 0.3) may actually be consistent with higher growth and the trade-off vanishes.

What is often overlooked is that both total GDP and its distribution among households and other claimants are determined by how transactions are shaped. Not only is the value of GDP defined as the sum of value added created in transactions, but its distribution (who gets what?) depends on how the exchange process functions. A better understanding of how the various exchange configurations operate allows one to recommend policies and institutions to improve their efficiency and equity. There is a direct link between improving the exchange process and furthering broad-based socio-economic development.

In the foregoing chapters we argued that the form and content of transactions are shaped by relevant aspects of the three exchange elements, items, environment and actors. But actors stand out among the exchange elements because of their exclusive capacity to activate transactions. The decisions they take – whether or not to engage in transactions and under which conditions, and the nature of transactions they select – determine the value added created. The overall result depends on their abilities, assets and motivation. The characteristics of these actors vary strongly among individuals within any country as well as among countries.

A similar argument applies to the pace of economic development. As Chapter 7 emphasized, actors play a vital role also in the dynamics of exchange. Their response to moves by other actors, to new opportunities (that may or may not be due to government policies) and to external events shape the course of development and this applies with particular force to strategic moves that actors devise.

In other words, economic development depends, first and probably foremost, on people, that is on individual actors, workers and members of families. Actors plan, initiate, activate and enter into transactions or fail to do so. The intensity and success of their activities drive economic progress. Governments and other public institutions can facilitate, stimulate and provide the right set of incentives, but the actions of private actors are decisive. This message has not received enough attention in the development economics literature with its emphasis on public policy and international aid.

It has been stated above that the decisions and actions taken by actors determine in the last instance the outcome and dynamics of exchange configurations. Public actors (governments) cannot guarantee economic growth. But these assertions do not diminish in any way the immense importance of government policies for economic exchange: where governments are lacking in performance, actors cannot exploit their potential. In this context it is useful to keep in mind the asymmetry of the impact of governments: while they cannot enforce growth, they are perfectly capable of destroying it. Too many failed states with absent, ineffective, or malfunctioning governments due to civil war, plunder, looting, corruption or stifling bureaucracy provide an illustration of the economic disasters that result. In such cases the primary task of new governments clearly is to drastically improve their public sectors' functioning and reduce their baleful influence.[1]

In other cases governments do perform their well-known, traditional functions. Pure and impure public goods – such as defence, police and road systems – possess characteristics that prevent supply by private parties. By providing such goods the public sector not only contributes to the satisfaction of consumers' wants and to producers' potential, but also to exchange opportunities. Other public goods, having an institutional character, are even primarily concerned with exchange conditions. Examples are the formulation of rules regulating exchange, land registration and parts of judicial systems. Institutions are of particular importance in a dynamic setting as they strongly affect the intensity and direction of economic incentives. These and other public goods are all aspects of the exchange environment and have been discussed in some detail in earlier chapters. Especially in developing countries, many of them need to be strongly improved or even to be introduced. Another pressing matter in many developing countries relates to highly unequal distributions of income, assets, education, culturally defined rights and, as a result of all these, of negotiating power. As a result, many market, intra-firm and intra-family transactions in developing countries not only generate and perpetuate unjust outcomes; unequal distributions also fail to realize the full growth potential as discussed above.

Analyses of exchange patterns in developing countries can reveal desirable policy areas motivating and enabling private actors in addition to the traditional ones listed here. Some of these policy areas are highlighted in Subsection 8.2.6 as an outcome of a comparison of neoclassical growth theory with an exchange-oriented approach.

### 8.2.4    The Vital Role of Learning in the Dynamics of Exchange

In the neoclassical literature learning is introduced only in connection with technological innovation and human-capital formation (see Subsection 8.2.6 below). These types of learning are obviously of great significance, but other types, at least as important for economic activities, are overlooked in the neoclassical approach, where economic actors are assumed to be always fully informed. Here follow examples of learning processes with a direct bearing on the dynamics of economic exchange. The message they are meant to convey is that exchange dynamics derives from decisions by actors which are all preceded by one or another type of learning.

Many learning processes merely consist of checking whether earlier acquired information still obtains and continues to be valid. The significance of this kind of learning derives from the possible need to change one's exchange patterns in the face of new developments or new insights. Examples are the collecting of information by private actors about the economic climate, about moves by competitors and colleagues, about the reliability of clients and suppliers and about the performance of employees. All these learning processes are characterized by a relatively low level of ambition. If they lead to a reaction, it is mostly of a tactical or adaptive nature. Still, due to the sheer magnitude of their numbers, their impact on the dynamics of exchange is enormous.

Strategic moves, taken individually, tend to have a more profound effect than tactical moves because they are meant to change certain aspects of exchange elements. Therefore also they tend to be preceded by more demanding, creative learning processes. Economic actors know that there are always unused gainful opportunities. Static efficiency is a purely theoretical concept that never obtains in reality. Hence the continuous search for sales opportunities among new consumer groups, new adaptations or new combinations of existing products, new uses for existing materials, and so on. All such moves alter particular aspects of exchange elements and, therefore, may well provoke reactions by other actors. As they entail uncertainty and significant costs they deserve careful preparation, among others by collecting and analyzing relevant information.

The importance of learning holds a fortiori for projects aiming at full-scale innovation of new and existing products and/or production technologies. Such innovative activities are the most ambitious strategic moves in terms of creative effort, funding and uncertainty, so they will be embarked upon only after rigorous analysis of marketing opportunities. In order to improve the probability of commercial success firms engaged in innovation projects can be seen to cooperate with their counterparts in exchange relations (see Nooteboom, 1992).

### 8.2.5 The Contemporary Global Financial Crisis Explored Within the Exchange-configuration Approach

**The genesis of the global financial crisis**
The crisis started in 2007 and reached its full destructive power in 2008 when it spilled over to the real economy to cause a worldwide economic

recession. It is widely asserted that an important cause of this global recession was the failure of a relatively specific financial configuration, namely, that for credit default swaps (CDS). The latter is a form of derivative that insures the holder of commercial papers or bonds issued by a corporation against the possibility of bankruptcy. Thus, for example, a large insurance company, say AIG, can issue a CDS to Deutsche Bank to protect the latter against possible default and collect a premium. Starting in the early 2000s, swaps were being used to encourage investors to buy into risky emerging markets such as Latin America and Russia by insuring the debt of developing countries. Later, after corporate blowouts like Enron and WorldCom, it became clear there was a big need for protection against company implosions, and credit default swaps proved just the tool.[2]

This was followed by the housing boom. As the Federal Reserve System cut interest rates and Americans started buying homes in record numbers, mortgage-backed securities became the hot new investment. Normally, mortgages are not readily transferable, but now mortgage portfolios were pooled together, and sliced and diced (securitized) into bonds that were bought by just about every financial and nonfinancial institution imaginable: investment banks, commercial banks, hedge funds, pension funds. Obviously, underlying risks became less easily assessable. Banks created separate 'special-purpose vehicles', escaping supervision by monetary authorities, in order to engage in the highly profitable trade in the new financial instruments. For many of those mortgage-backed securities, credit default swaps were taken out to protect against default. Financial institutions grossly underestimated the risks involved, also the risk that parties insuring against default should themselves be unable to honor their commitments, and allowed their reserve ratios to drop significantly.

The US biggest insurance company, AIG, had to be bailed out by American taxpayers after it defaulted on US$14 billion worth of credit default swaps it had made to investment banks, insurance companies and scores of other entities. The consensus opinion is that the collapse of the financial sector and the ensuing credit freeze can be traced back to credit default swaps, which ballooned into a US$62 trillion market at their high point, nearly four times the value of all stocks traded on the New York Stock Exchange.

### Characteristics of items exchanged, actors and environment
The financial market outlined above fits neatly into the exchange-configuration framework. Let us first describe a typical set of transactions. Home-loan borrowers receive mortgages from mortgage banks. The latter sell these mortgages to securitizers (such as Fannie Mae and Freddie Mac). Next, these securitizers package the mortgages into mortgage-

backed securities as described above, and sell them to financial institutions such as commercial and investment banks. At this stage, the financial institutions can insure those bonds by purchasing CDS from other financial institutions such as AIG. The above transactions can be couched and analyzed within the exchange-configuration framework. The items traded are mortgages, mortgage-backed securities and CDS. The actors are home-loan borrowers, mortgage banks, securitizers and other financial institutions. The environment is that of Wall Street and global 'high finance'. Markets are almost totally unregulated at both the international and national levels. The supervisory role of the state is conspicuous by its absence. Next, some of the more relevant characteristics of financial items, financial actors and the financial environment are described.

Financial *items* (instruments), in general, share some important common characteristics. A first characteristic is that their value depends on expectations regarding a future performance by other actors than the owners (for example, commercial credit, mortgage loans, shares). Clearly, the risk of considerable financial loss is always present. This also applies to financial derivatives, which are the assets deriving their value from other assets, possibly other financial assets. The higher the order of derivatives, the more opaque and complex they become; consequently, the risk gets more difficult to assess. A second characteristic concerns the fact that financial transactions can often be concluded at low cost across the continents, resulting in close financial connections between innumerable transactors in different parts of the world. Finally, financial assets traded in global financial markets have strong external effects as they influence directly the level and pace of economic activity worldwide.

*Actors* in the global financial market (commercial banks, mortgage banks, hedge funds, securitizers, pension funds, insurance companies) are closely interconnected through mutual buying and selling operations. Also, financial institutions are prone to confidence crises because of the nature of the items they deal with (see above). This means that there is always the risk of a systemic breakdown of the financial sector as a whole as the collapse of one actor can bring on the collapse of other actors. In fact, precisely this kind of risk caused the CDS market to collapse. Further, many actors in the global financial market had become extremely large, in fact, too large to fail. Since a possible collapse of such an institution could threaten the functioning of the entire system there is a strong tendency for supervisory institutions to prevent bankruptcies through bail-out operations. This phenomenon tends to corrupt the traditionally prudent attitude of decision makers in the respective financial institutions and create a moral hazard. The change in attitude was amplified by a general shift in emphasis towards maximization of short-run profits (and corresponding remuneration for decision makers) with an increasing disregard of threats to the continued viability of the organization. One of the results was an increased preference for high-leverage financing making use of low interest rates. Decision makers did not fully understand the intricacies of new financial instruments; their very high profitability was what counted most.

Next, we describe the financial *environment*. Most organizations operating in global financial markets finance their activities with funds from other actors with low tolerance for risk. Hence, the many-layered rules and regulations that are meant to enforce the prudential use of these funds. The task of supervising institutions such as central banks is to ensure that the rules are obeyed. Unfortunately, however, the rules mostly have only a national, or even sub-national reach and the same applies to the supervisors. This fact contrasts strongly with the extensive international operations of large financial institutions. It implies that the contemporary supervisory system is severely flawed. Another problem was that the new, massively traded financial products were typically not subject to the prudential regulations; in any case their inherent risk was not well understood by the supervisors. Moreover, rating agencies, which are meant to assess the riskiness of financial instruments objectively, failed to accurately evaluate and report potential risks. And, finally, the prevailing norms and values in the business world in general, including the financial world, also played a role. In the decades before the financial crisis the confidence in the beneficial effect of market forces had risen to remarkable heights exemplified by the waves of privatizations of previously public enterprises and activities the world over. This renewed belief in the merits of market processes and in the self-regulating and self-correcting powers of markets (which typically goes against the arguments of bounded rationality due to limited information and limited cognitive power of all individuals, including decision makers in financial institutions) gave excessive freedom of action to actors in the global financial market and often led to a form of irrational exuberance.

**Dynamics of the global financial crisis**
The dynamics that led to the massive failure of this exchange configuration are clear. AIG and other financial institutions over-extended and over-leveraged their capital base. When housing prices could no longer rise and the bubble burst, the CDS on the balance sheets of the financial institutions became 'toxic assets'. AIG became liable for hundreds of billions of dollars of losses incurred by corporations that had insured themselves

against just such contingencies. Lenders panicked and credit froze world-wide. When AIG could not cover its losses, the US Government was forced to intervene belatedly with a massive rescue package to help prevent an even worse global financial crisis

The financial crisis and the ensuing recession in the world economy did not have one single cause. It was the above-described particular mix of characteristics of exchange elements that proved to be explosive. The collapse of the housing market in the United States with its severe consequences for the subprime-mortgage market only provided the ignition spark. The main lessons to be learned are that a minimum set of rules of the game and regulations are called for at both the national and international levels to raise the transparency of derivatives and CDS (especially to protect against the possibility of unlikely, but catastrophic outcomes), and that adequate crushable zones are established and controls put in place such that no institution makes commitments that it can not honour.

### 8.2.6 How Does the Exchange Configuration Approach Differ from and Contribute to the Neoclassical Framework?

In the opening sentences of this book we emphasized the importance of economic exchange as a determinant of the state and pace of economic development. In Chapter 7 we listed the forces of change underlying the dynamics of exchange configurations and, thereby, of entire systems of exchange such as national economies. The nature and origin of these forces of change appeared to differ widely. Some were found to be exogenous and unintended, like acts of nature, others were exogenous and intended, like public policies, but the most telling forces of change were the endogenous forces which emanate directly or indirectly from decisions by actors in exchange configurations. Among the latter type of forces of change we distinguished between actors' tactics and strategies on one hand and feedbacks on the other.

The views propounded in Chapter 7 rested on the various assumptions and theories that form the basis of the exchange-configuration approach. Among the most prominent assumptions figured those relating to actors' bounded rationality, their satisficing rather than maximizing behaviour, their possibly opportunistic behaviour, the prevalence of uncertainty and risk and of transaction costs and the importance of institutions in this regard. Each of these assumptions implies a departure from a strict interpretation of the neoclassical approach. From this it follows that the picture of economic dynamics as painted in Chapter 7 differs in fundamental ways from the outcomes of neoclassical growth theory. The following paragraphs highlight the differences between the two approaches. Firstly, we summarize the neoclassical growth model. Thereafter we compare the policy recommendations of the neoclassical with those of the exchange-configuration approach.

## The neoclassical growth model

In the neoclassical Solow–Swan model of economic growth[3] (Solow, 1956; Swan, 1956) the savings rate does not affect the rate of economic growth; it only determines the level of income in the steady state. Any growth of per capita income beyond the steady state derives exclusively from technological progress, an exogenous variable. Further, since technological knowledge has the characteristics of a public good, the model predicts a very strong tendency towards convergence of incomes per head in different countries. Ultimately, any remaining variation in levels of income can only result from differences in national savings rates.

A new generation of models that emerged after a few decades addressed some of the weaknesses of the Solow–Swan model. In these models growth became 'endogenous'. By incorporating the generation of technological innovations one major shortcoming of the Solow–Swan model, namely exogeneity of the only source of continuing growth, could be overcome (Romer, 1986). Further, the introduction of human capital allowed an escape from the shackles of diminishing returns. If workers who improve their skills create a spill-over effect by raising not only their own productivity but also that of their co-workers, diminishing returns may be avoided (Lucas, 1988). As a result income can continue to grow through accumulation of production factors. And if rich countries can grow in much the same way as poor countries, the tendency towards convergence of incomes per head is much reduced.

However, new growth models share the mechanical patterns characteristic of the original Solow–Swan model; they tackle the shortcomings of the earlier model merely by adding relations that relax some of the latter's mathematical restrictions. Thus, new technological knowledge is obtained simply by adding a production function fueled by capital and labour inputs. The accumulation of human capital is modelled in much the same way. Workers devote a part of their time to the production of regular output and another part to the creation of human capital which is a function of the time invested in it. Any possible practical complications regarding transaction costs, motivation, empowerment, decision making and implementation are ignored.

The growth recommendations one can derive from neoclassical growth theory are extremely simple. In essence they stress the importance of increased investments in fixed and human capital, of spending on R&D

and of savings to provide the means for investment expenditures. There is, of course, nothing wrong with these recommendations and their simplicity has a strong appeal. But the recommendations are lacking in a number of very important ways, mostly because they overlook the complications arising in real-world exchange processes.

Not surprisingly, the performance of the neoclassical model in explaining inter-country differences in productivity levels is weak. For example, Lucas (1990) shows that, according to the Solow–Swan model, the marginal product of capital in India must have been approximately 58-times higher than in the United States by the end of the 1980s. Obviously, such an outcome cannot be correct. In another well-known exercise Hall and Jones (1999) applied a new growth model which incorporates the accumulation of human capital. In a comparison of five countries with high levels of output per worker with five countries with low levels, approximately 15 per cent of the difference in output per worker can be attributed to differences in capital-output ratios, 18 per cent to differences in human capital per worker, and 67 per cent to variation in productivity.[4] It seems very unlikely, however, that the state of technology, characterized by its public-good properties, can fully account for this difference.

Under the neoclassical paradigm exchange does not jeopardize opportunities for economic growth in any way, so it can be overlooked. But the growth perspective changes dramatically once it is recognized that exchange is a laborious, imperfect, costly, frictional and uncertain process. In fact, it may well be argued generally that the idiosyncrasies of exchange complicate the development process to such an extent that the analysis of the process does not lend itself to mathematical reduction. This argument seems to apply indeed to the neoclassical growth model.[5] In that case the advantages of mathematical representation may not outweigh the disadvantages of oversimplification.

### Exchange-related factors to promote growth

The difference between the neoclassical model and the exchange-configuration approach in the study of economic growth follows readily from the above discussion: the latter approach emphasizes the need to identify the (parts of) exchange processes that hamper or facilitate economic growth, and provides the tools for a detailed analysis. Contrary to the neoclassical model which assumes a fully informed, frictionless world, the exchange-configuration approach allows for the fact that private actors do not (often also cannot) actually exploit all prevailing opportunities for economic gain and growth. Further, it is unthinkable in the exchange-configuration approach that one overarching growth policy can fit all countries. Exchange processes are shaped by the characteristics of the three exchange elements, which often differ widely among regions and countries. The differences preclude uniform prescriptions.

Exchange is at the heart of economic activity. But exchange can be riddled with imperfections obstructing a desirable allocation of resources and failing to motivate economic actors into desirable activities. Thus, two groups of growth-promoting factors can be distinguished: one group enabling actors and another group motivating actors to take action. All of these factors are, in fact, aspects of exchange elements. Below these factors are mentioned only briefly as many have been described in earlier chapters. It will be seen that the neoclassical model emphasizes some (but not all) of the enabling factors. However, motivating factors are typically ignored in the neoclassical approach.

**Enabling factors**
One group of enabling factors aims at expanding, maintaining and upgrading factors of production to improve overall production potential. Thus, generally speaking, larger amounts of productive assets held by private actors allow an increase in production and the same applies to the introduction of more efficient assets. Another important enabling factor is, of course, physical infrastructure. Productive capacity further depends on education, directly as well as indirectly through the positive impact on productivity of other workers. Hence the importance of improvements in educational systems, such as providing access to schools to all layers of the population also in the countryside, and raising the quality of education in terms of the amount and kind of knowledge students must absorb. In order to see the relevance of education at an early age, recall that the capacity to learn (that is, to acquire new knowledge) depends on the extent of prior knowledge. Finally, the standard of health has an impact on the physical and intellectual capacity of a work force.

This particular group of enabling factors is what the neoclassical growth model is about. But, given the complexities of real-world exchange, it must be recognized that many actors do not have access to available production factors. It follows that there is a need to examine enabling factors at much lower levels of aggregation. Listed below are some examples of obstacles that confront multitudes of actors in many developing countries. Elimination or, at least, reduction of such obstructions enables actors to increase their productivity and their contribution to economic growth.

Specific types of actors do not have access to formal credit markets in developing countries as we have seen on several occasions in earlier chapters. Thus, many itinerant merchants cannot achieve an efficient volume of trade, many producers in the informal sector cannot buy the tools and equipment to improve their productivity and many farmers are unable to obtain the fertilizer and improved seeds that would allow a yield increase. In the agricultural sector imperfections in the markets for labour and draft animals create further obstacles. Also the operation of land markets is less than optimal. As a result the distribution of land ownership appears to impact on growth, where skewer distributions correlate with lower growth rates, as Alesina and Rodrik (1994) have shown.[6] It must be added that land reform, a very complex strategy in its own right, requires coordinated action for optimal results (See Hoff and Stiglitz, 2001). After a land-reform programme new landowners have new tasks and responsibilities. An adult-education programme should help new landowners prepare themselves for their new positions and opportunities. Further, poorly functioning or even absent land register systems preclude the possibility to use land as collateral and impede the start of new firms. Still other impediments are of a cultural nature when they create gender- or caste-related restrictions to productive opportunities. A final example relates to the economic isolation of villages and communities in developing countries due to the absence of even low-tech connecting roads causing unevenly distributed market power.

**Motivating factors**

Well-directed motivation of economic actors is a necessary condition for economic growth. But there is no reason to assume, as is done in neo-classical theory, that human condition and human environment ensure that this condition is always and automatically fulfilled. Hence the need to emphasize that an economy's performance in terms of efficient use of scarce resources and pace of development depends on the strength and direction of incentives[7] and the response they elicit from economic actors. Institutions play a major role in this regard. Or, as Helpman (2004, p. 139) put it,

> Countries that start with similar endowments can follow different developmental paths as a result of differences in institutional structures, because institutions affect the incentives to innovate and to develop new technologies, the incentives to reorganize production and distribution in order to exploit new opportunities, and the incentives to accumulate physical and human capital. For these reasons institutions are more fundamental than R&D, or capital accumulation, human or physical.

In our approach, institutions are key components of the exchange environment that help shape the various exchange configurations.

While strength and direction of motivation are partly innate aspects of actors, another part derives from culture. Families, as vehicles of culture, are particularly important in this respect. The ways in which families bring up children and the values they convey often leave a lasting imprint. Further, organizations by their nature often aim to establish an internal culture promoting the common goal (see Subsection 4.5.1). The educational system – as defined by educational targets and content of educational material – also deserves to be mentioned here.

Given their impact on motivation, it is important to realize that aspects of culture can facilitate or, alternatively, slow down the pace of development. In any case, it is difficult to change cultural values and norms and make them more responsive to public policy measures. Even then, much can be gained in many developing countries from efforts by governments to improve the developmental incentives and motivation of their subjects. This opportunity derives from the fact that many public-policy measures in the past have had the opposite, that is a blunting effect.

A novel view on public policy in many developing countries, even if they do not belong to the separate category of failed states, is needed in order to correct and remedy earlier public policies and bad habits that demotivate actors or create wrong incentives. Such forms of public appropriation as the inflation tax and forced delivery of goods at depressed prices through marketing boards are cases in point. Other public policies generate various types of rent-seeking activities. Where direct price intervention leads to black markets, actors cash in on the wedge that has been driven between prices and scarcity ratios. Corruption misuses power to extract resources from its victims. Rents also derive from patronage systems by which privileges, such as jobs in the public sector, are handed out in return for political support. Legal, but still undesirable, forms of rent also exist. The latter arise, for example, when protection against foreign competition allows monopolies to extract rents from their counterparts in the market. The problem in all these cases is that countries may remain locked into rent-seeking systems, not only because those who profit will do their utmost to maintain it, but also because some of the major rent-seeking activities erode morality and, thus, become self-reinforcing (see Van de Mortel and Cornelisse, 1994).

## NOTES

1. In this connection Ndulu and O'Connel, 2008, refer to what they call 'anti-growth syndromes'. They estimate that these syndromes in African countries account for more than half of the 3.5 per cent gap in per capita annual GDP growth as compared with other developing countries during the period from 1960 to 2000.
2. As *Newsweek* reported: 'There's a reason Warren Buffett called these instruments "financial weapons of mass destruction". Since credit default swaps are privately negotiated

contracts between two parties and aren't regulated by the government, there's no central reporting mechanism to determine their value. That has clouded up the markets with billions of dollars' worth of opaque "dark matter", as some economists like to say. Like rogue nukes, they've proliferated around the world and now lie hiding, waiting, to blow up the balance sheets of countless other financial institutions', Matthew Philips in *Newsweek*, October 6, 2008.

3. The following equations capture the essence of the original model:

$$Y = AK^{\alpha}L^{1-\alpha}, \text{ where } 0 < \alpha < 1 \tag{8.1}$$

$$S = sY \tag{8.2}$$

$$\Delta L = nL \tag{8.3}$$

$$\Delta K = sY - \delta K \tag{8.4}$$

where $Y$ represents total output; $A$ the state of technology; $K$ the capital stock; $L$ the number of workers; and $S$ savings.

4. Already in 1942, using data for four developed countries from the decades before the First World War, Tinbergen suggested that capital and labour growth explain only a small portion of the growth of production; Tinbergen, 1942.

5. This point is forcefully made in Kohn, 2004.

6. We have included land ownership under enabling factors, because, as an asset, it widens owners' productive opportunities and improves access to credit. But ownership of land may also be seen as a motivating factor.

7. This is the central theme in Easterly, 2001.

# REFERENCES

Alesina, A. and D. Rodrik (1994), 'Distributive politics and economic growth', *Quarterly Journal of Economics*, **109** (2), 465–490.

Easterly, W. (2001), *The Elusive Quest for Growth: Economists' Adventures and Misadventures in the Tropics*, Cambridge, MA: MIT Press.

Hall, R.E. and C.I. Jones (1999), 'Why do some countries produce so much more output per worker than others?', *Quarterly Journal of Economics*, **114** (1), 83–116.

Helpman, E. (2004), *The Mystery of Economic Growth*, Cambridge, MA: Harvard University Press.

Hoff, K. and J.E. Stiglitz (2001), 'Modern economic theory and development', in G.M. Meier and J.E. Stiglitz (eds.), *Frontiers of Development Economics*, Oxford, UK: Oxford University Press, pp. 389–459.

Kohn, M. (2004), 'Value and exchange', *Cato Journal*, **24** (3), 303–339.

Lucas, R.E. (1988), 'On the mechanics of economic development', *Journal of Monetary Economics*, **22** (1), 3–42.

Lucas, R.E. (1990), 'Why doesn't capital flow from rich to poor countries?', *American Economic Review*, **80**, (2), 92–96.

van de Mortel, E.G. and P.A. Cornelisse (1994), 'The dynamics of black markets and corruption: an application of catastrophe theory, *Public Finance*, **49**, 195–208.

Ndulu, B.J. and S.A. O'Connell (2008), 'Policy plus: African growth performance',

Chapter 1 in B.J. Ndulu, S.A. O'Connell, R.H. Bates, P. Collier and C.C. Soludo (eds.), *The Political Economy of Economic Growth in Africa, 1960–2000*, Cambridge, UK: Cambridge University Press.

Nooteboom, B. (1992), 'Towards a dynamic theory of transactions', *Journal of Evolutionary Economics*, **2**, (4), 281–299.

Philips, M. (2008), 'The monster that ate Wall Street', *Newsweek*, **152** (14).

Romer, P.M. (1986), 'Increasing returns and long-run growth', *Journal of Political Economy*, **94** (5), 1002–1037.

Solow, R.M. (1956), 'A contribution to the theory of economic growth', *Quarterly Journal of Economics*, **70** (1), 65–94.

Swan, T.W. (1956), 'Economic growth and capital accumulation', *Economic Record*, **32** (3), 334–361.

Tinbergen, J. (1942), 'Zur Theorie der Langfristigen Wirtschaftsentwicklung' (On the theory of long-term economic growth), *Weltwirtschaftliches Archiv*, **55**, 511–549.

# Index

uncertainty 61, 69, 123, 221
   fundamental, genuine, Knightian 61,
     64, 185
understanding 79
UNDP Human Development
   Index 1
urban bias 112, 113

Veblen, T. 126

wars 177
wheat-market transactions 32–4
Williamson, O.E. 58, 64, 66, 68, 70, 75

Zak, P.J. 108